584608

FRANCOIS DE FENELON

FÉNELON

AFTER THE PORTRAIT BY PHILIPPE DE CHAMPAGNE IN HERTFORD HOUSE

FRANCOIS DE FENELON

BY

VISCOUNT ST CYRES

WITH EIGHT ILLUSTRATIONS

KENNIKAT PRESS
Port Washington, N. Y./London

FRANÇOIS DE FENELON

First published in 1901
Reissued in 1970 by Kennikat Press
Library of Congress Catalog Card No: 72-113319
ISBN 0-8046-0998-5

Manufactured by Taylor Publishing Company   Dallas, Texas

PREFACE

THIS little book is an attempt to review the whole Life and Works of Fénelon from a standpoint somewhat more impartial than that of his biographers in France. There the ship of his reputation has always sailed under a Party flag. To contemporary admirers such as de Ramsai he is pre-eminently a Saint; a generation later comes the rise of sentimentalism, when Rousseau and La Harpe forget the Churchman in the prophet of philanthropy and the Rights of Man. During the Napoleonic era appears the great official Life by Cardinal Bausset, where Fénelon is pictured as the typical enlightened priest, blessing the typical enlightened despotism—though only to be elevated, thirty years later, to a very different pedestal, when Lamennais hails him as the champion of a progressive Papacy at war with illiberal Kings and Bishops. Lastly, in our own day has come the inevitable reaction, and in the various writings of M. Brunetière, but especially in the monumental *Fénelon et Bossuet* of M. Crouslé, the shifty womanish malcontent at Cambrai, a vague cosmopolitan and a friend of Rome, is everywhere unfavourably contrasted with the frank and manly Bossuet at Meaux, national in his faith and politics as in his genius and good sense.

That there is truth in each of these views, but not the whole truth, it has been my endeavour to show. Fénelon will appear in these pages as the father of eighteenth century sentimentalism—witness his politics and philosophy, his educational and literary theories—but also as an upholder of seventeenth century rationality, and of the most ruthlessly stoical of mysticisms—a disciple sometimes worthy, sometimes dilettantist, and sometimes morbid, of the great Spanish ascetic St John of the Cross. And in pursuance of this theme I have departed a little from traditional lines, and dealt with subjects usually dismissed more cavalierly, such as Fénelon's relation to the Jansenists and Papacy, to the philosophy of Malebranche and the Classical School of literature. Inasmuch, however, as these abstract matters may prove a weariness to many, I would advise readers interested only in the history of his life to pass rapidly over my 11th chapter, and omit the 6th, 12th, and 13th altogether.

It remains only to express my great indebtedness to preceding biographers, and to the long list of other writers on Fénelon, whose names are given on a later page. Also to the authorities of the British Museum for sanctioning the reproduction of three scarce engravings, respectively of the Duke of Burgundy, of Cambrai City, and of Malebranche. And more especial thanks are due to Sir John Murray Scott and the Trustees of the Wallace Collection at Hertford House, who have generously broken through their usual rule, and allowed the reproduction of the portrait of Fénelon by Philippe de Champagne, which serves as a frontispiece to this book.

CONTENTS

CHAPTER I
FÉNELON'S YOUTH . . . . PAGE 1

CHAPTER II
TOLERATION AND THE PROTESTANTS 16

CHAPTER III
EARLY OCCUPATIONS AND FRIENDSHIPS . . . 30

CHAPTER IV
THE EDUCATION OF GIRLS 52

CHAPTER V
THE COURT PRECEPTORATE 72

CHAPTER VI
MYSTICISM AND THE MAXIMS OF THE SAINTS . . . 87

CHAPTER VII
MME. GUYON 121

CHAPTER VIII
AT WAR WITH BOSSUET 144

CONTENTS

CHAPTER IX
TÉLÉMAQUE 178

CHAPTER X
CAMBRAI 203

CHAPTER XI
JANSENISM 227

CHAPTER XII
FÉNELON AMONG THE PHILOSOPHERS 248

CHAPTER XIII
THE LETTER TO THE ACADEMY 269

CHAPTER XIV
BURGUNDY AND POLITICAL REFORM 281

CHAPTER XV
THE END 296

LIST OF ILLUSTRATIONS

FÉNELON, *after the portrait by Philippe de Champagne in Hertford House* . . . . . *Frontispiece*

MME. DE MAINTENON, *from an engraving* . . . *facing* CHAP. iii.

THE DUKE OF BURGUNDY, *from an engraving by Edelinck* . ,, v.

MME. GUYON, *from an engraving* . . . . . ,, vii.

BOSSUET, *from an engraving after the portrait by Rigaud in the Louvre* . . . . . . ,, viii.

VIEW OF CAMBRAI, *from an engraving* . . . . ,, x.

MALEBRANCHE, *from an engraving* . . . . ,, xii.

FÉNELON, *from an engraving after Vivien* . . . ,, xiv.

CHAPTER I
FENELON'S YOUTH

Ce qui surnageoit dans toute sa personne, c'était surtout la noblesse.
—St Simon.

THE age of Fénelon coincides exactly with the second, disastrous, half of Louis the Fourteenth's reign. During the earlier part of that vast episode France had reached the zenith of her glories; her history was become the history of Europe, her king, as his subjects justly boasted, arbiter of all this portion of our hemisphere. Each decade brought a fresh successful war and more successful peace, with fresh enlargement of her frontiers; from the last triumph of Mazarin at the Pyrenees (A.D. 1659) the tide flowed on to Aix-la-Chapelle (A.D. 1668), and thence till the great Peace of Nymwegen (A.D. 1678) realized the ambition of two hundred years, and confirmed the conquest of Franche Comté. At home, with nobles and lawyers ruined by the Fronde, towns exhausted by the Religious Wars, and provinces destitute of even a language in common, Louis could bend the whole nation to his will, his monarchy, as M$^{me.}$ de Sévigné will tell us, exalted above all imagination could conceive.[1] It seemed as though a Golden Age were dawning; Justice was assured, the army reformed, finance and commerce organized by Colbert, and a strong navy set on foot, while Molière, La Fontaine, Racine and a host of lesser writers were ready with their pen to prove—

> Qu'on peut comparer sans être injuste
> Le siècle de Louis avec celui d'Auguste.

"All is new!" cries M$^{me.}$ de Sévigné again, "All is

[1] See the letter of 22nd August, 1675, and those of September, 1676.

wonderful. The fortunes of the French are greater than they have ever been."[1]

But in this triumphal procession there came a great break, fixed by most writers at the Revocation of the Edict of Nantes in 1685, or at the king's serious illness in the following year, but by Fénelon dated much earlier, from the beginning of the Dutch War of 1672.[2] Thenceforward appear all the vices arraigned in the famous Letter to the King; his foreign policy sank into unabashed robbery and chicane, he made war out of sheer vain-glory and pique at the caricaturists and libellers of Holland, twice shamelessly ravaged the Palatinate, (in 1674 and 1689), seized on Strasburg in time of peace (1681), becoming, like the Idiomeneus of Télémaque, a menace to the life of every neighbour. His neighbour's answer was the League of Augsburg, (1686) and the campaigns of William of Orange (1688-1697)—campaigns which at last made the sun of France stand still: at the great Peace of Ryswick, (1697) she was, for the first time, forced to restore ill-gotten goods.

And Louis' world-wide ambition, typified in his vaunting motto, *Nec Pluribus Impar*, reacted evilly at home. More of a king than a man, and "the greatest actor of monarchy that ever filled a throne,"[3] the official egoism of his kingship dwarfed all other qualities; Louis would have accepted in good earnest the theological formulas which St Simon applies to him in irony: like God, he could not love outside himself, but must make his own glory his final end. Hence the two mainsprings of his policy at home were belief that all authority of every kind must centre in the Crown, and that worship at its altar was the highest privilege of the subject. For this he turned his nobles into courtiers, the swarm of lazy, noisy drones, whom, a century later, satire was to thank for having given themselves the trouble to

---

[1] Letter of , 1689. [2] See his Works, vol. vii. p. 510.
[3] Bolingbroke, Seventh Letter on History, qu. Kitchen's Hist. of France, iii. p. 149.

be born. For this he persecuted, as possible rebels, the Huguenots and Jansenists, and kept the clergy in due subjection, his whole Church policy being summed up in the caution to an over-zealous preacher: "I like to take my part in a sermon, but will not have it pointed out to me."[1] For this he built up an omnipotent executive in Paris, and parcelled out the rest of the country under the charge of his Royal Intendants, the real masters of the kingdom, beside whom Governors and Parliaments, nobles and clergy, were as nothing.[2] That mouth-piece of humbler grievances, the Provincial Estates, was hurried into oblivion, the corporate life of the towns destroyed, the poor so oppressed by the load of taxation as to make one great writer declare that they could not live like men, another, that they feared to live at all. For Cæsarism ever demands its price in full, and for a 'glorious habit of conquering' the gods expect a heavy requital; every day Corneille's sombre prophecy was more abundantly justified—

> A vaincre si longtemps mes forces s'affaiblissent.
> L'Etat est florissant, mais les peuples gémissent.
> Leurs membres décharnés courbent sur mes hauts faits,
> Et la gloire du trône écrase les sujets.[3]

From such a system there must needs be reaction, and it is the chief glory of Fénelon to have been one of its first apostles, throughout his life the very embodiment of all that Louis did not like. In him, indeed, as in most reformers, good and evil are closely interwined; we shall hear much of contradiction and extravagance in this 'M. de Cambrai,' whom the world thought always so extreme in everything.[4] In politics, he will appeal from a hard-hearted, conquering, despotism, tempered by the capacity of middle-class

---

[1] J'aime à prendre ma part dans un sermon, mais je ne veux pas qu'on me la fasse.
[2] So at least thought the financial adventurer of the Regency, John Law. See Lotheissen, Gesch. der franz. Litt. im siebzehnten Jahrh., iv. p. 270.
[3] Qu. in Paul Albert's Littérature Française au dixseptième siècle, p. 74.
[4] Fénelon says himself: on crie que les Jésuites poursuivent un fantôme, avec M. l'Archevêque de Cambrai, *qui outre tout.* Wks. vii. p. 380.

Ministers, to a benevolent despotism still more rigorously searching, and tempered by the chivalrous incompetence of nobles, from Colbert's wasteful system of State-aided industry to agriculture and free-trade, but also to sumptuary laws. In religion, he upheld the Interior Life against a king, of whom his own wife said that he would never miss a sermon or a fast-day, but knew not the meaning of prayer or repentance—[1] yet this standard of piety verged on the morbid and the controversial, and in its interest he helped to persecute the very salt of France, the Jansenist supporters of Port Royal. A champion of the 'amiable simplicity' of Homer, he raised his trenchant protest against the bastard Classicism of Versailles, but what is to be made of a prophet of Romanticism who treats of Love as an indecency, whether in literature or life, and would like to banish verse from France, as unsuited to the genius of the tongue?

But, although each of his theories bears abundant marks of weakness, Fénelon was greater than any of his works; to-day we cannot afford, like Louis XIV., to call him the finest and most visionary thinker in the kingdom, nor, with a mightier future ruler of France, to dismiss his politics as mere 'rhapsody.'[2] A man of transition, what he lost in distinctness, he gains in significance; though he presents us with no finished canvas, he has designed many a picture for a later brush to paint. It was his mission to teach the Eighteenth Century to wield the weapons of the Seventeenth, to appropriate its reasonableness and harmony and order, while yet remembering what the closing age forgot—that clearness and logic are no end in themselves, that the workman cannot be forever polishing his tools, but, having learnt the How of things, must go on to ask the Why and Wherefore: *Gleich nach dem Wie? fragt man nach dem Wozu?*

Secondly, he was called to temper the intellectual asceticism of his age by restoring emotion to its rights—in litera-

---

[1] Geffroy, Mme. de Maintenon, i. p. 320.
[2] See Las Casas, Mémoires de Napoléon, III. vi. 3.

ture, to show that orator and poet must touch as well as prove and paint, in education, that pedantic exactitude offers a weaker leverage than pleasure, in politics, to teach an age which knew no patriotism save the service of its king, that there was no shame in being *infected* by devotion to the common weal.[1] Lastly, in religion, he is no prophet of stern, unbending dogma, but speaks to his penitents, each in turn, as a kindly friend and counsellor, bringing piety before them less as a duty than a means of happiness, and making them feel that their welfare was essential to his own.[2] In Fénelon the personal element is ever to the fore ; le moi, it has been well said, est au fond de toutes ses chimères, comme il inspire ses plus exquises conceptions,[3] and ours will be but a barren judgment of the work, unless we have made acquaintance with the man.

Francis de Salagnac de Lamothe Fénelon was born at the ' poor Gothic Ithaca of his fathers,' the Castle of Fénelon in Périgord, on the 6th of August 1651. He sprang from a younger branch of the distinguished family of Salagnac, a house of good and ancient nobility, says St Simon, and rich in the dim glories of half-forgotten ancestors, ' in governors of provinces and kings' chamberlains, in ambassadors to the leading courts of Europe. Its daughters had married into the noblest families of their provinces and its sons had filled every military office formerly open to men of gentle blood.'[4]

One name alone has survived in history, that of Bertrand de Fénelon, a distinguished soldier and diplomatist, and one of the earliest members of the illustrious Order of the Holy Ghost. Bertrand's fame rests largely on his connexion with our own country ; he was many years French Ambassador in London, where he tried hard to lure Queen Elizabeth into 'the gaping gulf of a popish marriage' with the Duc

---

[1] Ces gens-là, said Mme. de Motteville, lady-in-waiting to Louis' mother, speaking of the Frondeurs, étaient tous infectés de l'amour du bien public. qu. P. Albert, p. 153.
[2] See Bausset III., p. 133, for a good criticism by the Abbé Trublet.
[3] Lanson, Hist. de la Litt. Franç., p. 613.
[4] Fénelon to his Brother, Wks., vii. p. 405.

d'Alençon, younger brother of King Charles IX. But he also won the better opinion of our fellow-countrymen by curtly refusing to justify or extenuate his master's action in the matter of the Bartholomew Massacre. And he foreshadowed the future literary eminence of his name by writing an account of the famous siege of Metz by Charles V. in 1552, which has become a classic of military history.

These various dignities, however, brought little wealth to the Fénelons; perhaps, like other Southerners, they were better able to manage the affairs of the public than their own, or found, like their most famous representative, that a long rent-roll was the best road to debt. The future Archbishop of Cambrai, one of the youngest of many sons, did not escape the common lot; like other cadets of his family, he was forced to begin the world with little patrimony beyond an honoured name. But his poverty sat lightly enough upon him, embodiment as he was of that ideal aristocracy of Goethe's, whose aim in life is the perfecting of character rather than achievements or possessions, for it looks on wealth and talents and accomplishments as a mere external adornment, worthless except to set off a nicely balanced temperament, an unvarying self-control.[1] 'We shall have need of such things,' said Fénelon himself, in one of his spiritual discourses, 'if we are to live peaceably and honorably in the state to which God has called us, but we must take from them only so much as we are absolutely forced to take, just as a shrewd and careful steward keeps back no more of the income of his master's property than is sufficient for its needful repair.'[2]

Of Fénelon's parents or his early education scarcely anything is known. He was one of the offspring of an elderly father's second marriage with a youthful wife, Mlle. de St Arbre, sister of a celebrated lieutenant of Turenne, and said to have been a pious but somewhat ca.eless mother. His was a sickly childhood; once, at least, in early

---

[1] See Wilhelm Meister's Lehr-Jahre, Bk. V. chap. iii.
[2] Wks., vi. p. 141.

days his life was despaired of, and he only recovered to be for many years the victim of sleeplessness and other kindred ailments, aggravated, as he afterwards thought, by his own neglect, with a temperament very different from that of his great rival, the robust Burgundian Bossuet, to whom ' by God's mercy, sun, wind, rain—all were good.' But his intelligence developed very quickly, fed on a generous diet of those Greek and Latin classics, which were to become inseparable companions of his after-life. And it is to this early familiarity with the Ancients that his biographer traces the singular grace and ease of style that, with Fénelon, were no hard-won gain of age or experience, but seem to have sprung, already perfect, from his brain.[1]

At twelve years old he left his father's house to begin a three years' residence at the neighbouring University of Cahors. There he took his degrees in Arts, and at once set out for Paris to begin his preparation for the priesthood. Of the causes which determined him to this step Fénelon has left no record, perhaps because an ecclesiastical career seemed, to his relatives and himself, a simple matter of course. In the days of Louis XIV. a love of books and a want of bodily vigour must often enough have done duty for more interior signs of a vocation to the altar, more especially in such families as commanded some influence in the Church, or could point, like the Fénelons, to a neighbouring bishopric, then, as frequently beforehand, held by a bearer of their name.

Yet, if the Comte de Fénelon dreamed of mitres and rich abbeys for his studious child, these grosser arguments can have had but little weight on the imaginative and high-strung nature of his son. Fénelon was ambitious, but his ambition was of that rare and ethereal sort that can at first be scarcely distinguished from the more unselfish buoyancy of youth, and is at all times a desire to gain ascendancy over the wills of others rather than a lust after commoner earthly glories. Its full extent Fénelon hardly gauged

[1] Bausset, i. p. 9.

himself; it was an instinctive need of his nature, that defied his careful analysis,—no vice, says the kindly Lamartine, but a force mounting upwards of itself,[1]

> a power and will to dominate
> Which I must exercise; they hurt me else.

Again, Fénelon was proud, proud not only with the scholar's contempt for the unlearned, or the great Churchman's for the wretched Huguenot, or the philanthropic noble's disdainful kindness to the common folk, 'the people that is always the people, gross and credulous, blind and capricious, the enemy of its own best interests, to be driven like sheep before a master's will.'[2] There was all this in Fénelon and much more also; there was a pride of that imperial sort, which delights in being a law unto itself, in caring nothing for the praise or blame of men or for the standards of excellence recognised by others, but affects, in earlier and unchastened days, such singularities of thought as mark it out from among the common herd, till it learns, with time, to discard even this ironic subservience to public opinion and go forward on its own chosen path, looking neither to the right nor to the left.

There were not many who would have ventured, like Fénelon, to correspond on matters of religion with the infamous Duke of Orleans, afterwards Regent of France, a man so steeped in vices that even his infidelity loomed small beside them. And still fewer would have dared, in the face of the Church's condemnation of Comedy, to discuss in print the genius of Molière, or themselves give birth to a Télémaque, destined to shock the *censoria gravitas* of their intimates, and to be pronounced by Bossuet a frivolous work, unworthy of a Christian priest.

And Fénelon's temperament was curiously complex; art, even artifice, was its nature; it embraced within itself a great diversity of characters, the Christian, the prelate, the noble, the writer; it could travel at one and the same time along

---

[1] Fénelon, par A. de Lamartine (Paris, 1876), p. 57.
[2] See Wks., vi. p. 241.

several different planes of morality. Admirers have sought to blend these various elements into a single unity, but his friends did not know Fénelon as he knew himself—" When I examine into my mind," he wrote, " I seem to dream ; I am to my own conscience like a vision of the night." [1] Within him two opposite forces struggled for the mastery ; on the one side a passionate eagerness to become meek and humble and poor in spirit, to give himself 'the simplicity loved of God and man,' on the other, an all-powerful instinct of self-assertiveness, that could not move without involuntarily posing, or see the truth that made against its own advantage. Never was a mind more utterly subjective, never a horizon more quickly changed, and, changed, more over-clouded by a single idea ; prudence, logic, memory, must all give way before it, appearances were nothing to him, extravagance was welcome ; his religion must be more loving than love, his daily life more kind than kindness, his words be truer than truth itself. Everywhere the Self is the touch-stone, determines his opinions as well as his acts, places him, whether in life or writings, at the point where he can make the best display. " Little as I know my mind," he said, " one fault is lasting and easy to fix ; almost everywhere I think too much of self, am almost always guided by my own advantage." [2]

In short, Fénelon was far from being the saintly priest that legend has made him ; despite all his efforts, he remained to the end altogether lacking in the disinterested energy, the hardy singleness of purpose, that alone make possible the highest achievement. Only stupidity or pure genius—and sanctity is a form of genius—can bear confinement within narrow bounds; the rich many-coloured natures that belong, rather to talent, yet often rise above it, can never be entirely hidden under a cassock or a uniform, least of all when they are natures such as Fénelon's, abundant in graces rather than strength, ethereal rather than profound, and great chiefly in that they hold in concordant subjection

[1] Wks., vii. p. 348. [2] *Ibid.* viii. p. 589.

a large number of different, and often contradictory, qualities. Fénelon was never unfaithful to his sacred duties, never chafed under the many restrictions of his state, never slackened in the young enthusiasm that had seen in every priest "a mouth-piece of the Holy Ghost, a steward of the mysteries of God, whose time was his Creator's, whose worldly wealth was the portion of the poor and an atonement for the sins of the people."[1] If his life was not always attuned to this lofty pitch, if the feet of the courtier and writer sometimes stumbled on the narrow path of sacerdotal perfection, can we very greatly blame him?

His choice of a profession was certainly not unwelcome to the relative under whose guardianship he passed on coming to Paris. His father's brother, the Marquis Antoine de Fénelon, once a soldier of distinction, was ending his days in an atmosphere of austere military piety traced out for him by M. Olier, founder of the famous theological college of Saint Sulpice. Thither his nephew was transferred so soon as he had gone through a preliminary training in philosophy at the Collège du Plessy, and at Saint Sulpice, Fénelon was fated to spend the next ten years of his life, years associated in later days with the most pleasing memories. His devoted affection for the seminary never decayed; only the fear of compromising them with the King prevented him from entrusting his own college at Cambrai to Sulpician Fathers; on his death-bed he declared that he knew of no institution more venerable or more apostolic. Of his own tutor, M. Tronson, he spoke in even warmer terms: "Never have I known his equal," he wrote to Clement XI., "for piety and prudence, for love of discipline and insight into character; I glory in the thought that I was brought up under his wing."[2] Indeed M. Tronson won his pupil's confidence as no other man or woman ever succeeded in winning it, and remained ever afterwards his most trusted friend and counsellor. And, on the whole,

[1] Wks., v. p. 586.   [2] *Ibid.* vii. p. 613.

FENELON'S YOUTH

Fénelon's praises of St Sulpice were well deserved. The Seminary, then in the first flush of its enthusiasm, was far from being St Simon's home of ignorant Ultramontanism and trumpery devotions, far from M. Renan's school of voluntary mediocrity. A principal fruit of the great Catholic revival at the beginning of the century, it was an embodiment, a perpetuation in action, of all the forces of that movement, of its very real piety and earnestness on the one hand, of its frosty austerity and almost theatrical sentimentalism on the other. It was founded by a group of men sprung from that severe and orderly upper-middle class, that nobility of the ermine, which had furnished three-quarters of its great names to the Age of Louis Quatorze, and, in revenge, had stamped with its own characteristics the whole spirit of the age. An accident of his position—he was rector of a 'peculiar' immediately dependent on the Pope—working on a gentle visionary nature, had made M. Olier into an Ultramontane and coated his Seminary with a layer of somewhat feminine Italian devotion, but it had not robbed him and his colleagues of those essential qualities of their class, for which Jansenism became the natural expression. There was something of Port Royal's obstinate rationality at St Sulpice; there was a deep sense of moral responsibility, not to be tricked by the elegant chicanery of Jesuit casuists; there was a yearning after some closer union with the Divine than was afforded by the stiff official Catholicism brought into fashion by King Henry of Navarre.

This last want it was the special mission of St Sulpice to supply. The Seminary was to build up again the Interior Life in France, by devoting itself to the education of the priesthood 'not so much in theological science as in the practice of that science and in the virtues proper to the ecclesiastical state.' Asceticism, not learning, became the corner-stone of M. Olier's system, his house was to be like the hedge of the Gospel, which 'fences off the vineyard of the Lord, and pierces with its thorns the flesh of him who passes through it.' Not that he wished to revive the unlettered solitude or corporal austerities of a ruder age; knowledge, within certain limits, he held to be a most worthy support of piety, and to the torture of the body he preferred the mortification of the mind by renunciation of all earthly interests and ties, by entire surrender of the Will into the hands of a Director. For M. Olier set before his pupils an ideal of almost terrible severity. The good priest, he said, must become a model of all the virtues of every state; in him the Religious Orders and the laity must find the pattern of their several perfections.[1]

Lessons so exalted may doubtless have proved a useful spur to the languid piety of the many; they were no small danger to a highly self-conscious temperament, always prone to rush into extremes, and ill provided with that moral thickness of skin which deadens in coarser natures the effect of an oft-repeated shock. Fénelon had not been long at St Sulpice before their influence began to tell on him in the form of mysterious communications to his Director.—"I most earnestly wish," he wrote to the Marquis de Fénelon, "that I could enter into some detail to you of my conversations with M. Tronson, but, indeed, sir, I cannot do it. For, although my relation to you is very frank and open, I must confess—and I do so without fear of exciting your jealousy —that I am much more explicit with him, nor would it even be easy to describe to you the degree of union we have reached."[2]

It is likely enough that M. Tronson, no friend to spiritual extravagances, might have disapproved alike the tone of this letter and its account of his relations to his pupil; even M. Olier, though himself a visionary and a mystic, could deal in very trenchant fashion with outbursts of religious hysteria. Yet it is impossible to avoid the suspicion that St Sulpice, with its intense inwardness and scrupulosity, its love of Direction and probings of conscience, did much to foster the growth of that morbid

[1] See Faillon, Vie de M. Olier (Paris, 1873), iii. pp. 117-127.
[2] Wks., vii. p. 392.

element in Fénelon's character, which, twenty years later, made him a ready listener to M$^{me.}$ Guyon.

None the less, the Seminary did him great and lasting service. Its stubborn pedantic unworldliness, its straightforward singleness of purpose, were the best of disciplines for one whose leading characteristic was not simplicity, whose manifold talents needed the reminder that culture and brilliance are little enough without a moral foundation. Nay, the grave sweetness, the reasonable tenderness of the greater Spiritual Letters or the Education of Girls, is nothing other than the religion of M. Olier, softened by a larger knowledge of God and man, and moulded by an artist of transcendent power.

And in this home of piety and study Fénelon laid the foundations of that happy union of Greek with Christian antiquity, whose results will meet us in the Dialogues on Eloquence and Télémaque. There was even a time, soon after his ordination, when he dreamed of a missionary journey to the Levant, drawn thither ' not only by a desire to make the voice of the Apostle heard once more in the Church of Corinth, or to stand on that Areopagus from which St Paul had preached to the Sages of this world an unknown God, but also by a wish to breathe in among those precious monuments and ruins the very essence of the antique.' "After the Sacred comes the Profane; I do not scorn to descend from the Areopagus to the Piræus, where Socrates sketched the plan of his Republic; I shall mount to the double summit of Parnassus; I shall pluck the laurels of Delphi; I shall revel in the joys of Tempe."[1]

This project, however, was not doomed to be fulfilled. Fénelon abandoned it in deference to the wishes of his family, and devoted himself to work in the parish of St Sulpice, till, in 1678, he was appointed Superior of the New Catholics of Paris, a position soon to become of some importance. Meanwhile his relatives interested themselves

[1] Wks., vii. p. 491.

warmly in his fortunes; the Marquis de Fénelon received him into his house and hastened to introduce him to his friends; another uncle, the Bishop of Sarlat, tried to secure his election to the Assembly of the Clergy of 1675, as a Proctor for the Province of Bordeaux, and made over to him, a few years later, the little Deanery of Carénac, a sinecure, whose value—about £400 a year of modern money—was hardly proportionate to the pomp with which the new Dean took possession.

"I must certainly," wrote Fénelon to one of the ladies of his family, "be a man destined to make magnificent entries. A deputy of the local nobility, the Rector, the Prior of the Monastery, with a few farmers, representing the Third Estate, came to escort me in state from Sarlat to the port of Carénac. The quay was lined with masses of people; two boats, filled with the *élite* of the neighbourhood, approached me on arrival, and I noticed that the most warlike soldiery the place could furnish were hidden by a gallant stratagem in the pretty island you know well. Thence they marched forth in battle array, and saluted me with such a deafening roar of musketry that the air was filled with smoke, and my fiery steed would certainly have thrown himself into the water, had I not had the moderation to dismount. Everyone made instant way for me, every eye sought to read its owner's destiny in mine, as I proceeded to the Castle with slow and stately pace, the better to lend myself to the public curiosity. Drums and cheers accompanied my route; at least a thousand voices cried that I should certainly be the darling of my people. At the Castle gate the Consuls harangued me by the mouth of their Royal Orator, an officer whose eloquence was fully worthy of his exalted station. He compared me to the sun; soon afterwards I became the moon; every one of the more radiant stars had the honour of resembling me, and so we passed on through the Four Elements and the meteors, and finished up happily with the Creation of the World. By this time the sun had sunk to rest; and I, to complete my likeness to him, hastened to my bed-room and prepared to do the same." [1]

To this early period, also, belongs the beginning of Fénelon's intimacy with Bossuet, lately become the leading figure of the Church of France; and it was at Bossuet's instance that he embarked on his first serious work, a Refutation of some of the errors of the famous contemporary metaphysician, Father Malebranche.[2] By this friendship, however, he forfeited the good-will of his own diocesan, Archbishop de Harlai, who, incensed at the brilliant young Abbé's rare appearance at his levées, told him, on one occasion, that his wish to be forgotten would certainly be respected. But Fénelon's career was not to be made or marred by the dispositions of a profligate courtier, whose sun of favour was already setting before the rise of Mme de Maintenon; nor could de Harlai ever have been very zealously inclined towards a nephew of the stern old devotee, who had once publicly reminded him that Louis XIV. was not the only Master to whom prelates must give in an account of their stewardship. A road to favour, at once more sure and more congenial, was opened to Fénelon when he became acquainted, through the good offices of his uncle, with that devout section of the aristocracy, which M$^{me.}$ de Maintenon was soon to raise to power.

Meanwhile, the young Abbé, in his modest situation at the New Catholics, was being brought into the vortex of calamities and scandals, that eddied round the Revocation of the Edict of Nantes, and forced to take a side on one of the greatest questions of the age, the question of Religious Toleration.

[1] Wks., vii. p. 394.   [2] See below, c. xii.

CHAPTER II

TOLERATION AND THE PROTESTANTS

Truth is compared in Scripture to a streaming fountain; if her waters flow not in a perpetual progression, they sicken into a muddy pool of conformity and tradition.—MILTON, AREOPAGITICA.

HE would write imperfectly indeed on Fénelon's relation to the Protestants who did not begin by warning his readers against the legend of that churchman's tolerance invented by the eighteenth century. From the time when Voltaire said that M. de Cambrai, had he only been born in England, would have become a genuine thinker, and Rousseau wished to have been his footman, Fénelon has been a favourite with the philosophers, to be honoured not merely as a vague precursor of the modern world in general, but as the harbinger of each particular reform, and more especially of Liberty of Conscience. And the reason is not far to seek. Careless enough of history themselves, the French reformers knew their world, and saw how far more closely it listens to the Prophets who dimly foreshadowed a new gospel in the past, than to the Apostles, who, in the fulness of time, preach it in all its light and dignity. Hence their devotion to retrospective proselytism, to the furbishing up of a roll of such prophets, swept together by hasty zeal rather than by critical sagacity, as unconscious witnesses to the new Revelation; hence their crowning of many a great name with posthumous honours from which the living man would have shrunk, as from a brand of disgrace.

Strange and eclectic indeed are many of their lists of heroes. There Francis of Sales and Fénelon take high place, because they showed some kindness to misbelievers;

and by their side stand the philosophic sceptics, glorified because they could place Judaism or Islam on a level with the religion of Jesus. As though freedom of conscience had really been the work of a handful of priests, merciful in their strength to heterodox weakness, or of scornful Epicureans, to whom every religion was equally false and equally useful, and not of men to whom Liberty of Prophesying was as the very breath of God, the first article of Faith, a dogma more sacred than any creed of the Churches! These were the true Apostles of Toleration; among them is no place for Catholic prelates, nor for any that believed wrong theological opinions to be a deliberate insult to God, or heresy a natural punishment of sin.

The stage Fénelon of Revolutionary drama, who releases imprisoned nuns from their convents, and piteously bewails the bigotry that, during five reigns, had been the curse of France, is a being more wholly imaginary than most of the characters of his Télémaque; his tolerance is a *fata morgana*, projected, in part, indeed, from some real acts of kindness towards the Protestants, but chiefly from the political idealism of his writings, from his many points of likeness to the coming century, or from the tradition of his Saturnian reign at Cambrai. The real man, who in politics, education and literature, often saw a long way into the future, remained, in matters of ecclesiastical policy, a docile son of the Church.

And the Catholicism of the seventeenth century not only believed firmly in its inherited prerogative of correction, but was resolute to exercise its right. Bossuet, at once the oracle and the faithful echo of Gallican opinion, was far from showing towards heretics the unbending severity of a St Bernard, yet Bossuet's voice knew no uncertain tones when the time came to speak of the Revocation of the Edict of Nantes. One of his great sermons hails this infamy as 'the miracle of our days,' 'the greatest achievement of the second Constantine, and the true characteristic of his reign,' 'the proof that his merits even exceed his power'; while Fénelon, then actually engaged on a mission to the

Protestants, wrote to beg that his master's words might come to charm his provincial solitude, after confounding the rash criticisms of Paris.[1]

Again and again did Fénelon give the anticipatory lie to the legend of his tolerance. The word, in his mouth, is a synonym of godless impiety ; it means 'that cowardly indulgence, that false compassion, which could let the gangrene of disobedience creep over the whole body of the people, rather than nerve itself to sever the festering limb at one sharp blow.[2] The Church must use towards her stiff-necked children a remedial harshness, a terrible kindness, and herein her efforts must be seconded by the civil power : sword in hand, the Prince must stand at the gate of the sanctuary to protect her from her external enemies, so that she may freely pronounce, approve, correct, and to enforce her decrees on all innovators and contemners of her authority within the realm.'[3]

This is no grudging acceptance of an unwelcome dogma, but the frank avowal of an inward conviction. Even in Télémaque, Fénelon could not conceive of a Church unsupported by the secular arm. Idomeneus, no less than Louis, must force his subjects to obey the Etrurians, who are skilled in the oracles of the gods.[4] In truth, he was nearer to the Middle Ages than he thought for : God was still the feudal overlord of the sovereign and heresy a form of universal revolt, an impious defiance of the Heavenly Source, whence flowed all lawful power.

Then, too, his education and surroundings did much to harden Fénelon's heart against the Huguenot Dissenters. Puritanism, at its best, is an uncompanionable Faith, and the rugged sterling manly qualities, that marked, not only the inner life, but the very gait and dress and language of

---

[1] Wks. vii. p. 493. The sermon in question is the Oraison Funèbre du Chancelier le Tellier, who had drawn up the Edict of Revocation just before his death.

[2] *Ibid*, v. p. 182. Fénelon is here speaking of the Jansenists.

[3] *Ibid*, p. 606.   [4] Tél, bk. xvii. (Wks., vi. p. 552).

the Protestants of France, was of all qualities the most repugnant to the light-hearted genius of the nation. Their rude and uncourtly independence, their violent and insulting methods of controversy, their braggart austerity of life, excited the disgust of minds less squeamish than Fénelon's, and hid from eyes that were little disposed to seek it, all evidence of the noble qualities that lay beneath. By seventeenth century public opinion the Huguenot was pictured as a being offensive to God, pilloried as an outcast by the Law, and hardly deserving of compassion from his fellow-men, since the creed which set him apart was grounded on a blind and wilful prejudice, inexpugnable by reason, but generally yielding to a skilfully awakened cupidity or fear. The history of Northern Europe was an eternal warning against his errors; there the pretended Reformation had its root in pride, ran its troubled course through scandals, quarrels, and incertitude, till it ended in a godless indifference.[1]

But it would be unfair to set down the whole of Fénelon's antipathy to social prejudice; beneath it lay a deep conviction of the necessary and essential wickedness of Protestantism. In one of his sermons he declares it hard to explain why the Divine Mercy should suffer its longer continuance; and we, who have read the sermon, shall find it easy to see how a good man could bring himself, not only to persecute, but to proselytize.

"Trembling we must adore that inscrutable counsel, that unfathomable judgment of God, which delivers over to heresy so many young children, who, at an age so tender, suck in poison with their mother's milk, whose misfortune is brought about by the blind tenderness of the parents whom God hath appointed for them, so that their very docility leads them astray. Yet, since we know that God is the Father of all men, and wills the destruction of none, we must suppose that His Eye has detected in their heart a secret corruption, invisible to our human sight, which is inured to

[1] Wks., i. p. 203.

grosser sin. He marks the deadly seriousness, which shows itself in innocent childish pastimes, the feeble reason that believes itself to be strong, the presumptuousness that nought can check, the blind love of self that teaches idolatry, and it is this which He strikes with blindness."[1]

Nevertheless good men find it easier to utter bad maxims than to act up to them. Bossuet remonstrated successfully against some of the most odious clauses in the Edict of Revocation; Fénelon told the Elector of Cologne that correction, like those medicines with which poison was mingled, must be used sparingly and with infinite precaution. Rigour stirred up the last vestiges of pride and left in the heart a secret and quickly mortifying wound; the guide of souls would find a better though a slower, road to success in kindly insinuation care and patience, since he must win the affection and confidence of his penitents before he could hope to lead them to the Love of God.[2]

These words describe the method which Fénelon sought to follow in all his dealings with the Protestants, but especially in the scenes of his earliest missionary activity, the convents of New Catholics in Paris. If his conduct often fell below this standard, the fault lay not so much with himself, or even his ecclesiastical superiors, as with the iron-handed tyranny of ministers who 'played the Bishop' and themselves directed the whole business of conversion.

Even the New Catholics was far more of a Government establishment than a religious society; it was managed and subsidized by the administration in furtherance of its old policy of sapping the foundations of Protestantism. Long before Louis XIV. had begun to persecute in earnest, his government had encouraged persecution by private effort, mostly in the form of legally kidnapping Huguenot children in order to bring them up in the State religion.[3] This

---

[1] Sermon preached at the taking of the veil by a newly converted Protestant.— Wks., v. p. 655.
[2] Vol. v. p. 613.   [3] Douen, Intolérance de Fénelon, p. 11.

abominable practice had brought the 'New Catholic' sisterhood into being; their convents were the workshops, in which Protestant girls, snatched from their homes against their own wish and without their parents' consent, were transformed into Catholics as expeditiously as possible. It is true that official language otherwise described them—they were "salutary retreats for the newly converted from the persecution of their relatives and the artifices of the heretics"[1]—but, in practice, the only actual converts to Rome were a small number of ladies whose abjuration of Calvinism had been so flagrantly insincere as to fail to satisfy the consciences of the police.[2] The bulk of the inmates were Protestants, committed to the charge of the Mother Superior by a Secretary of State, and ordered, in some cases, to make their submission to the Church within a fortnight of their entry, on pain of incurring the royal displeasure.[3] Those who were careless of these threats and deaf to the persuasive eloquence of Fénelon—and they were not a few—were removed to other convents or subjected to the sharper discipline of a fortress or a prison; the oldest were banished the kingdom as irreclaimable.[4]

It is not likely that Fénelon had a large share in these horrors. He seems to have been little more than Warden or Visitor of the convent, its concerns being entirely managed by the Mother Superior, acting under the minute direction of the Government. Whatever his position, he was powerless for good or ill; mild counsels would not be attended to, and might even draw down suspicion on himself; severities would only breed hypocrisy and endanger his influence with his charges.

But, at the worst, severity was only for those who would not hear him; for the rest was never teacher more gracious. They were no longer under the ban of Protestantism, but souls which it was his bounden duty to save, hearts which his nature, always greedy of affection, longed to fill with love of himself. And therefore all his gifts were at their

[1] Douen, p. 8. [2] *Ibid.* p. 84. [3] *Ibid.* p. 66. [4] *Ibid.* p. 81.

service—that marvellous power of fascination, against which St Simon, his enemy, struggled almost in vain, the gravely facile manner that could set the most awkward at their ease, the intellectual tact that brought clearness and simplicity into the thorniest subjects and quickly found the level of his dullest hearer's comprehension.[1]

And we may fancy that, like his own Mentor, all that he said was short, precise, and nervous. He never repeated himself, was never decoyed into side-issues ; but, if he must return more than once to the same matter, it was always in a different fashion, with new and striking metaphors, with fresh appeals to the imagination.[2] There was no straining or importunity, but a gentle, constant pressure, quick to seize on every passing mood, every moment of weakness, and slow to give up its once-gained advantage.[3] Then, too, the perfect courtesy, always master of itself, that so often put to the blush the snappish impertinences of Protestant controversialists,[4] must have had a double charm when it flowed straight from his lips in answer to some objection, or robbed of its sting, but not of its point, the delicate raillery that lightly pricked the bubbles of the Calvinistic argument. For Fénelon had an art beyond the satirist : he did not care to make his adversary seem odious or foolish in the minds of others : he wished to make him feel ashamed of himself. It is to the conscience of the Huguenot, and not to the plaudits of the Catholic gallery, that he is appealing when he dwells on the absurdity of a Church, whose voice is ' as the discordant shrieking of many contradictory sects, of a Body of Christ that is not a body, but a monstrous amalgam of independent and quarrelsome members, of a City of God built up by pride and confusion of tongues, of a Bride of Christ, who receives into her bosom a host of adulterers and corrupted sects, from the impious

---

[1] St Simon, xi. p. 59.   [2] See Télémaque, bk. ix.   Wks. vi. p. 467.
[3] See Wks., vii. p. 500.
[4] *Cf.* His treatment of Jurieu, Wks. i. pp. 199 and *ff.*, in the Treatise on the Ministry of Pastors, published in 1688, a work on the Apostolic Succession, of no very general interest.

Arian, who denies his Lord, down to the Papist, less tolerable in his idolatry than the heathen.'[1]

Yet Fénelon was far too wise to strike always at his enemy's weakest point; he knew that attack is far more deadly when it can afford to praise where praise is due. And therefore he does full justice, as he thinks, to the more impressive side of Protestantism; he speaks with respect of its zeal for learning, of its striking prayers and sermons, its imposing psalmody; he praises its severity of discipline, its hatred of the coarser vices, its steadfast resistance to abuses.

And he could do so truthfully, since, in his view, the best qualities of Protestantism were a distorted reflexion of Catholic virtues, stray fragments of the Church's scheme of holiness, but cast and moulded in an alien furnace, till their original significance was lost. For their mainspring was not humility, but pride, pride duly ordered and turned to account and christened with more seemly names, yet, none the less, giving its moroseness to the Protestant's courage, its bitterness to his enthusiasm, its Pharisaical gall to his austere morality. Between the difference of dogmas lay a deeper difference of spirit; the life of the Protestant was argument, but the life of the Catholic was prayer; the one tried hard to reform the Church; the other was satisfied if he could reform himself. The Protestant spoke to men of God, the Catholic spoke to God for men, praying Him to accomplish, in His own good pleasure, that which no feebler hand could bring about.[2]

And so Fénelon draws out his chain of antitheses between the natural piety of the New Faith and the supernatural piety of the Old; nor ever dreamed that a later world, securely judging, might reverse his verdict, and hold that creed highest which could be natural and supernatural alike, not a Catholicism of fixed collective laws, external to and far above mankind, but the Protestantism

---

[1] Wks., i. p. 200.
[2] See the Letters on the Church, Wks., i. p. 202 and *ff*.

of inward individual Freedom, that enters into the very marrow of man's being, becomes bone of his bone, and flesh of his flesh.

Such was Fénelon in his dealings with individual souls, the tenderest and most persuasive of monitors: it is only in contact with large masses of persons that the darker shades in his Catholicism appear, to mark the difference between a Church grounded on "pure reasoning" and one that is built on "pure authority."

In 1685, Louis XIV., by revoking the Edict of Nantes, put an end to the legal existence of Protestantism in France, and thereby made a long step towards the attainment of his cherished project, the levelling of every independent element in the national life. For it was not only his bigotry that hated the Protestants—Louis cared little for the glory of God, unless it was associated with the glory of the King of France—but he believed that religious uniformity was the best road to political absolutism, and that its worst enemy was 'the sect which had become a state within the state, dependent on the King no more than it chose, always loud in complaints, and ready, on the slightest pretext, to embroil the whole kingdom by an appeal to arms.'[1] For about ten years penal edicts had been falling thick and fast, and now that the King found himself at peace with his neighbours, yet with a large army idle on his hands, he was easily persuaded to strike the final blow. Grossly misinformed as to the numbers and courage of the Huguenots, he believed that their conversion would be easily effected; 'force a little more than moral' would soon crush the resistance of a dying sect, and then, as Mme. de Maintenon said, even if there were some hypocrisy among the adults, their children, would, at anyrate, be gained to the Church.[2]

The Government's plan was alternate force and moral suasion, missionaries in cassocks following on the heels of

[1] St Simon, xiii. p. 86.   [2] Geffroy, i. pp. 298-299.

missionaries in spurs. A military force was drafted into each of the infected districts, quartered on the Protestant householders, and encouraged to neglect no means of terrifying its involuntary hosts out of their heterodox beliefs. As soon as a satisfactory number had been converted—and the process was rapid, twenty-four hours often sufficing to conduct the proselyte from torture to abjuration, and from abjuration to Communion—the soldiers were withdrawn and replaced by eminent preachers from the capital. "Father Bourdaloue," wrote M$^{me.}$ de Sévigné, "is going to preach at Montpelier, where so many have been converted without knowing why; but the Father will explain it all, and will make good Catholics of them. Hitherto the Dragoons have been excellent missionaries, but the clergy, now to be sent, will complete the work."

What the Jesuit orator was to do in the South, the young Superior of the New Catholics was to carry out on the west of Saintonge, in and about the famous Protestant citadel of La Rochelle. The ground had been well prepared by *dragonades*; the chapels were closed, the pastors all imprisoned, and soldiers were still at work in the neighbourhood when Fénelon arrived, in December, 1685, at the head of a number of priests.[1] The mission lasted till the harvest-time of the next year, July, 1686, and was renewed for a few months in the year next following, May to July, 1687.

Fénelon reports the people in a state of heart-rending agitation, clinging 'with terrible obstinacy' to their creed, and turning a deaf ear to the voice of the Roman enchantress, yet so panic-stricken at the sight of a soldier that they would embrace the Koran to be rid of him.[2] The most sanguine longed for the appearance of a delivering fleet from Holland, the rest were eager to fly the country at the first opportunity; escape, even with the sailors, was becoming a point of honour, and every deserter, sooner or

---

[1] Douen, p. 120. [2] Wks., vii. p. 498.

later, dragged his family after him.¹ Hunger, too, was conspiring with the Government to make their state more miserable; they had lost their alms from the Protestant consistory; they were oppressed with new taxes; the salt-trade, their one resource, was at an end; foolish interference was ruining even the commerce of La Rochelle. Fénelon's first demands were for a largess of corn, the best form of argument for the famine-struck, and for a redoubling of the coast-guard to prevent desertion; but there could be, he said, no hope of spiritual progress till it had become more agreeable to remain in the country than it was dangerous to leave it.²

Against a vile enemy vile arms. Fénelon was not content to alleviate Protestant misery; forgetting one of the noblest maxims of his Télémaque,³ he threw himself into the work of encouraging conversion by the use of the very earthliest means. He sang the praises of Cardinal Pellisson, once a Huguenot, and now conscience-broker to the Court, for 'employing the graces of his Prince to rescue his brethren from error;[4] among his proselytes he promoted wholesale dissimulation, bribery and espionage; he improvised farcical disputations for the edification of Huguenot gentlemen, in which he himself, in the character of Protestant advocate, was gloriously routed by one of his subordinate priests.⁵ Nay, finding the people much encouraged by the pastoral letters which their great leader, Jurieu, addressed them from abroad, he advised his Government to employ a Dutch Socinian enemy of the great Huguenot to write libellous pamphlets against him, such as would find their way to France in the guise of genuine Protestant literature.⁶

¹ Douen, p. 333. The letters from which I here quote were first published by the Abbé Verlaque in 1874, very incorrectly. The texts were amended by M. Gazier in the same year, and are printed in the corrected form by Douen in the second edition of his book under the heading of Appendices viii. and ix.

² Wks., vii. pp. 196, 198.

³ See Télémaque's speech in bk. xv. on honour and good faith. Wks., vi. p. 532.   ⁴ Wks. vi. p. 607.

⁵ Wks. vii. p. 199.   ⁶ Douen, p. 335.

TOLERATION AND PROTESTANTS

Nevertheless they were happy who, in that evil time, fell into the hands of Fénelon. He had vast patience, he had a statesman's eye, he had an abundant horror of sacrilege. Only one class was beyond the pale of his charity—to the deserters and irreclaimable heretics he would show no mercy; for them there was the *rigeur des peines*, solitary confinement, deportation to other provinces, where they might serve as hostages on the good behaviour of their families, even deportation to Canada.[1] Their steadfastness won no admiration from him. Others might be unpleasantly reminded by their tortures of the sufferings of the Early Church, but Fénelon was only struck by the different bearing of the victims: the martyrs had been humble and fearless and without dissimulation; the Huguenots were stubborn and cowardly, and ready for any hypocrisy.[2]

The remainder he would treat with a cautious kindness, with a severity that was not rigour. Like disobedient children they must see the rod always uplifted over them; their conventicles must be prohibited, their heretical literature taken away. Their children must be forced to go to Catholic schools; they themselves must be driven to Mass by vague threats, to sermon by fines large enough to be galling but insufficient to cause desertion.[3] On the other hand Fénelon begged for certain graces from the Government; their clergy must be equal in capacity and learning to the ejected pastors; the State must furnish supplies and competent teachers for their schools; there must be free distribution of New Testaments and books of Catholic piety printed in large type; alms should be given to the well-disposed according to the excellent system of the Consistories.[4] And Fénelon even brought down suspicion on his head by leaving out of his sermons the customary Invocation to the Virgin, and by proposing that some special prayers and Bible-reading should be added to the religious services attended by the heretics.[5]

---

[1] Douen, p. 331.   [2] Wks., vii. p. 493.   [3] Douen, p. 332.
[4] p. 328.   [5] Wks., vii. p. 196, see p. 494.

But he knew that the harvest was still far from ripe. Very few were really converted, though the opinions of all were profoundly shaken, and many held back out of mere shame-facedness or irresolution. The resistance of these last, he thought, would be overcome by a few little civilities and indulgences on the part of the Government, but with the majority progress would be slow indeed—there was no hope but patient perseverance.[1] Weariness of their present state and confidence in their clergy would do much, but habit would do more; they would in time become accustomed to the Catholic services, and—such is human nature!—would be ashamed of going to church only to save payment of a fine.[2] But there must be no forcing of consciences, no throwing of the body into a sewer because a man had died without the sacraments; such violence might make them crowd to the altar, but it would be only at the price of appalling sacrilege and hypocrisy.[3]

To us this measure of clemency seems bare and scanty enough; in Fénelon's own time it was both unusual and effective. His counsels of mercy had weight with the Minister, and led to the suppression of various abuses, civil as well as ecclesiastical; they manifestly gained for him the affection of his proselytes, and, stirring up against him the bile of the more rigid Catholics, seem to have stood in the way of his early promotion to a Bishopric.

Yet the Saintonge Mission, on the whole, is a dark page in Fénelon's life. Those whose view of history is still "a study in snow and ink, tender innocents on the one side, and on the other bloody persecutors," will not long hesitate over their verdict; and even more tolerant spirits may find something unpleasing in this young ecclesiastical statesman, so fertile in expedients, so ready to base his counsels of mercy, not on Christian feeling, but on policy, so keen to make his wisdom and successes tell in his own favour at the Court. Or they may ask, with Fénelon's greatest living critic, whether his zealous approval of the Revocation shows

---

[1] Douen, p. 323.   [2] p. 327.   [3] p. 316.

a really high degree of statesmanship, whether the extermination of these sturdy religionists made in the best interests of Catholicism itself, whether the "purely metaphysical delight of hearing God's praises sung everywhere in Latin" was worth the loss of the strongest nerve in French morality.[1]

[1] See Brunetière, Études Critiques, v. pp. 212 and *ff*.

CHAPTER III

EARLY OCCUPATIONS AND FRIENDSHIPS

Both our nature and condition require, that each particular man should make particular provision for himself.—BISHOP BUTLER, TWELFTH SERMON.

"YOU will be unfaithful to God," once wrote Fénelon to Mme. de Maintenon, "if you hide under a bushel the light He has set upon a candle-stick," and certainly the lack of a reasonable worldly self-assertiveness is one of the last 'infidelities' that can be laid to Fénelon's own account. As evidence to the contrary, all his solemn disclaimers, his energetic preachings of Humility, go for nothing: was there ever a born diplomatist, more especially if he were a *méridional*, a son of the quick-blooded boastful South of France, who did not declare that only main force had dragged him to Court, away out of a beloved obscurity and refinement; or is it upon his own failings and vices that the lash of the honest preacher falls least heavily? Surprise Fénelon in a moment of confidence, and he will answer that the world still flatters him a little, much as he hates and despises it;[1] he will advise his favourite nephew to be detached from it by religion, yet understand the need of keeping it his friend, to choose his companions, 'not for their virtue only, but for merit set off by social position, or even a certain rank.'[2]

From his youth up, he held it his duty—and later, when he was old and far from the Court, it became his much-loved nephew's after him—to build up once more the shattered fortunes of their house. For the Fénelons were many and poor, most of them, too, feeble ineffectual creatures, who

---

[1] Wks., vii. p. 348. [2] *Ibid.*, pp. 432, 447.

MME. DE MAINTENON

FROM AN ENGRAVING

hung on to their distinguished relative's skirts, and begged him to help set their affairs in order, or get them some little favour from the King. Moreover, the young Churchman's heart was leavened with not a little pride of birth, scoff as he might from the pulpit at ancient names and pedigrees and titles, "honours won by ancestors long ago forgotten, and now often enough dragged through the mud by their unworthy heirs."[1] He was not ill-pleased, while tutor to the Duke of Burgundy, to be allowed a place at his pupil's table and in his carriage, privileges that had been denied to the middle-class Bossuet, while Preceptor to the little Prince's father, the Dauphin. There was much correspondence, also, with a favourite cousin as to whether a certain office at Court was 'honourable enough for her name of Laval,' and Fénelon's history, rich in trivial surprises, has none more curious than his estrangement from this very lady over the question of her son's beginning his service in the army. "Your boy is much to be pitied," wrote this author of Télémaque, this apostle of universal peace and brotherhood, in words that shocked her fond maternal tenderness, "for he has not yet been gazetted to a regiment, though he is close on twenty, an age at which most young men of his rank have been through two or three campaigns. Even if you have good reasons for keeping him at home, as I, of course, am ready to believe, scarcely a soul will understand them, for they are very extraordinary, and opposed to the strongest prejudices of the nation. Two painful courses, therefore, lie before your son, either to cast aside all filial duty and serve, or else to let himself be governed by you, and be for ever dishonoured in the public eye."[2]

But Fénelon knew his countrymen far too well to value their good opinion at more than its proper worth. If he lived in outward obedience to their standards, and forced his penitents 'to give the world whatever they could not well refuse it,' in return he held the world tightly to its part of the bargain, and expected, as the price of his conformity,

[1] Wks., v. p. 695.   [2] *Ibid.*, vii. p. 427.

to reap full measure of its advantages. And their agreement had reference only to matters external; Fénelon would never suffer his inner thoughts and fancies to be domineered over by the dry unimaginative commonsense of commonplace profundity—a slavery, as it seemed to him, 'even worse than bondage to the passions.'

But, within these limits, Fénelon gave himself free rein, knew what it was to 'grovel before those who are in the fashion,' caught 'a little air of easy playful raillery,' that was respectful, and even flattering, to the great, watched, with a vigilance as tactful as untiring, for every opportunity to please them, or to do them service. Christian scruple, perhaps, checked him from aiming directly at any particular place. "Your friends," wrote the wise old Superior of St Sulpice, M. Tronson, on Fénelon's nomination to the Court-Preceptorate, "will doubtless tell you that you did not ask for the appointment, and that is certainly just matter for rejoicing, though you must not pride yourself too much thereon. We have often more part in our own elevation than we think for; we do not deliberately seek it, but, half-unthinkingly, we smoothe away obstacles, and show ourselves in the most favourable light to persons in authority, and thus we can never be quite sure that we did not call ourselves to the office.[1] But Fénelon held on his course, M. Tronson notwithstanding, and told his conscience that it was not mere ambition or vanity that moved him —only an honourable zeal for his own and his family's advancement.

And truly Fénelon, at his very worst, was far from being the shameless scheming flatterer some of his enemies have made him. Worldly successes he pursued with much of the lively eager disinterestedness of the sportsman, looked on them as a comedy, a game of cards, as a refuge from the heavy clouds of gloom and *ennui* that hung about him in the background. "In this world of vanities," he said, "the truest wisdom is to let oneself be hoodwinked, to find amusement

[1] Wks., vii. p. 498.

in little childish trifles, for, if our days are short, our hours are long."[1]

Moreover, to Fénelon's rare combination of talents such triumphs came almost for the asking. For proof of this we need go no farther than that jovial, downright, gossiping Bavarian, the Duchess of Orleans, and her sketches of the brilliant young Churchman 'with deep-set eyes and ugly face all skin and bone, who talked and laughed quite unaffectedly and easily,'[2] or to Saint Simon's full-length portrait of our hero, as he appeared about the time of his appointment to Cambrai, tall, thin, well-built, pale with the exceeding pallor that has been called *pulchrum virorum illustrium colorem* by a Father of the Church, with a great nose, eyes from which fire and genius poured in torrents, a face curious and unlike any other, yet so striking and attractive that, once seen, it could never again be forgotten. There were to be found the most contradictory qualities in perfect agreement with one another, gravity and courtliness, earnestness and gaiety, the man of learning, the great noble and the bishop, but, above all, an air of high-bred dignity, of graceful, polished seemliness and wit—it cost an effort to turn away one's eyes.[3]

And Chancellor d'Aguesseau, the greatest lawyer of his age, falls also under Fénelon's spell, and speaks in wonder of his 'noble singularity, an indescribable compound of simplicity and grandeur, that gave him an almost prophetic air.' Yet, with all this, he was neither passionate nor masterful; though in reality he governed others, it was always by seeming to give way, and he reigned in society as much by the attraction of his manners as by the superior virtue of his parts. Under his hand the most trifling subjects gained a new importance, yet he treated the gravest with a touch so light that he seemed to have invented the sciences rather

---

[1] 127th Sp. Let. Wks., viii. p. 541.   [2] See her Letters, ed. Jaeglé, ii. p. 86.
[3] St Simon, xi. p. 58. St Simon was born in 1675, and presented at Court in 1691. His acquaintance with Fénelon was very slight, and they never met after 1697.

than learned them, for he was always a creator, always original, and himself was imitable of none.[1]

After the lawyer and the noble comes the man of letters; our last statutory witness must be La Bruyère, delivering his Inaugural Lecture to the French Academy. That solemn moment allowed of no expanse of detail, nor was the author of *Les Caractères* the most sympathetic of men; but he pays due passing homage to the powers of that rare genius, who was always master of the hearts and intellects of his hearers, whose ease and charm and greatness none could envy, for, whether he was explaining himself in conversation, or preaching a studied sermon, or holding an impromptu discourse, their only interest was to listen, to hear what he said and how he said it.

It was by means of his powers of speech that Fénelon first hoped to make his way in the world. During these earlier years he delivered nearly all his published sermons, and entered upon a serious study of the art of preaching, whose results he has embodied in his Dialogues on Eloquence.

For Eloquence, in the days of Bossuet and Bourdaloue, meant the oratory of the pulpit. In this field the Church reigned without a rival; there were no popular assemblies, the language of the Academy was stilted and unnatural, the great leaders of the Bar were absorbed in chamber-practice, and of the style of popular pleadings one of Fénelon's letters gives a sufficient account.

" I stayed an extra day at Sarlat to hear the provincial Ciceros argue out a famous cause. They began with the Creation of the World, and, after some remarks about the Flood, descended straight to the matter in hand, which was to ask the Court for a dole of bread for some orphans who had none. Their appetite was alluded to in a number of graceful euphuisms, mingled with a few sterner references to the Code, and every spectator of taste applauded the

[1] Wks., xiii. pp. 167 and *ff.*

OCCUPATIONS AND FRIENDSHIPS

artistic fashion in which their counsel passed from the Metamorphoses of Ovid to some of the most terrible passages of Holy Writ. We all thought that the children were sure of their dole, and that so rare an eloquence would keep their kitchen-fire forever alight. But alas for the inconstancy of fortune! Though the lawyer got plenty of praises, the children got no bread. The cause was adjourned, which means that the poor little wretches will have to plead again on an empty stomach, while the Bench went gravely to dinner."[1]

And even the Church had not escaped a taste for 'figures ill-paired and similes unlike.' The spirit of the Ciceros of Sarlat still spoke through the mouth of many a popular preacher of the capital, for, as La Bruyère will tell us, profane eloquence had quitted its true home, the Bar, to mount the pulpit, where it had no place. Sermons were become a mere display, to the preacher a means of advancement more rapid, though not less hazardous, than the profession of arms, to his hearers one among the thousand amusements of fashionable life. They came to criticize, not to learn; he strove to interest, not to teach; it was much if he remembered, by an afterthought, to slip in a word or two of praise to God.[2]

Formerly it had been necessary to have enormous learning in order to preach so badly, and country congregations were still edified by sermons in which there was more Greek and Latin than French. But now every curate was an orator, though he had neither wit nor piety nor eloquence, though he must fly for refuge to a Concordance or an Anthology, or else sew together ill-fitting passages from old sermons he had bought. However lacking he might be in solid theology, it was easy to abound in phrases and epigrams and showy misapplications of Scripture, in a network of reasoning all the more brilliant, because superficial and probably false.[3]

---

[1] Wks., vii. p. 395, and see the remarks of Lotheissen, iii. p. 395.
[2] See La Bruyère, De la Chaire, *passim*. [3] Fén. Wks., vi. p. 578.

Nor did the evils of the filagree style of pulpit oratory rest within that School itself; like all other such absurdities, it provoked a violent reaction. Under pretence of apostolic simplicity, numbers of zealous young men forswore eloquence altogether, and, with it, learning and lucidity and order; they did not even soberly expound the Scriptures, but 'froze our blood with their perspiring efforts,' as they roared and ranted, filling their sermons with the Devil and Hell, and thinking they had failed in their duty, unless they left the pulpit breathless and exhausted.[1]

But far above these pygmies rose the two giants Bossuet and Bourdaloue, differing much from one another, and leaders of rival schools of oratory, but alike in their perfect moderation of language, in their clearness and simplicity, in their recognition that "the highest law of the pulpit was the service of the children of God."[2]

Bossuet's was the oratory of Scripture. He was above all things a divine, one who made of his eloquence a stately, willing vassal of theology, though it found God tributaries in every realm of thought and feeling, in poetry, philosophy and history. Bourdaloue stood at the head of a colder school. Far poorer than Bossuet in natural gifts, less daring in thought, less splendid in imagination, he was a logician and a moralist, a great searcher of the human heart, busied with practice rather than dogmas, quicker to analyze than to teach: his sermons, said Fénelon, were magnificent reasonings about Christianity, but they were not religion.[1]

For Fénelon leaves no doubt about his sympathies; the Dialogues are through and through a plea for Bossuet, at the expense of the great Jesuit, who had supplanted him in popular favour. Bourdaloue is brought almost maliciously before the reader's eye, as he stood in his pulpit with eyes shut fast, his arms continually sawing the air, his voice

---

[1] p. 597.
[2] Bossuet, Sermon on the Conception of the Virgin: qu. Lanson, p. 102.

OCCUPATIONS AND FRIENDSHIPS 37

melodious but badly managed, with no more variety than a peal of bells. And his style is pronounced no less monotonous than his delivery; never for a moment easy or familiar, never tender, never grand or sublime, he ploughed his way through closely serried arguments and portraits of contemporary vices, often rousing by his logic the opposition of the intellect, but leaving the springs of passion untouched. And therefore his critic denies him the very title of orator: " He is a great man; he has done much for the pulpit, has delivered it from the rhetoricians, but—he has not eloquence."[1]

A judgment so sweeping, passed on one of the greatest orators that ever adorned the Church of France, might well seem a mere freak of juvenile impertinence. But Fénelon, who, all his life, was to keep much of the visionary hopefulness and extravagance of youth, had none of its irresponsible iconoclasm; ageless self-confidence had early given him an adult seriousness of mind, which, little as it cared for established reputations, was never at pains to attack them without just cause.

But with Bourdaloue and his following there was cause enough. Their colourless sense and solid exactitude grated at every step on Fénelon's more emotional nerves; his simpler palate was offended by their artificiality, by the rounded periods and polished aphorisms, that told of a long imprisonment in the study, to the neglect of the preacher's holier calls;[2] their brilliant useless moral sketches, which converted no one, and were listened to less like a sermon than a satire or a farce, came as a scandal to this stern young censor, who held that only virtuous which was useful.[3]

Against them he invokes his masters, the great orators of Greece and Rome. For he had studied with Demosthenes, who fired and swayed the heart, filled even to self-forgetfulness with love of his Republic, and much also with the

[1] p. 584. At the end of his life Fénelon spoke more kindly of Bourdaloue. See p. 615.   [2] p. 599.   [3] p. 572.

poets, for 'poetry only differs from eloquence in that it paints more boldly and with enthusiasm.'¹ From Homer he had learnt to prize the 'antique simplicity, for which we have lost all relish,' that preferred facts to reasons, details to generalities, and proved the greatness of such a man as Cyrus, not by any wealth of arguments or adjectives, but by telling the plain story of his life.² In Plato reason had forestalled religion to show how pleasure is the means of working, but virtue the final end of art, how all that stops short at mere diversion must be banished from the true Republic.³

And Bourdaloue's critic carried his appeal to loftier tribunals yet. Akin to the Greek in form and movement, almost in narrative and substance, was another literature still higher; Demosthenes must yield place to St Paul, and Homer to Moses and the Prophets, for the Scriptures, in their grand simplicity, were the true, the Divine, model of Christian eloquence.⁴

And so it was Fénelon came to wage his war on behalf of the Scriptural natural style of Bossuet, lord of his language, not the slave of its machinery, who needed no anxious preparation, no committal to memory of his phrases, but dare abandon himself to the impulse of the moment, and speak out of the abundance of his heart.⁵

Into a closer analysis of his master's genius Fénelon was too wise to enter, still less to try to reduce it to a code of formal rules. Eloquence, he held, was not to be learnt from books on Rhetoric; from Aristotle's 'dry and curious precepts' the pupil must turn to Longinus and his living, real examples, and 'study the Sublime sublimely' among those great ancient and modern masters, whose art it was to have no art.⁶ For Fénelon was of the same opinion as Erasmus,

---

[1] p. 581.
[2] p. 591, referring to the Cyropædia of Xenophon, afterwards (p. 646) seen to be a 'philosophical romance.'
[3] p. 571. [4] p. 596. [5] p. 587.
[6] p. 570. The Classics, however, are only a counsel of perfection: on peut s'en passer (p. 598). Longinus had been translated by Boileau in 1674.

OCCUPATIONS AND FRIENDSHIPS 39

who once bade men of letters despise the art of writing, after they had learned to write—"The whole secret of eloquence," he said, "lies in carefully watching what Nature does, when she is unconstrained."[1]

And already in the Dialogues are traces of a wish, afterwards more fully realized, to carry simplicity and naturalness to a still higher point than Bossuet; Fénelon, like La Bruyère, looks back wistfully to the Early Church and the informal homilies and pastoral instructions, whose day was now gone by.[2] These were far better suited to his genius than more elaborate discourses, for Fénelon had but little grasp of the majestic qualities of eloquence; on the few State occasions when he preached he was clearly cowed and ill at ease among surroundings that would have given Bossuet new strength, and there results therefrom a frigid, academic sermon, a polished, but lifeless, imitation of his master.[3]

And, as Fénelon's character developed, their differences became more clear. Bossuet was the Handel of oratory, the interpreter of grand, universal, ideas of Providence and Death and Immortality; he took his station far above mankind, judging and not being judged of men; they went away from his tribunal, more guilty, if not more virtuous, than they came. But Fénelon set before himself a higher model than Daniel or Ezekiel. Even the Apostles, he said, stumbled under the burden of their message, but Jesus Christ had all the calmness of a master. He needed no effort, but said whatsoever He would; He spoke of the Kingdom of Heaven as His Father's House. The glories that fill us with awe, were to Him a matter of course; He had been born among them, and told men only what He had seen Himself.[4]

The thought was not a new one: Pascal had bidden men notice how Jesus said great things so simply that He scarcely seemed to have thought of them, and yet so clearly

---
[1] p. 585.   [2] p. 603.
[3] See M. Gustave Merlet's introduction to his edition of the Epiphany Sermon. Paris: Hachette, 1880.   [4] p. 596.

that it was easy to see what He thought of them ; and to many Fénelon's love of simple directness will always seem a little suspect, as being not the perfection of art, but a refinement the more, not the child-like golden negligence he praised in La Fontaine, but the studied *naïveté* of the literary craftsman. But it served him as a guide, more especially after trouble and experience had deepened this early, somewhat dilettante, piety into a holier feeling ; it taught him the one secret unknown to Bossuet, the secret of that purely Christian eloquence whose only law is sympathy, that speaks to the people, not sternly as a prophet, but with the tenderness of a fellow-bondsman, who does not separate his lot from theirs, and has himself first reached the spiritual haven, into which he beseeches them to enter.[1]

Bossuet again preached a single sermon, clear and precise and incapable of misunderstanding, every word the exact translation of his thought : he spoke to great multitudes of great things, and left the invisible Monitor within to apply the lesson to each hearer's needs. But Fénelon's language, in the informal letters and discourses that are his truest sermons, has the curiously clinging elasticity peculiar to the mystics, who commonly will not imprison their meaning within a single definite formula, but give each phrase a double and a treble sense, turning and returning it till it can be seen in all its length and breadth, till each hearer can discover the application most suited to himself, and fancy that the preacher is addressing him alone. As Cardinal Bausset rightly says, it was just because Fénelon laid aside all general maxims and abstractions, because he coloured all his writings, now with one shade, now another, of his own most complex personality, that he found so many ready listeners ; for he had learned that 'Wisdom of the Spirit,' which has no rigid form or substance of its own, but measures its words by others' needs, instead of by its

---

[1] See the fine quotation from Massillon in Paul Albert, p. 282.

own enlightenment, and tells them just so much as they are able to bear.[1]

Endowed with these rare gifts of social tact and grace and sympathy, Fénelon's path lay clear before him. Why should he waste his powers on fruitless strivings in the pulpit, when it was his real vocation to be a great Director of Consciences? And the opportunity for the exercise of his talents was not long in coming. While still quite young he had been made known through the good offices of his uncle, the Marquis de Fénelon, to the two men who were destined to be his early patrons in the world, and life-long disciples in the Spirit, the Dukes of Beauvilliers and Chevreuse.

These two noblemen and their wives were characteristic figures of the age of M$^{me.}$ de Maintenon, a period when France was atoning for the loss of her earlier literary and political brilliance in the practice of an assiduous and often morbid piety. The cloister, it is true, had ceased to be the only home of religion; after a life of unbridled license, men no longer threw themselves into a Carthusian habit, like the Catholic Leaguers of the previous century, the better to make their peace with God; though the doors of a convent still stood widely open to the desolate or repentant woman of the world. But, in revenge, the monastic spirit had put off its peculiar dress, and come out into the world, there to embody itself in the Duke of Beauvilliers, of whom his ardent friend, St Simon, records that he was early touched by God, and never lost His Presence, but lived entirely in the future world, indifferent to places and cabals and worldly advantage, content, when called to the Council-Board, simply to state his true opinion, without much caring whether it was followed or no, but sitting there like a monk who should be exemplary in his attendance at the offices, yet think it enough to repeat the Psalms in their accustomed rhythm, bringing little of his heart or his attention to bear thereon.[2]

[1] See the 25th Spir. Letter. Wks., viii. p. 461.
[2] St Simon, vii. pp. 10 and *ff*.

Not that he was deliberately neglectful of his public or private duties; his were the virtues of the monk doubled on those of the perfect official. Punctual and orderly to excess, he controlled his household with an almost too vigilant kindness, managed his property with the most scrupulous care, and laid on his shoulders, as the King himself bore witness, a load of administrative detail, that would have killed four other men.[1]

But he was wretchedly unfit for any high position, narrow and bigoted in his views, especially in all that affected the Church, so timid that he treated the King, 'not with reverence, but with positive idolatry,' cowed in the presence of those who disagreed with him, unless his conscience or his prejudices were deeply roused, when he would flame forth, sometimes into real decision and statesmanship, sometimes into an unreasoning warmth and obstinacy, the fruits, as Fénelon used to tell him, of an overheated imagination.[2]

And, in Society, his natural shyness, fostered by a neglected education and an intensely Christian wish to set a guard upon his eyes and ears and lips, made the Court a very desert to him; so that even when, as a principal minister, he was the observed of all observers, when Princes and nobles were thronging around him, he stood aside in timid lofty shyness, freezing all who came across him by his solemn primness and reserve.[3]

Dull, decorous and prudent, he was the very opposite of his brother-in-law, the far more interesting and original Duke of Chevreuse; though the two lived together so intimately that there seemed only one set of thoughts between them, nor, says St Simon, did Providence ever interfere in this arrangement, except to prevent Beauvilliers from putting one of Chevreuse's magnificent plans into execution. For Chevreuse, although as devout as his brother-in-law,

---

[1] Proyart, Vie du Dauphin, Père de Louis XV., i. p. 8.
[2] St Simon ix., p. 4; see Fén. Wks., vii. p. 244.
[3] St Simon, x. p. 276.

OCCUPATIONS AND FRIENDSHIPS 43

but broader-minded, and much more able and well-informed, was the most erratic figure at Versailles, a kind of logical Don Quixote, 'always ill of reasoning, the greatest distiller of quintessences there ever was.'[1] Revelling in the most far-fetched and impracticable paradoxes, he had wit and flow of language enough to give his sophisms an appearance of perfect clearness and good sense; let him advance the simplest proposition, and his hearer was vanquished —laugh as he might at the absurdity of the Duke's conclusions, he could find no joint in his argumentative armour.[2]

His whole life was laid out on abstract geometrical principles. Such was his desire to live by Reason alone, that he could not come to the most trifling decision without brooding for hours over the state of his mind, to make sure that the intellectual purity of his motives was not in any way dimmed by passion or caprice.[3] Of delicate health and a sufferer from gout, he doctored himself on 'speculative principles of medicine,' eating little, but consuming quinine in inordinate quantities, and ready to poison himself with chicory-water at dinner, rather than forego his bumper of spiced wine at dessert.[4]

His property, managed entirely by himself, and according to the strictest axioms of mathematics, fared even worse than his health; had it not been for the King, he must have died a beggar, for he had little of his own, and his wife's large fortune was wasted on costly, but futile, experiments, such as the canals, made at enormous expense, to float down the timber from woods which he sold, before ever a tree was felled.[5]

Always behind-hand, always lost among details and side-issues, he began many things, but never finished one. He had no fixed days or hours for anything, found it as hard to go to bed as it was to get up in the morning, seldom arrived at dinner before the fruits were on the table, would

---

[1] St Simon ix. p. 122. [2] *Ibid.* p. 382.
[3] Fén. Wks., vii. p. 223. [4] St Simon, ix. p. 383. [5] *Ibid.* p. 349.

keep his carriage waiting for a dozen hours at a stretch. Yet, with all this, says St Simon, he was not simply loved, but adored, by his family and friends and servants. Throughout his troubles—and they were many—he was never for a moment cast down, but offered up his all to God, and fixed his eyes on Him. No man possessed his soul in greater peace than he: as the Scripture says, he carried it in his hand.[1]

The lack of social capacity in the two Dukes—for Chevreuse, though more accessible than Beauvilliers, was stiff and shy to those who did not know him well, was in some degree atoned for by their wives, both daughters of the famous minister, Colbert. Brusque and imperious, yet kindly and self-controlled, with a caustic wit that sparkled in her eyes, even when her piety forbade its utterance, and finer taste and intellect than any other woman of her time, $M^{me.}$ de Beauvilliers, had she chosen, might have had the whole Court at her feet.[2] And $M^{me.}$ de Chevreuse did so choose; far less gifted than her sister, she had all the charms of face and figure, that in $M^{me.}$ de Beauvilliers were rather conspicuously wanting, as well as the little social graces, which the elder Duchess despised. Introduced immediately on her marriage to the gaieties of the Court, she had, says St Simon, a freedom and uprightness quite peculiar to herself, yet always managed to be on good terms with the King, the Queen, the mistresses, and that not only without truckling, but without the slightest effort. Her extraordinary virtue and piety were another source of favour, for the King and $M^{me.}$ de Maintenon were proud of having in their train a prodigy of saintliness, whose godly doings passed all belief, even of those who had her continually before their eyes.[3]

Yet it was not their religion only that brought these pious persons into royal favour; to the King, Beauvilliers'

---

[1] St Simon, pp. 383-4. See x. p. 292.
[2] x. p. 294; and see Fén. Wks., vii. p. 296.
[3] ix. pp. 387, etc.

OCCUPATIONS AND FRIENDSHIPS 45

merits were hardly more endearing than his defects. Himself of slender intellect, but with boundless powers of application, ambitious enough and firm of purpose, yet woefully narrow in his ideas, Louis was ready to sacrifice everything to the fetish of his own authority, loving to govern for the sake of governing, to stretch out the tendrils of his power over the farthest corners of his Kingdom, and suck up, in return, into his own incomparable dignity every excellence, every fine achievement, of his people's life. For years he had been thwarted by the will of Ministers stronger than himself—Chevreuse, says St Simon, was the only wise and witty man with whom he really felt at ease, for he was reassured by that air of trembling modesty, which was also the chief merit of Beauvilliers.[1] But Colbert died in 1683; the happy year, 1691, delivered him of two men grown most intolerable, Louvois, the great War Minister, last of the tyrannical giants, and Seignelai, Colbert's brilliant son: thenceforward he could reign alone, supreme over a ministry of titled clerks. Beauvilliers was called to the Treasury in 1685, to the Council Board in 1691; Chevreuse, though he held no seals, was consulted about most departments, Louis finding both interest and amusement in the outbursts of tumultuous verbiage that the Duke was apt to take for inspirations from on High.[2]

But Louis alone did not make the Beauvilliers; they would scarcely have raised themselves out of the ruck of virtuous unimportant courtiers, had they not gained the special favour of the lady, into whose hands the keeping of the royal conscience passed. Their rise coincides exactly with the beginning of the reign of M$^{me.}$ de Maintenon, that strange grand-child of the sturdy old Huguenot, Agrippa d'Aubigné, whose unexampled career,[3] beginning in her father's prison, was to lead her, first, into marriage with the

---

[1] v. p. 402.   [2] Fén. Wks., vii. p. 238.
[3] M$^{me.}$ de Maintenon was born in Niort gaol in 1635, became a Catholic, 1649, married Scarron, 1652, left a widow, 1660, became governess to Montespan's children, 1670, gradually ousted Montespan 1677-1679. In 1683 the Queen died, and (probably in the next year) M$^{me.}$ de Maintenon was married to Louis.

poet Scarron, next into the post of governess to the King's children by Mme. de Montespan, and left her, after she had supplanted her friend in the royal affections, not the mistress, but the lawful wife, of the proudest King in Christendom. It was the anomaly of her situation that first drew Mme. de Maintenon to the Beauvilliers, for the austere little circle had notoriously refused to bow down before the royal mistresses, and their friendship, therefore, bore serviceable testimony to the honour of this uncrowned queen.[1] But there was also a natural alliance between the Dukes' monastic piety and Mme. de Maintenon's own devotional trend, alive as this was with the whole spirit of seventeenth century religion in its severest, most orderly and moral form. Differences there were, it is true, between them, hidden at present, though the Quietist controversy later brought them to light: there was in Mme. de Maintenon a practical sense that was wanting in the Beauvilliers; she, born a Protestant, took a lawful generous pride in her reason, while they were wholly, ecstatically Catholic, zealots who gloried in the 'folly of the Cross.'

To the keen-eyed Catholic, again, self-respect is a thing intolerable, "an evil, cries Fénelon, far worse than long silly vanity,"[2] "vanity," echoes his great nineteenth century analogue, "changed into a more dangerous self-conceit, as being checked in its natural eruption."[3] But Mme. de Maintenon's character was built up on a double basis, on her religion firstly, and secondly on her honour, on a *bonne gloire* that covets the praises of the virtuous, delights in the knowledge of its own moderation, in the thought that its merits are beyond its rewards. "I never wished to be loved by any particular person," she wrote, late in life, "I wished to be thought well of by all. I cared nothing for riches, I was far above self-seeking; all I wanted was honour. Honour was my folly, honour was my idol, for which,

---

[1] See the Souvenirs of Mme. de Caylus (Maestricht, 1789), p. 123.
[2] See his letter to Mme. de Maintenon. Wks., viii. p. 483.
[3] J. H. Newman. Idea of a University, p. 208.

perhaps, I am not punished by excess of greatness. Would to God I had done as much for Him as I have for my own reputation ! "[1]

And so this Queen of Prudence held her way, regardless of priestly remonstrances, and made of her *bonne gloire* at once a weapon, a protection and a charm, the safeguard of her chastity in days when it was perilous for an attractive woman to walk alone, the mainspring of those companionable qualities, which, as she said, gained her the suffrage of every society, of the women, because she was gentle and kept in the background, of the men, because she had kept some of the natural graces of youth, of all, because she thought only of what might give them pleasure.[2] Her spirit was always clear and equable, the mind of one who —thanks be to God!—had neither passions nor hatreds nor ambitions, nothing to fear, nothing to hide, and nothing to regret.[3] Chary of speech, for 'those who talk much most often talk nonsense,' she was prompt and lively in conversation, an excellent listener and easily taken with new ideas; yet at bottom her judgment was solid and cautious, her powers of conception puny, her intellect narrow, though strong; the vice of originality never pierced beneath the surface, and left her "witty enough for the brilliant Montespan, and not too clever for the King." To her Louis came for refuge, exhausted by the tempestuous beauty of his mistress, her jealousies and love-philtres, her rage, her crushing wit, her arrogance; for this new guide could lead him into an unknown country, into an intercourse of friendship and conversation, where there was no intriguing and no constraint.[4]

"Providence," cried the neglected Queen, Maria Terese, "has raised up Mme. de Maintenon to bring my husband back to me," and this new favourite who was not a mistress believed abundantly in the divine nature of her mission.

---

[1] Geffroy, i. pp. 20, 21, and see the admirable Section iii. of his Introduction.
[2] *Ibid.* p. 22.   [3] See i. p. 108, ii. p. 176.
[4] Mme. de Sévigné. Letter of 17th July 1680.

To attract the King's notice she schemed and plotted, not only for the joy of ousting Montespan; she 'accepted his friendship to give him good counsels, and end his slavery to vice.'[1] The care of his salvation became the first and most absorbing of her duties; she held herself a monitress, charged to encourage and console him, or, if it were God's pleasure, to grieve him with reproaches that none but she dare utter;[2] she was his disinterested adviser, *Votre Solidité*, 'Your Seriousness,' as he used to call her, who never annoyed him with opposition, never encroached, had no will of her own, but became, as it were, the King's conception of his better self, his second conscience, a magnet quick to draw him, sometimes into the really worthier of two possible courses, always into the more ecclesiastically virtuous.

Out of this personal sphere she did not travel; public affairs were barred to her by lack alike of genius, taste, and opportunity.[3] She was not made to be 'a sentinel in the midst of Israel'; the little policy that she had, as Fénelon, after their estrangement, bitterly declared, was made up, half of feminine prejudice and humours, half of anxiety to shield the King from worry by always making for the easiest and simplest course.[4]

But it was part of her system to encourage Louis' attraction to pious persons like Beauvilliers, for the King, strong in the primary instincts of absolutism, was weak in the adaptive ingenuity that carries them out; his conduct, followed no settled lines of policy, but was guided by the ideas of those around him, so that—as Fénelon once told her, in the days of their friendship—he would never be brought to a knowledge of his duties till he was blockaded by an army of virtuous men.[5]

And there was a time when Fénelon himself hoped to command such an army, and to make the King's wife and minister his instruments of political reform. While still

---

[1] Geffroy, i. p. 103. [2] *Ibid*. p. 208, and see ii. p. 177.
[3] ii. p. 232. [4] Fén. Wks., vii. p. 375.
[5] Wks., viii. p. 486.

quite young, he had been accepted by Beauvilliers and Chevreuse, not as Director merely, but as spiritual master— as the mind of their mind, says St Simon, the soul of their soul, the sovereign ruler of their heart and conscience; and a few years later, under circumstances that belong more particularly to the history of Quietism, he had been admitted to close intimacy with Mme. de Maintenon herself.[1] And the power thus gained he wished to turn to the general advantage, to force the great lady and the Minister out of their present 'feeble timidity' into taking a more resolute part in public affairs, into opening the King's eyes, that had so long been closed by flatterers, to the bitter truth of France's extremity. For it was a strange contradiction of his nature that this apostle of the most self-centred of mysticisms should have been throughout life an ardent political reformer, endowed with all the boiling sensibility and reckless indifference to established order, with the alternate cool clear-sightedness and blurred extravagance of vision that give the great philanthropist his weakness and his strength. And still stranger is it to find him laying down, in the plenitude of his spiritual authority, schemes of social endeavour as means of grace for his friends, when in his own mind, thanks to his mysticism, religion and philanthropy were kept widely apart, and left each to pursue its separate road, the one the reconciling of the individual soul with God, the other the altruistic service of its neighbour. And the division extends to their very foundations; Fénelon's was never a mere *Politique tirée de l'Écriture Sainte*, but sought for its principles outside Catholicism on a wider field of natural rights and natural feelings, pressing them with a desperate earnestness that knew little of the sobriety of the Gospel—nay, rather foreshadows that new religion of emotional humanity, which was, in days already dawning, to offer deadly battle to the Church. There is more of Rousseau than of Bossuet in Fénelon's great appeal to the conscience of his patrons, the tremendous Letter to the King.

[1] See below, ch. vii.

They must set bounds, he said, to the unscrupulous tyranny of the Ministers, the real masters of the kingdom, between whom Louis floated powerless in everything, except to determine the limits of their rival jurisdictions ; they must save him, also, from more shameful servitude to his Confessor, Père La Chaise, that dull, lax, jealous, silly Religious, who was become a Minister of State. And they must work for the limiting of an autocracy, which had much to say of the Sovereign and his pleasure, but little of the Commonwealth and the laws, for the reversal of a policy of violence and chicanery, that went to war out of sheer vaingloriousness and love of conquest, that robbed the weak, stamped on its treaties, turned every ally into a slave, till the very names of France and Louis were become intolerable to every nation in Europe. They must cast down the idol of false glory, which the King loved more than peace or justice, more than the prosperity of his Kingdom, more than his own salvation ; they must show him the miseries of a land become nothing other than a vast hospital, desolate and without the necessaries of life, where the numbers of the people were daily diminishing, commerce was bankrupt, the fields were untilled ; wretched and mutinous, the poor were daily dying of hunger, the nobles lived only on doles from the King. Such was the great realm of France, once so flourishing, under a Prince of just and noble nature, who, even yet, was hailed by courtiers as the darling of the nation, though now, corrupted by the schemes of wicked men, he hardened his heart and ground his people down, tearing the very bread from their mouths to pay for his frivolous conquests, till they cared no more for his splendour or victories, but their lips were filled with treasonable murmurings, their hearts with bitterness and despair.[1]

[1] Wks., vii. pp. 508, 513. Of course the Letter was not intended for the King's eye, but for Mme· de Maintenon's and Beauvilliers', and Louis' name is only put at the top, in order to avoid the inconvenience of addressing severe reproaches directly to them. For an excellent criticism of the Letter, see Henri Martin, xiv. pp. 109 and ff.

OCCUPATIONS AND FRIENDSHIPS 51

Such criticisms are indeed the manifesto of a new school of statesmanship, no distant forerunners of the book that tells how man was everywhere born free, and yet is everywhere in chains. They are a Télémaque in little, big with all the faults and merits of that famous dream, and uttered, it might almost seem, to bear out Louis' own description of their author, as the finest and most visionary thinker in his Kingdom. For, with much that is grand, there enters into them much that is unreasonable, and more that is unjust, not only to Louis, but also to his Ministers, from the dead Louis at the top, to the *bonhomme* La Chaise at the bottom of the scale ; there is an utter disregard of historic possibilities, of the guilt which the nation must share with its rulers in sowing the seeds of its own decay.

Yet the Letter contains far more ugly truths than fancies. It was in vain that M$^{me.}$ de Maintenon and her friend tried to console themselves by agreeing to call Fénelon's strictures too harsh.[1] In vain she listened to a little of his teaching, and wrote—patriot as she was—after the victories of Steinkerk and Namur, that what pleased her most in the recent successes was that they had not shaken the King in his real desire for peace ; none of his people's woes were hid from him, and he would strain every nerve to set them right.[2] Matters were long past Louis' mending ; already through Fénelon's Letter rings the *Dies Iræ* of the old régime, already the *débâcle* was begun.

[1] Geffroy, i. p. 262.
[2] *Ibid.* p. 229. These victories—Steinkerk, at least, a very barren one—were gained in the summer of 1692.

CHAPTER IV

THE EDUCATION OF GIRLS

Es ist sonderbar, rief Lothario aus, dass man es dem Manne verargt, der eine Frau an die höchste Stelle setzen will, die sie einzunehmen fähig est : und welche ist höher als das Regiment des Hauses ?—GOETHE.

FÉNELON and the Beauvilliers had not been long acquainted before the Duchess, mother of many daughters, begged him to put down on paper some rules for the guidance of their education. Under his hand the work swelled out into a larger compass, and, indeed, applies, in all that concerns early childhood, to the other sex as well. It was written soon after Fénelon went to the New Catholics, and first published in 1687.

"Nothing is more neglected than the Education of Girls." Fénelon in his opening words draws an indictment against more ages than his own. The question had not failed to attract the notice of many earlier writers, or to draw from them some general counsels, valuable, for the most part, as proofs of real sympathy for the neglected sex rather than as any practical assistance to their education. In zeal and moral beauty Fénelon is not always ahead of his predecessors. Xenophon and Plutarch had as chivalrous a respect for women ; St Augustine as real a tenderness ; Erasmus and his pupil, Vivès, were even more valiant in the discrediting of that monstrous aphorism, which makes ignorance the mother of feminine good behaviour.[1] But Fénelon brought to the task a finer insight and a firmer grasp than was within the power of any earlier thinker ; he moved with a freedom unknown to the Middle Ages, yet

[1] See a fine passage in Vivès Ausgew : Schriften, ed. Wychgram, p. 214.

with a precision of aim which marked his distance from the age of universal ferment and New Learning. And he was the first to grapple with the question in its entirety, the first to lay down a code, based on the whole duty of woman, whereby the education of girls might be guided from the cradle till their entry into the greater world.

The times were ripe for such a Treatise. The seventeenth century loved to argue about women's rights and women's position, to discuss whether their true place was the kitchen or the drawing-room, whether they were born to be the slaves of a household or the cherished ornaments of society, to whom no language might be offered, save that of respectful adoration. There were still many who held by the ideas of the past, by Duke John of Brittany and his saying that a wife knew enough when she could distinguish her husband's doublet from his trunk-hose, who believed, like some characters of Molière, that women were lower and irresponsible beings, playthings or drudges of men, to be trusted with no tool but a needle or a saucepan, lest it turn in their hands to evil uses, to be held under *couvert-baron* in more than a lawyer's sense, and taught above all things to " fear and obey their lord and do his commands, were they good or were they evil."[1] These men would hear of no education for their daughters; they preferred, said Fénelon, to leave them to the neglect of a foolish and indiscreet mother.

Such were the ideas of the upper *bourgeoisie,* in M$^{me.}$ de Maintenon's opinion the worst educated class of any, and even of the rank Fénelon more especially had in view, the poorer provincial nobility. In the great families a certain worldly and superficial education had been in vogue since the beginning of the previous century, since Francis I., for the first time in the history of France, had thrown open the doors of his Court to a sex " whose beauty enhanced the

---

[1] Rousselot, Histoire de l'Education des Femmes en France, i. p. 66, quoting the Chevalier de la Tour-Landry, a fourteenth century writer. See Molière, Femmes Savantes, ii. 7, and Ecole des Maris, i. 2.

splendour of his pomps, whose amiability spread courtesy and refinement around them, and awakened noble and generous feelings in every well-fashioned heart.[1]

The movement was not wholly frivolous; there was real progress both in manners and intelligence when the licentious Court-life of the sixteenth century broadened into the more orderly salon-life of the seventeenth, when the royal patronage of the New Learning began an alliance between women and Letters, which gave its meaning to that salon-life. It was something that Vaugelas, most infallible of grammarians, should pronounce women better guardians of their tongue than men; it was much more when Molière and the great scholar, Bishop Huet, could boast that a certain generous freedom of intercourse between the sexes was rich in benefits to both, softening and correcting the natural roughness of the man and teaching the woman to find within her own heart a bulwark of honour safer than any bolts and bars.[2]

Nevertheless there was but slow advance in that moral estimation of women on which all else depended. M[me.] de Rémusat, writing at the beginning of the nineteenth century, supplies some grim comments on their outward triumphs, on the rigid Court etiquette, which, if it saved them from a fall, also prevented a higher rise, on a leadership of society, purchased always at the sacrifice of their higher feelings, often of their self-respect, not seldom of their honour.[3] And to the unrealities of their position corresponded a worthless education. M[me.] de Maintenon has drawn its outline—"The young girl's wit," she says, "was carefully embellished; she learnt a thousand things by heart, that she might shine in company to the delight of her parents and the credit of her governess, but no one thought of strengthening her reason or her judgment, nor was it certain that she would possess

[1] Mézérai, the seventeenth century historian, quoted Rousselot, i. p. 81.
[2] Molière, Ecole des Maris, i. 2; for Huet, see Rousselot, i. p. 211.
[3] Qu. Sallwürk, p. 348.

the humblest elements of knowledge."[1] In Fénelon's day few girls could read aloud without stumbling or mispronouncing, or write legibly and correctly, or cast up the simplest household account without falling into confusion,[2] while his friend, the Abbé Fleury, feared that he would gain a reputation for paradox, if he proposed to carry their education beyond the customary point, beyond 'the Catechism, needlework and a few small accomplishments, singing, dancing and the art of dress, deportment and polite conversation.'[3]

The first light in this darkness had been kindled by the Précieuses, the official patronesses of reform both in Letters and Education, and the extreme representatives, the caricature, of the literary movements of their age. They were apostles of the Sublime and the Beautiful, more especially as those words are understood by maiden ladies of tender heart and strong attraction to all that is romantic or out of the common groove, creations of that mysterious law of nature which sends euphuists in one age, sentimentalists in another, and believers in art for art's sake in a third. Yet they did not wholly eschew common sense; no one protested more forcibly than M$^{lle.}$ de Scudéry, novelist and leader of préciosité, against the absurdity of an education which devoted twelve years to the dancing-master, in order that the young lady might figure at balls for half that period, and no years at all to the formation of sound habits of thought, though she would be expected to speak sensibly and act discreetly all the days of her life. How, she asked, could girls be otherwise than coquettish and empty-headed, when their education fitted them for nothing but to sleep, to grow fat, to look pretty and to say silly things?[4]

Yet in that age of gallantry and pastorals the Précieuse could not keep her feet; a torrent of rose-water sweeps her

---

[1] Gréard, Maintenon Extraits, p. 4.
[2] Educ. des Filles, ch. xii. Wks., v. p. 593.
[3] Traité du Choix et de la Méthode des Etudes. Opuscules (ed. of 1780), ii. p. 117.   [4] Rousselot, i. p. 225.

away when she would approach the relation between the sexes. She revived the mediæval Courts of Love, yet shuddered at the thought of a husband; she was the geographer of the tender passion, yet held that marriage was its grave; she sang the praises of melancholy, the Vestal who keeps the flame of love eternally alight, yet sighed after a spiritual union with philosophy, rather than carnal slavery to a man.[1] At the bottom of her heart she agreed with that eccentric priest, Poulain de la Barre, who, after conversion to Protestantism and a wife, had come forward to preach the equality of the sexes; man, she vowed, only clung to his exclusive property in intellect out of dread lest women's powers should prove more than a match for his.[2]

Encumbered by these extravagances, the Précieuse could do little for Education. She had survived into the time of Fénelon, after martyrdom at the cruel hands of Molière, only to be the object of his ridicule and contempt, a busy meddler in theology, who left her servant's accounts unaudited, that she might discuss the doctrine of Grace, or a visionary dreamer, wrapped in a fanciful kingdom of heroes and princesses and marvellous adventures, when she would some day have to descend to the homely, tedious duties of a household.[3]

The Education of Girls leads the way into a higher world. Fénelon interposed between the Précieuses and their opponents, not to patch up a shallow compromise between them, but to raise the debate into a higher atmosphere, to remind them of principles which both had failed to apply. All considerations of mere elegance or utility drop out of sight; women, Fénelon argued, had rights and duties of their own, which lay at the root of all human existence; the aim of their education could only be to fit

[1] Lotheissen, iii. p. 53. See Molière Précieuses Ridicules, sc. 5.
[2] Rousselot, i. pp. 266 and *ff.* And see p. 218.
[3] E. F., ch. ii. Wks., v. p. 565.

them for the performance of their tasks. To the enemies of their education he answered that virtue was the same for women as for men; they were a half of that human race which Jesus Christ had ransomed with his blood.[1] He replied to the Précieuses that a woman's best ornament was the happiness and good order of her family and household —nay, in the godly upbringing of her children the mother uttered her best and surest prayer; had not St Paul declared that through them she would work out her own salvation?[2]

For Fénelon made religion the groundwork of all education. He could not resolve it into a training of the intellect, though that was indispensable, nor into the formation of virtuous habits, though that must not be omitted; he could not, like Locke, make it a supremely important branch of natural history, nor did he hope, like Rousseau, to call by its means into existence a new impossible world, that should redress the balance of the old. As close an observer as the first, and a dreamer of political dreams like the second, Fénelon differed by the whole breadth of heaven from both; to him education was one of the most sacred, one of the most terrible of human responsibilities, whose goal lay, not in this, but in the future world, whose final end was the saving of souls.

As a Christian priest, he was bound to believe in the intense reality of sin, in its presence everywhere, in the need for a steady search through all the windings of a childish brain, after those hidden roots of evil, which else might some day bear their bitter fruit. He knew the need of constant watchfulness, the vanity of those surface medicines, which elaborately cure the symptom, and leave untouched the inward disease. Yet he was no Jansenist, no fanatic of man's original wickedness, to believe that a little girl's heart is a mass of festering sores, poisoned by envy, malice, and self-will; he could not bind responsibility and its frightful burdens on the weak shoulders of the child. Nay,

---

[1] ch. i. p. 564. [2] ch. xi. p. 591, *sic interpr*: 1 Timothy ii. 15.

the Jansenist himself lacked courage fully to carry his theory into practice; the Little Schools of Port Royal were overshadowed by ascetic gloom enough, and by the haunting fear of wrath to come, yet even there it was the Master who descended into the arena, and fought with Satan in his charge's place.[1] And Fénelon carried the vicarious principle still farther, till he almost forgot that the child was already a moral agent; for him all was sweetness, all was light; virtue must show herself with a smiling face, and vice under its most hideous aspect; no priest's black robe must give him sombre notions of religion. It was the mother who must make herself God's sentinel, and teach, forestall, correct, must gain and keep authority over her children without losing their affection or their confidence.[2]

Fénelon knew how much he was asking, how few mothers had the talent fully to carry out such an undertaking, how difficult was success, even to these few, had they more than one child. But he did not write a book on Education only to give imperfect rules; our efforts, he thought, will be none the worse if we aim at a mark beyond our range. Nor did his little book call for any great ability on the part of the teacher, it was enough if she could understand its general sense, and avoid the worse mistakes of which it spoke. Or with its aid mothers of scanty leisure could train up a governess in the right methods of education, and five or six such governesses might set themselves to prepare a great number of others, and thus relieve the mothers of families from their present great embarrassment.[3]

For Fénelon had broken entirely with the ideas of the Catholic Revival and its love of mediæval models. If, himself the Superior of a nunnery, he was bound to think well of a good convent, he thought still better of a good mother, who could give her whole attention to her child, and gradually wean her to the ways of a world which the

---

[1] Rousselot i. pp. 350 and *ff*. [2] E.F. chs. iii. xi. Wks., v. pp. 566, 590.
[3] E.F. ch. xiii. pp. 596 and *ff*.

THE EDUCATION OF GIRLS 59

nun had once and for all renounced. For he knew that the more effectually a convent wall shuts out all knowledge of misery and evil, the ruder will be the awakening when the time of happy ignorance is past, and the young girl is cast out, all in a moment, into the world, deafened by its roar and blinded by its glare, like one who has been brought up in the gloom of a dark cavern, and is suddenly dragged forth into the light of day.[1]

He knew, also, that many a convent did not keep its Rule, that there vanity was held in honour, the world looked upon as an enchanted place, its pleasures over-valued, its disappointments over-looked, that luxury and petty vices flourished rankly on its soil, that its education was of the poorest, often leaving the pupil to learn for herself, at the price of irreparable blunders, all she should have known before her entry into the world.[2]

And therefore he echoed the judgment passed on convents by the grand-daughter of the foundress of the Visitation, the most famous teaching Order of the time. "Keep Pauline at home," wrote M$^{me.}$ de Sévigné, "and do not think that a convent will mend her education, either in matters of religion—of which the good sisters know nothing—or in any other subject. She will learn far more from you, if you talk to her freely, and make her read good books."[3] And all the wiser mothers of the coming century agreed with M$^{me.}$ de Sévigné.

Yet better the most mediocre convent than an unhappy home; many a mother was herself the worst obstacle to her children's education. And of such mothers Fénelon gives a dreary catalogue—the scolding housewife who made every excuse for herself and none for her daughters, and vented all her ill-humour on their heads[4]; the worldly

---

[1] See the Avis à une Dame de Qualité, printed as an appendix to the E.F. Wks. v., p. 600.
[2] *Ibid.* p. 599.
[3] Letter to M$^{me.}$ de Grignan of 24th Jan. 1689. The Visitation was founded by M$^{me.}$ de Chantal in 1610.
[4] E.F., ch. ii. p. 564.

mother who passed her whole time at cards and scandal, and thought she had fulfilled her whole duty to her children, if she had on her lips a few excellent maxims, each one of which she outraged by her own behaviour.[1] Or there was the mother whose coldness taught her girls to love no human being, so that they suspected her of a wish to be rid of them, and saw the gates of a convent opening wide.[2] Or they were left to the charge of a vulgar, gossiping servant, miscalled a governess, who made her own convenience their standard of morality, and disgusted them with true religion by exhibitions of her sensual, grovelling, hypocrisy.[3]

On such corrupt trees grew only evil fruit. The first step forward was to educate the mothers, to purify and sweeten the surroundings of the young, and thus enlist for virtue that faculty of imitativeness, given them that their hearts might be turned the more readily towards the practice of the Good.[4]

In his method of teaching Fénelon was a thorough reformer. Like M$^{me.}$ de Maintenon, like his friend the Abbé Fleury, like even the Jansenist masters at Port Royal, he had drawn his inspiration from the Cartesian philosophy, then the ruling educational influence of France.

Teachers were indebted to Descartes for two things, a method and an enthusiasm. His method sounded the knell of the old scholastic learning. Logic ceased to be a matter of memory and formulas, of verbal traps and hair-splitting dialectic; it became the art of clear thinking and exact expression, of turning all the powers of the mind towards the attainment of truth.[5] For the master's *fiat* had gone forth: henceforward nothing was to be believed, except it were wholly clear and distinct; men must dig away the

---

[1] ch. xiii. p. 598.   [2] ch. ix., p. 587.
[3] Avis, p. 600.   [4] ch. iv. p. 568.
[5] See the quotation from Fleury in Sallwürk, p. 37, note, and Sallwürk's Introduction.

THE EDUCATION OF GIRLS 61

drift and sand of doubtful opinion until they reached the rock of certainty at the bottom of their mind.[1]

The enthusiasm was all for truth and reason, a powerful conviction, common to philosophers and to many, who, like M$^{me.}$ de Maintenon, had never opened a text-book of metaphysics, that 'we cannot be reasonable too soon, nor overmuch.'[2] Reason had come into her own again; by means of Reason man could break through the cloudy wall of phantasms, that separated him from Truth, could learn to know himself and God and the world around him; by means of Reason he could escape from bondage to his passions, and advance to moral goodness. "Of all the qualities of children," says Fénelon, "there is only one on which we can surely count, and that one is Right Reason."[3]

With these principles as a reaping-hook Fénelon and his fellows began, perhaps more thoroughly than they thought for, to mow down the tares of mediæval education. Henceforward human nature was to be trained and aided, not crushed and moulded into another shape; punishment ceased to be a second name for improvement; the child could no longer be beaten, as in Erasmus' story, simply to make him humble. For the wells were no more poisoned by a crushingly real belief in man's original wickedness; the reign of Giant Metaphysical Sin was over, and 'children were born without any natural trend to good or evil.'[4]

And from post-natal sin they had in their Reason a means of regeneration which every Churchman could recognize as co-operative with Grace. And Grace itself came with no violent arbitrary shock from outside, but grew out of a hidden secret germ, implanted in the soul at birth, and only distinguishable from Reason when it began to put forth buds and roots. "This formless and secret germ is the beginning

---

[1] Descartes, Disc. de la Méthode, chs. ii. iii.
[2] Extraits (Ed. Gréard) p. 7, and see pp. 196, 197.
[3] E. F., ch. v. p. 573.   [4] ch. iii. p. 566.

of the New Man. It is not Reason alone; it is not Nature left to herself; it is Grace concealing itself under Nature, to redress it little by little."[1]

For Fénelon had no sympathy with those more extravagant Cartesians, who were accused of identifying Reason with Virtue. His was the aim of Mme de Maintenon, to 'inspire nothing but Christianity and Reason,' but the second was only a means to the first. If he makes much of mental clearness as a chief pre-requisite of moral excellence, it was because his School held firmly to a truism, too true to be always, even now, remembered, that virtuous conduct is only the outward expression of reasonable ideas, and reasonable ideas the fruit of a well-ordered intellect.[2] Moreover, his mystical philosophy taught him that the God of Truth is very really present to our mind under the form of those Clear Ideas, which are the sure foundation, the abiding touch-stone, of all thought, so that man, in a more than metaphysical sense, holds actual communion with the Divine, not only when he prays, but also when he thinks.

And for this reason Fénelon and his School of *Vernunft Pädagogik* would hear nothing of the flaccid modern distinction between the moral and the intellectual virtues of truth. It is the just boast of their descendants that the great scholars of the sixteenth century introduced into the world a conception of literary veracity, hitherto unparalleled in strictness, and that this conscientiousness, learnt in the study, extended itself thence over all the affairs of life. But the Cartesians would spare their pupil the toil of his apprenticeship, and demanded that, from the very first, he should be brought up to aim at perfect clearness of thought and expression, to have "that absolute belief in the force of language, which finally is belief in thought, belief in men." The beginnings of education were not completed till the child had arrived at a complete understanding of every syllable uttered, of every syllable heard, till he had learned

---

[1] Wks., i. p. 136.   [2] See Sallwürk, p. 26.

THE EDUCATION OF GIRLS 63

to express himself shortly and to the point, and knew how to say much in a small number of words.¹

And so our grave young Churchman would reform the nursery with a severity of reasonableness that is itself sometimes almost unreasonable, as not more ruthless to a real defect than to its mystic *Halb Kinderspiel, halb Gott im Herzen*. Away, he cries, with all the petty abuses that breed untruth or slovenliness of thought, with the folly of those silly women who delight in a child's nonsensical chatter, with the hobgoblins invented by nurse-maids to scare their charges into right-doing, with the shows of forced, unreal, affection, by which these are taught to repay a kindness, with the odious habit of praising them for some neat little bit of deceit!² Away, also, with the clumsy glosses, by which elders think to hide their own failings from the sharp sight of youth, with the self-indulgent harshness of those teachers who demand of their pupil an exactitude of thought of which they are themselves incapable, with whom all is silence, uncomfortable postures, threats, and punishment.³

Such pedantry as this Fénelon held to be the death of education. It destroyed the child's confidence, bred hatred of all learning, replaced the free organic growth of his faculties by subservience to an authority, always arbitrary and external, often a mere excuse for severity. It outraged the Golden Rule of Teaching, which was to excite the pupil's interest in his studies, let him see the How and the Why of his education, the bearing of one kind of knowledge upon another, the bearing of any kind of knowledge on practical life. It destroyed his sense of the justice of his education, in that it gave to his punishments an appearance of caprice, not of a natural following on his fault.⁴

But, long before a child's Reason is fully awake, the work of education has begun. While it still slumbers, the master

---
[1] chs. iii., ix. pp. 565, 587.
[2] chs. iii., ix. pp. 566, 587, 588, and see ch. v. p. 574.
[3] chs. iv., v. pp. 567, 570.   [4] ch v. p. 569 and *ff*.

must become, as it were, its ambassador, and stand between his pupil and the external world, to correct the impressions that it made upon him, and see that each conveyed the appropriate moral lesson. "We must make haste to write upon the tablets of a childish brain while it is still soft and easy to our hand, yet making careful choice of the characters we engrave thereon; into a vessel so precious and so small we must pour only exquisite things."[1] Thus the teacher will 'follow and assist Nature,'[2] watching diligently for the appearance of each constituent element in the mind, and preparing beds for the torrent of passions, whose inrush it would be hopeless to resist. Each of them will serve some useful purpose, curiosity lead on to valuable instruction, imitativeness be turned to virtuous uses; jealousy wears another aspect, when it is called emulation; out of a well bound, gilt-edged, volume vanity quickly learns to read.[3] The Imagination will serve our purpose in religious teaching. "God, who knows the hearts of His creatures better than any man, has put the whole of religion into popular facts, which lodge without effort in the memory. And we have only to follow the methods of Scripture with our children, awaken their interest, and let pleasure do all."[4]

Pleasure, indeed, is one of Fénelon's watch-words, and that for reasons as well physiological as moral. The pedantic Humanists of Montaigne's time had educated 'minds, not men,' but Fénelon had learned wisdom from the Essayist, and was resolved to give even the despised body its share of attention. Doubtless his science is not ours—he would have been perfect, cries an admiring modern physician, had he had any real knowledge of medicine—but it was enough to show him that the brain moves quickest when it is kept at an even temperature of moderate happiness, and allowed to refresh itself by many digressions. " A child's mind is like a candle exposed to the wind. He asks you a question, and, before you can answer him, his

[1] ch. v. p. 568.
[3] *Ib.* p. 568, and see p. 571.
[2] ch. iii. p. 567.
[4] ch. vi, p. 576.

THE EDUCATION OF GIRLS

eyes have wandered to the ceiling, and he is counting the figures painted there, or the number of panes in the window. If you try to bring him back to his question, you will harass him as much as if you kept him in prison."[1]

For this reason matters of diet fall within the teacher's province. Young blood is hot and easily excited, and he must keep it cool by means of moderate fare and simple habits, must see, too, to balls and kites and bodily exercise : with Fénelon and Fleury games for the first time take their place in Christian education.[2]

But Fénelon had other uses for Pleasure than simply sweetening the blood. In this field also he was a reformer, charged to break down the ancient brutal system, that thought more of rules than moral sentiments, and turned education into the art of hindering.[3] Already over the Education of Girls is cast the shadow of the eighteenth century ; we hear but little of the claims of law or discipline, of the good of troubles bravely encountered and overcome : Fénelon would make the whole world partaker of his own serenity ; all should " do Duty's work and know it not," all should

> in love and truth,
> Where no misgiving is, rely
> Upon the genial sense of youth,
> When love is an unerring light
> And joy its own security.

"We must avoid," he says, "the faults of ordinary teachers, who let the child associate nothing but tedium with his studies, nothing but amusement with his hours of play. We must make learning and virtue agreeable, hiding away our lessons under an appearance of liberty and enjoyment.[4] And, with the exaltation of Pleasure, comes that of its correlative, Feeling. Fénelon was too impatient to

---

[1] ch. v. p. 569.   [2] Sallwürk, p. 35.   See Fén. ch. v. pp. 572 and *ff*.
[3] See his disciple, Mme. Necker, Sallwürk, p. 390.
[4] ch. v. p. 571.

remain forever in the School of Reason, and hurries on to prepare a way for the sentimentalists, for the coming of Rousseau and Bernardin de St Pierre. Passion, indeed, is not yet sovereign; we have still far to travel to the doctrine of *Émile*, that Goodness, Justice, Law, are empty words, except they find their sanction in the natural, uncorrupted human heart; nor has a sacrilegious hand yet meddled with the best-known of Cartesian formulas, to change it to ' I Feel, and therefore Am.'

But, if Reason still is master in the house, Feeling has become its mistress. Emotion, in Fénelon's later pages, has ceased to be merely the raw material of future thought, and been pronounced of all educational levers the most important; unless the teacher can carry it with him, he will convince, but he will not persuade.[1] Affection, on the other hand, will make the pupil do all that is required of him; Feeling is a goad that may be used to rouse his indolence, awaken his interest, prick on his self-respect; he should learn to take pleasure in his honour, in the cleanness of his conscience, in a Stoical contempt for all that weakens the body.[2] By means of Feeling, we can shame the girl out of her unworthy habit of shuddering at a dream, at the upsetting of a salt-cellar, at the thought of death; we can teach her that no Christian, of any age or sex, may dare to be a coward.[3] . . . Fénelon's appeals to the Feelings will be neither prurient nor mawkish; if we think their tone a little too delicate, too cloistered for a "mortal race that must be run through dust and heat," that is no more than may be said of his whole theory of Education.

In the last pages of his book Fénelon deals with girls alone. On this more delicate ground his principles remain the same, but some of the earlier kindliness has vanished; this friend of many women could not forget that their brain was even feebler and more trivial than that of man; this father of sentimentalists was also a priest, an inheritor of

[1] p. 573.   [2] ch. vii. p. 580.   [3] *Ibid.* p. 583.

THE EDUCATION OF GIRLS

some of that traditional Catholic disdain, which once, speaking through the mouth of Bossuet, had called Eve's daughters "the painted dust, for whose adornment almost all Creation must travail, almost every trade must toil, almost every hour be spent." For, if his religion often sharpened Fénelon's eyesight, there were times also when it warped his judgment. In his horror of préciosité or theology in petticoats he would have women shrink from learning almost as from vice; knowledge only made them long to raise themselves above the common groove; it emboldened them to have an opinion on every subject, to join in every dispute.[1] Or in its name they embarked on Italian and Spanish, on secular music, plays and novels, on all the dangerous and corrupting studies that told of earthly love, clothing it in the full splendour of worldly generosity and grace, till it lost its true character of a detestable vice, and caught many a heedless conscience off its guard.[2]

But such atavism is rare. Fénelon was a priest who disbelieved in total depravity, and meant to make the best of human nature as it was. The strain of sacerdotal aloofness is more than balanced by a patient interest and understanding; women were no longer 'a mere afterthought to God's scheme of Creation, formed out of Adam's superfluous rib,' but a sex worthy of almost as close an attention as men. And, for his own part, he had studied them at every stage and in all their occupations, and learned to base reform, not on the reckless, abstract censures of theology, but on accurate distinction of the deeps and shallows of their character. To the natural follies of their age he is merciful enough: to take wild, unreasoning likes and dislikes, and live habitually in the superlative is a transitory privilege of youth, that Reason and experience will set right.[3] But it was otherwise with their rooted defects—the curiosity that turns the clever girl into a

---
[1] chs. vii., x. pp. 580, 590.
[2] ch. xii. p. 595, and see the Sermon on St Teresa, p. 640.
[3] ch. v. p. 574.

précieuse, and her duller sister into an inquisitive gossip, agape for the last new novel or the last new piece of news, the violent desire to please that makes a national question out of a ribbon or a ringlet or the choice of a colour, the slyness that is ever ready with its little ruses and its tears.[1] Or there are indolence and frivolity, to give wrong notions of religion: girls look on prayer as a tedious exercise, on their Creator as an austere Judge; they behave in His Presence as though they were in the company of one whom they respect, but rarely see, and that only on the most formal occasions; they are weary, they are ill at ease, they long to make their escape.[2]

Having traced these various vices to a common root in ignorance and ennui, Fénelon proposes, as his remedy, some healthy practical interest; like M$^{me.}$ de Maintenon at St Cyr, he thought the best employment for a girl was management of a few small household concerns.[3] But the two bring domesticity before their scholars in very different terms—M$^{me.}$ de Maintenon, as a drudgery, an evil consequence of their want of fortune, if not as a penance for their fathers' sins: Fénelon, as the daughter's best bond of union with her mother, her sacrament of initiation into the essential duties of her sex. For was it not woman's mission in life to ruin or sustain a household, and thus make or mar the characters of nearly all the world? And is not the virtuous woman of Scripture she who "worketh willingly with her hands"?

Not that he wholly eschewed the petty social graces and accomplishments, on which the foundress of St Cyr had laid so heavy a hand. He willingly allows such literature as "purifies the feelings without exciting the passions," ancient history, the history of France, "which also has its beauties," music within jealous limits, singing, and painting. Art he would even turn to practical account: classical sculpture might set before girls the careless ease and majesty of

---

[1] chs. ix., x., *passim*.   [2] Avis., p. 603.
[3] ch. xii. p. 593.

THE EDUCATION OF GIRLS

Greek and Roman dress; a knowledge of drawing would bring into their embroideries a much-needed harmony and design.[1]

But Fénelon's ideal lady cares little for accomplishments; her heart was in her still-room and her nursery. Essentially of noble birth, though condemned by her poverty to live in the country, among unpolished neighbours and occupations that were not delightful, she had learnt to be homely with those who were homely, and not to think fastidiousness a sign of lively sensibility.[2] Within doors she was neat and orderly, but not to excess, a careful stewardess of her fortune, yet firm against all avarice and unintelligent economy, willing, on occasion, to spend largely in the hope of future profit, and never so absorbed in the counting of her candles that the steward had liberty to rob on every side.[3] A knowledge of the use and prices of commodities saved her alike from being cheated and from becoming the plague of her household: she was no Pharaoh of her kitchen, to expect that preserves should be made without sugar.[4] Hers was the difficult art of managing servants; she treated them neither as beasts of burden, nor yet with an excessive laxity, well knowing that, if carelessness on her part spoiled the servant, too great excellence in serving spoiled the mistress. And she remembered that the meanest among them was a fellow-Christian, placed in an unnatural state, and therefore specially deserving of patient counsel and of charity.[4]

And before the heiress Fénelon lays a wider programme. Many a future mistress of a country house, he says, knows no more of rural life than of the habits of the savages in Canada; she thinks economy and estate-management utterly beneath her; she does not even know enough of the ways of Justice to avoid going to law.[5] Yet how easy to give her some little notion of her duties! She might learn what was meant by Lord of the Manor, Tithe Impro-

[1] p. 595. [2] ch. x. p. 590. [3] ch. xi. p. 592.
[4] ch. xii. p. 593. [5] ch. xi. p. 591.

priation, Rents and Fines; and she should know something of the moral obligations of a landowner, how to prevent the violence and chicanery so common in the country, should found little schools, provide food for the starving and care for the sick, and, above all things, ensure for all her dependants a solid instruction and Christian control.[1]

Thus Fénelon had done much, if he had not done all. He stood far ahead of all other contemporary reformers, above Port Royal in his humanity, in his insistence on the social duties, as well of education as religion, above M$^{me.}$ de Maintenon in his adaptiveness, in his wish to soften down the outlines of a training rigorously practical and domestic, by some little touch of wider, more artistic culture. Nor need he fear competition with a later world. "When we turn to modern literature from Fénelon's pages," says Mr Morley, "who does not feel that the world has lost a sacred accent, as if some ineffable essence had passed out from our hearts?"[2]

Gaps there are, and contradictions and extravagances. Fénelon is open to the charge, so often brought against the Jansenists, of first teaching girls to think for themselves, and then forbidding them to express their thoughts. We might have wished his intellectual programme a little broader. Thirty years later, within his own lifetime, his correspondent and admirer, M$^{me.}$ de Lambert, was already chafing at its narrowness; unless their minds were better stocked with serious knowledge, girls, she feared, would find their way back to the 'delicious poison of Society.'[3] And it was long before another disciple, M$^{me.}$ de Rémusat, broadened his timid conception of a house-wife, busied with much serving in the background, into the worthier ideal of a wife, whose glory it was to be the mother and the consort of a citizen, ready, though herself holding no cards in the game of life, to sit as a counsellor beside the players, to

---

[1] ch. xii. p. 594. [2] Rousseau, ii. p. 249.
[3] Sallwürk, p. 98.

THE EDUCATION OF GIRLS 71

share in their victories, and console their defeats.[1] Yet it was from the Education of Girls that these later reformers started; from Fénelon they learned to turn "all their knowledge into character, all their wisdom into virtue."[2]

[1] Sallwürk, p. 351.
[2] Mme. de Lambert, qu. Gréard, Introduction, p. liii.

CHAPTER V

THE COURT PRECEPTORATE

Tu modo nascenti puero, quo ferrea primum
Desinet ac toto surget gens aurea mundo,
Casta, fave, Lucina.—VIRGIL.

THE Education of Girls was destined to bring its author something more than literary glories. On the 20th of August, 1689, the Duke of Beauvilliers was gazetted Governor to the little Duke of Burgundy, eldest son of the Dauphin, and the Abbé de Fénelon, on Beauvilliers' recommendation, was appointed his Preceptor. On the following day M$^{me.}$ de Sévigné wrote that the King had made three men out of one Duke,[1] which was quite as it should be—St Louis could not have made a better choice. This Abbé de Fénelon too was a man of rare merit for intelligence, knowledge and piety.

The appointment was received with general satisfaction. Louis the Great, it was said, had once more outshone all earlier monarchs, and shown himself wiser than Philip of Macedon when he appointed Aristotle tutor to his son.[2] Bossuet was overjoyed at the good fortune of Church and State, and regretted only that the Marquis de Fénelon had not lived to see the elevation of a merit which hid itself with so much care.[3] But M. Tronson, the wise old tutor from St Sulpice, wrote that his joy was mixed with fear; he was afraid lest prudence and charity should reconcile his old pupil only too easily to the ways of a world where the Gospel was but little known.[4]

---

[1] In allusion to Beauvilliers' three offices, Governor, First Gentleman of the Chamber, and sinecure President of the Council of Finance.
[2] Proyart, Vie du Dauphin, Père de Louis XV., i. p. 22.
[3] Fén. Wks., vii. p. 497.   [4] *Ibid.* p. 498.

THE DUKE OF BURGUNDY
FROM AN ENGRAVING BY EDELINCK

THE COURT PRECEPTORATE 73

Beauvilliers and Fénelon had a hard task before them: they were called upon to do for the son what Bossuet and the Duke of Montausier—a man no less excellent than Beauvilliers—had failed in doing for the father. The education of the Dauphin, says St Simon, had been so severe that, after it was finished, he never opened a book and read nothing but the birth and marriage announcements in the newspaper.[1] The severity indeed, came not from the Preceptor, who believed in other methods, but from the Governor and the King; Louis had often been flogged himself, and saw no reason why his son should not be scourged as soundly as the least pupil of a Jesuit college. But, in any case, Bossuet's herculean efforts must have been wasted on his pupil, a crass, obstinate, idle boy, who grew up to be a taciturn, stubborn, indolent man, timid and awkward, except among his servants, though a brave soldier and a mighty sportsman. His personality was wholly absorbed into that of his father: before the King had spoken, the Dauphin never dared to have an opinion; after Louis had delivered himself, his only anxiety was to agree.

Burgundy was a very different being from his father; he inherited most of his qualities from his mother, Mary Anne of Bavaria, a delicate, melancholy, unattractive princess, passionate and proud and caustic, terribly neglected by her husband, and unpopular at Court owing to the political misdeeds of her brother, the Bavarian Elector, and her own unsocial habits. Palace customs allowed her little voice in the education of her children; we only know that she highly approved the appointment of Beauvilliers, and died soon afterwards, bitterly regretted by her eldest son.[2]

And Burgundy himself was a frail, unhealthy creature,

---

[1] viii. p. 262. See the Comte d'Haussonville's article on Burgundy in the Revue des Deux Mondes for Feb. 1897. At six years old, says Mme. de Maintenon, the Dauphin knew a thousand words of Latin, each one of which he had forgotten before he grew up. Geffroy, ii. p. 368.

[2] Haussonville, Ibidem. Geffroy, i. p. 203.

a valetudinarian even as a child, always thinking that 'his soul was about to take her flight into his pocket-handkerchief,' and 'kingly neither in face nor carriage.'[1] His body lacked symmetry as much as his mind. One shoulder very early outgrew the other, defying the most cruel efforts of the surgeons to set it right, and probably doing far more serious mischief to his general health than was suspected at the time.[2]

And the hurricanes of passion, which his contemporaries mistook for vice, seem to be more easily accounted for by some derangement of his nervous system. He was born terrible, says St Simon, and in his youth made all men tremble. The least contradiction made him furious; he would fall into ungovernable fits of rage even against inanimate objects, would break the clock that summoned him to some unwelcome duty, or storm at the rain, when it prevented him from going out. He had an insatiable appetite for all sorts of pleasure, but especially for eating and drinking, for music and for games, at which it was dangerous to beat him. His pride and arrogance were indescribable; mankind he looked upon as atoms, with which he had nothing in common; his brothers were only intermediate beings between him and the human race. He had a savage, cruel temper, and a biting wit, that spared no one, and always hit the mark. His quickness and penetration, even during his transports of rage, were astounding; his liveliness of thought was so great that he must always be doing two things at one time. He often reasoned more quickly than his masters; his memory was so good that he would remind them of things they had once taught him, and afterwards forgotten. He readily stiffened himself against threats; against flattery he was always on his guard; the only influence he would ever obey was reason, and he was not always disposed to listen to that. Often, when it reasserted itself after one of his tornadoes, he was

---

[1] Proyart, i. p. 90.
[2] See the letter of Mme. de Maintenon after his *post-mortem*. Geffroy, ii. p. 307.

THE COURT PRECEPTORATE 75

so much ashamed of himself that he fell into a new fit of rage. From the very beginning, however, he was frank and truthful to a fault.[1]

Such is St Simon's earliest portrait of the Prince who afterwards became his prodigy of saintliness, too virtuous for this wicked world. And truly Burgundy's was a remarkable nature, even if much in the portrait be discounted by St Simon's wish to magnify his hero's intellect, and more by his Jansenist belief in miracle and the "thunderbolt of Grace." But he who would learn to know Burgundy aright, must study him in the pages of Fénelon.

For it was on the Preceptor that the real burden of his education rested, although the formal responsibility lay with Beauvilliers; he appointed the subordinate officers, to him they reported, at his hands the Princes received their rare punishments.[2] The King, to his later sorrow, interfered little in the management of his grandsons, the Dauphin not at all; he had not even been consulted on the choice of a Governor, and Beauvilliers was one of the few men he really disliked. And of other outside influences there was only Chevreuse, called in occasionally at leisure moments to mingle instruction with amusement.

Thus the Governor and Preceptor were quite untrammelled (for Fleury and the other Household officers were mere subordinates), and could peaceably bring up their Princes according to the methods of the Education of Girls —a book, be it remembered, written originally for Beauvilliers' wife. To the great scandal of the Court Physicians, the Duke carried out Fénelon's prescription of simple food and much exercise in the open air; the Princes were brought up "just like common people," eating and drinking as much as they pleased, but only of dishes plainly dressed,

---

[1] St Simon, vii. pp. 370 and *ff*; and see Proyart, i. pp. 10 and *ff*.
[2] For all details see Louville's Memoir on the Education of the Princes in Fén. Wks., vii. pp. 519 and *ff*. Louville was one of the equerries to the Princes, and wrote in 1696: Burgundy was educated in company with his two brothers, the Duke of Anjou, afterwards Philip V. of Spain, and the Duke of Berry.

running and riding in all weathers, and always with uncovered heads. Louis XIV. had suffered terrible things at his doctors' hands—*quicquid delirant medici, plectuntur reges*, said a contemporary satirist—but the Princes had no need of medicine, nor ever seriously complained of an ailment.

It was Fénelon who made their hours of study so agreeable that they entered the schoolroom almost as readily as they left it, Burgundy saying that he should remember all his life the pleasure of having worked without constraint.[1] Indeed his master kindled in him a hunger after knowledge so absorbing as afterwards to become a matter for reproach. St Simon compares him to a watchmaker who should be so much absorbed in the making of his tools as to forget when the time came to turn them to account.

For this Fénelon was not to blame. Always and everywhere an enemy of pedantry, he hated it most of all in a Prince. "Better," says Louville, "that a King should know nothing of Art or Letters than that he should play the poet or the philosopher on the throne. The staple of a royal education is History, Politics, and the Art of War; a Prince needs only such garnish of general knowledge as will enable him to outshine his courtiers in a conversation."[2]

The voice is the voice of the courtly Louville, but the thoughts are the thoughts of Fénelon, and Fénelon's also was the system, which made the Princes' hours of study as desultory and informal as possible. Burgundy was encouraged to break off from the matter in hand to any subject that interested him, and History was taught him in a kind of debate; masters and pupil discussed together the faults committed by kings in the past and the reasons for committing them, and the Prince was made to give his opinion the first. In this way it was hoped that his judgment would be strengthened, and a power of rapidly seizing on important points be brought into being; moreover, Fénelon and St Simon were agreed that the Art of Con-

---
[1] Fén. Wks., viii. p. 123.   [2] Louville, p. 521.

versation was more useful to kings than many statelier accomplishments; it was in familiar talk that men's little foibles and vanities most certainly appeared, and their master learned to know them as they were.[1]

Perhaps it is to be regretted that there was not more systematic education, more teaching by rule and less by ear, more mental discipline and less enjoyment. But the time was short, and the curriculum long; moreover, the dread reproach of Pedantry fastened on all such subjects as were not immediately useful; while for metaphysics, which every Cartesian thought a practical study, the pupil was held to be too impatient and too imaginative—a fault not wholly unpardonable in one not yet fourteen.[2] And Burgundy, too, was grandson of that Idomeneus, who, though wise and enlightened, was always absorbed in little things, too busy over the parts to comprehend the whole, too fond of arranging atoms when he should have been conceiving a system. And Fénelon was resolved that his pupil should have the mind, not of a shopkeeper, but of a king; he must learn to leave the care of detail to others, and be content with governing those who governed in his name.[3]

The real centre, therefore, of Burgundy's education was his direct preparation for the throne, and, more especially, the magnificent code of moral lessons, the Fables, the Dialogues of the Dead, and Télémaque, which were timed to keep place with his gradual development, and lead him from fairy-stories to History, and from History to the heights of a political Utopia.

There is small trace in the Fables of Fénelon's enthusiastic admiration for La Fontaine; his little fishes always talk like moralists of the sounder school of Æsop. Nearly every story has a personal application; much is made of the danger of life at Court, of the evils of tyranny and bad faith, of the insufficiency of riches and grandeur without virtue. More than once Burgundy's sense of humour

---

[1] See esp. Fén. Wks., vii. p. 95. [2] *Ibid.*, 518.
[3] Télémaque, bk. xvii. Wks., vi. p. 548.

is turned against his own defects, as in the story of how the child Bacchus, while learning to read, was annoyed by a Faun, who laughed at his mistakes. " How dare you mock the son of Jove ? " exclaims the angry little god. But the irreverent Faun replies unmoved : " How dare the son of Jove make a mistake ? "[1]

Or else Fénelon sketches his pupil on a larger canvas, as in the fable Master Whimsical.[2] "What has happened to Melanthus ? "—" Nothing without ; everything within. There was a wrinkle in his stocking this morning, and we shall all have to suffer for it. He cries, he roars, he alarms, he moves pity. Don't speak to him of what he likes best ; for that very reason he won't hear a word in its favour. He contradicts others and tries to annoy them ; he is furious that they will not be angry. Or else he turns on himself, is wretched, and will not be consoled. He wishes for solitude, but he cannot bear to be alone ; he comes back to us, and at once quarrels with us all. We must not be silent, we must not talk, we must not laugh, we must not be sad. There is nothing to do but wait until he recovers.

" Sometimes he will suddenly drop his rage, and be amused at his own fury ; he forgets what has annoyed him—all he knows is that he is angry, and is going to remain so. Or, rather, it is we who are angry ; the whole world is yellow, because the jaundice is in his own eyes. He spares no one, but rushes on the first-comer, just to vent his rage. Take care what you say to him, for he has not lost control of his wits—if you say something foolish, he will become reasonable, just to convince you of your folly. . . . But stay—he has changed again ; he avows his fault, laughs at his own absurdities, and imitates them for our amusement. Now he is full of affection, caresses and cajoles those he has offended, till you would think that he could never lose his temper again—you are wrong ; there will be another outbreak to-night, at which he will

[1] Wks., vi. p. 213.   [2] *Ibid.* p. 335

laugh in the morning, but without the least thought of amendment."

The same method is pursued in the earliest Dialogues of the Dead. The valetudinarian Prince Bilious mistakes a slight indigestion for gout in the stomach; Achilles, lamenting to Chiron that he has often broken his promise of good behaviour, is comforted by the assurance that, after long centuries he will be born again, and have another Chiron at his side. But, for the most part, the stage is crowded with the great figures of ancient and modern history, each intent on teaching his own lesson of wisdom. Herodotus tells Lucian that too much belief is better than too little; Plato upholds against Aristotle his Eternal Ideas; Parrhasius and Lionardo da Vinci criticize the art of Poussin. And at their heels follow the great Kings and tyrants and statesmen of the past, disputing together, sombrely enough— " We ghosts," says Sulla, " want no wit or phrasings, but only what is serious "—as they stand forth to be judged in that land of shadows which is also the land of Truth, where flatteries and railing accusations are alike unknown.[1] Sometimes the good is simply placed side by side with the bad, Numa Pompilius by Romulus, Leonidas by Xerxes, the Black Prince by that 'priest's bastard' Richard II., Louis XII. by Louis XI. and Francis I.; sometimes Rhadamanthus calls up culprits to his bar. But most of the combatants are more equally matched; each can overwhelm the other with reproaches, and wring confessions out of him, till of his vices and defects not one remains concealed.

For Fénelon, in his great desire to make God's and the people's enemies look foolish, becomes, like his own Cato the Censor, " too ardent against all the world"; Bossuet scarcely overshot the mark when he complained that M. de Cambrai's dead did nothing but insult each other.[2] He looks on History as the hand-maid of philan-

[1] p. 248.   [2] Le Dieu, ii. p. 22.

thropy, a pillory for scarecrow heroes, conquerors and despots, made to show—

> by what wretched steps their glory grows
> From dirt and seaweed as proud Venice rose;
> In each how guilt and greatness equal ran,
> And all that raised the hero, sunk the man.

His Alexander is a madman, Julius Cæsar a mere adventurer, climbing to power on the shoulders of his creditors and of garrulous and licentious women, Louis XI. a pettifogging trickster, Richelieu an odious tyrant, an apostate, and a murderer. The whole book is tainted with a strain of narrowness, rooted not indeed in the harsh fatuity of commoner priests, but in the arrogant unreason of dogmatic sentimentalism. All the weaker, womanish qualities of Télémaque appear; personal virtue is proclaimed the first criterion of statesmanship; conquest and territorial expansion are everywhere condemned, on lines which make the feudal land-law identical with the Law of God.

Yet there are times when Fénelon himself deserves the compliment that Virgil in his Dialogue pays to Horace, of writing with such delicate brevity and wit as to give new meanings to old words.[1] There is real political wisdom in the aphorisms of his Socrates or Solon, real humour in his 'mar-plot Alcibiades,' a lively Libertine more French than Greek, or in the pedantry of Cardinal Bessarion, excusing himself by the ὕστερον πρότερον of Greek philosophy for having visited the Duke of Burgundy before the King of France. And there is vigour in his portrait of the last wretched Valois, Henry III., with his monks and his Macchiavelli and his painted face, as again, in that of the founder of Burgundy's own line, Henry of Navarre, a prince 'whose ears were never too fine to hear things called by their names.'[2]

Thus, both in their virtues and defects, the Dialogues form a historical introduction to Télémaque, a kind of

[1] p. 298. [2] p. 315.

THE COURT PRECEPTORATE   81

foretaste of its principal lesson. For the last, but not the least sharply criticized, figure in the long gallery is Cardinal Mazarin, dead little more than thirty years, and once principal Minister to Louis XIV. himself. And, if Burgundy were taught that his grandfather's famous adviser was 'feeble and timid, treacherous and untrustworthy, a great comedian but not a great man,'[1] was not this an encouragement to raise his eyes still higher, and ask whether *now* the laws ruled, and not the man, whether flattery and self-indulgence were today unknown at Versailles, whether Louis' only aim in life was the well-being of his people?

To teach the little Duke to criticize his grandfather was an error not wholly unpardonable in a young and zealous philanthropist; it is less easy to acquit the tutor of a dangerous extravagance in the moral and spiritual education of his pupil.

In principle nothing could be better than Fénelon's method. Louville finds nothing to say of the religious training of Burgundy and his brothers, "because it is always and everywhere going on. It is known throughout all Europe that no Princes have had a more Christian education than ours." They were initiated into the strict and sober piety preached in the Education of Girls, taught that ceremonies were instituted as an aid to man's weakness, not for God's glory,[2] and strictly forbidden the little trivial "devotions," the agnuses and reliquaries and trumpery convent-amusements, that M$^{me.}$ de Maintenon was banishing from her great girls' school at St Cyr.[3] And in this article Fénelon had his reward; Burgundy's religion was often thought austere and obtrusive in his later years, but it was always innocent of fetishism.

Nevertheless, the Preceptor had the defects of his qualities. An apostle of the Interior Life in an age of formalism, he was inclined to refer everything to the

[1] p. 329.   [2] Wks., v. p. 584.   [3] Maintenon, Extracts, p. 28.

conscience, to guide his pupil less by a healthy outside discipline than by the inward sting of conscience and remorse. Burgundy's tornadoes of passion were received in perfect silence; his books and playthings were taken away, and he was left to himself till the reproaches of conscience overmastered him, and he fell at his tutor's feet, promising never to offend again. More than once he gave a written promise "on my princely honour to do all that M. l'Abbé de Fénelon bids, and in default, to submit to all manner of punishments and disgrace."[1] And Fénelon carried this principle to lengths from which our blunter English Protestantism recoils, creating where should have been a crop of salutary faults 'a sense of religion so strong as to force him to the most painful avowals.' Once, he says, when the Prince wished to hide something from me, I adjured him in the Name of God to tell the truth. Whereupon he burst out: "Why do you ask me in God's Name? That forces me to answer truly."[2] Do we not already see the reason of that cry of despair, which afterwards burst so strangely from a Jansenist's lips: "The Duke of Burgundy has so ruined his reputation with all men by his religious excesses, that he may well have to answer at the Bar of Heaven for having been too virtuous!"[3]

Still, the Preceptor knew the real Burgundy far better than we can ever know his fugitive shadow, and it is possible that these appeals to the heart and conscience may have been the only means of reaching him. St Simon and the Abbé Proyart talk lightly of his Reason, but Fénelon shows us a Télémaque whose mind was utterly deranged by the violence of his passions, his feeble will tossed powerlessly from side to side by forces which listened to one only voice, obeyed the only guiding hand—it was the hand of Mentor.[4] And Fleury says that Télémaque's original was hard to educate, though easy enough to teach; intelligence and penetration he had in plenty, but little of

[1] Bausset, i. p. 188. [2] Fén. Wks., viii. p. 123.
[3] St Simon, vii. p. 365. [4] Tél. Wks., xiii. Wks., vi. p. 504.

THE COURT PRECEPTORATE

the only quality on which it is possible to count; his *Vernunft*, that higher Reason which is also character, developed but slowly; he was twenty before it got the upper hand.[1]

Much, no doubt, must be set down to the count of his environment. Versailles, truly, was not the place where healthy freedom of thought and will could flourish abundantly; it is no wonder that M. de Broglie looks wistfully away from Louville's stuffy details to the mountain-air of Béarn, where Henry of Navarre first learnt to be a man. As Fénelon well knew, his pupil's great wealth of affection was slowly starving to death in that vast ice-chamber of a Court, where, as the preacher said, even at midsummer all was frozen. He had no mother; his father cared little for any of his children, and least of all for him; of his grandfather he stood, not in fear, but in positive dread. What was more natural than that Fénelon should eagerly dig a channel for the warm affections thus running grievously to waste—what more inevitable than that, in doing so, he should overlook the claims of the more masculine qualities, and unconsciously lead to himself what was meant for God, till he later turned in alarm at their tumultuous outflow, and bade Télémaque be less tender and more courageous in his love of one who would not always be with him, and learn to seek out truth and virtue for himself, rather than lean for ever on his guide?[2]

Excellently as he could discourse on the following and assisting of Nature, Fénelon himself was wanting in this supreme gift of his profession; neither as teacher nor as spiritual counsellor could he lead men onward while respecting their individuality, while preserving what St Francis of Sales has called the 'particular difference' of each mind. St Francis held each soul to be a little world, existing in and for itself as completely as the whole universe; but Fénelon saw in a new soul only a fresh world to conquer. His persuasiveness, says St Simon, had been

[1] Sallwürk, p. 57.   [2] Télémaque, bk. x. Wks., vi. p. 475.

spoilt by its own success, till it could bear no longer with resistance ; to be an oracle had become with him a kind of second nature ; over great things and small he must rule as an autocrat, commanding, but giving his reasons to none.[1] A bitter after-experience was to show him his mistake, to prove what helpless, clinging things the feelings and the conscience are, how vain was the hope of teaching Burgundy by their means to be " a son of valour and to fight the battles of the Lord."[2]

And this intensely personal education was disturbed by no influence from without. The Dauphin had had three or four little 'Children of Honour' always round him, but Burgundy and his brothers were only allowed youthful companions out of doors, and neither to them nor to one another might they speak apart or in a whisper. For Fénelon and Beauvilliers had early seen in their Prince the Ezra, who was to restore the Temple and the People of God after the present Babylonish Captivity, and they were resolved to keep him unspotted from that heathen world, where the Gospel was but little known.[3]

Not that Fénelon had in view the monkish youth that Burgundy, under other influences, actually became ; their little Prince, he told Beauvilliers, must, above all men, *bien faire vers le monde sans y tenir*.[4] But it was his mistake to fancy that he could do the whole work alone, that, with no assistance from the outside world, he could transfuse his own incomparable mastery over social graces into a Télémaque, who was by nature good and thoughtful, but not gracious, slow to think of what would give pleasure to others, ignorant how to make a present.[5] It was well enough to bid Burgundy be gay without folly, dignified without arrogance, amiable without weakness, and appear to give himself to all, while in reality he gave himself to none :[6] it was impossible to enforce these lessons, when the pupil's

---

[1] St Simon, x. p. 287.
[2] See below, ch. xiv.
[3] St Simon, viii. p. 424.
[4] Fén. Wks., vii. p. 240.
[5] Bk. x. Wks., vi. p. 504.
[6] Wks., vii. p. 291.

inborn awkwardness and love of solitude were being daily intensified by all the surroundings of his life.

And, in a larger sense, it may be said of Fénelon that he aimed wrongly at a great ideal. *Saint Louis se sanctifia en grand roi*,[1] wrote the Preceptor to his pupil, and Burgundy was to emulate alike the spiritual grandeur of his ancestor and the temporal glories of that other Christian hero, Charlemagne, was so to balance and contrive his two ideals that each would lend assistance to the other: his sanctity would call forth new qualities of greatness, and greatness, in its turn, become a means of sanctity.

But Fénelon blundered in that he did not carry on the two halves of his moral ideal side by side. Our popular axiom grounds the truest unworldliness on knowledge of the world, but Burgundy's knowledge of the world was to be grafted on unworldliness; firmly as Fénelon was resolved to give his pupil 'the royal wisdom of a Solomon, and a heart as large as the sea,'[2] it was only after education had made him a Saint that his master could think of making him a man and King.

And it was here that time and fortune failed him. In the midst of his work he was called away to Cambrai, and, two years later, was banished from the Court, while the inheritance of his labours fell to Chevreuse and Beauvilliers, poor but willing substitutes, and to the Jesuit Confessor, Father Martineau, an influence both grotesque and harmful. Thus the Burgundy that we know is the result of a hazardous experiment only half completed, or, rather, finished by bungling apprentices while the master-spirit was no longer by. Every trait in his character witnesses to a suddenly arrested development: his piety had all the feverishness of adolescence; he offended the prudes by an awkward schoolboy devotion to his wife, behaved in the presence of ladies "like a seminarist on his holidays," in camp was helpless, undecided and given to nursery pastimes; even Chevreuse, so late as 1709, found him indolent, childish, wanting in

[1] p. 235.   [2] pp. 320, 343.

vigour and tact and knowledge of men. Except in the one article of piety, where he developed strongly in a wrong direction, he remained—alike to his master's glory and his shame—exactly where that master had left him, a living monument to the vast capabilities of education, a warning also, against its dangers, when the whole of virtue, knowledge and religion is summed up in the person of a single Mentor.

CHAPTER VI

MYSTICISM AND THE MAXIMS OF THE SAINTS

> O Deus, ego amo te
> Nec amo te, ut salves me,
> Aut quia non amantes te
> Æterno punis igne.
>
> Sed sieut tu amasti me
> Sie amo et amabo te,
> Solum quia Rex meus es,
> Et solum quia Deus es.—St Francis Xavier.

FROM the Preceptorate of Burgundy and the Letter to the King is a long step to the Maxims of the Saints. As a buoyant reforming energy marks the one, so nervous despondency in search of rest is the characteristic of the other; and the reader must be warned to suspend judgment on the whole man, till he has passed from the sanguine outward Fénelon of society and the schoolroom to the inner Fénelon of the oratory, trembling before his God. Of the present chapter this second, less known, Fénelon is the subject, more especially in relation to those wrangles over Quietism, of which his Maxims was at once an outcome and a cause. Inasmuch, however, as that ill-starred volume is little comprehensible in itself, to the account of it has been prefaced a brief outline of the earlier mystical theories, out of which it took its rise.

In the Catholic Church Mystical Theology has always borne a special and restricted meaning, that often differs as widely from our vague *a priori* notion of mysticism as a hand-book of Chancery practice from our idea of natural equity. We loosely give the name of mystical to every vivid feeling of the Presence of the Divine, whether it be the poet who comes to God through His first Sacrament of Nature, seeing in the whole Creation Him everywhere and Him alone, or some platonising fancy that finds Him in the realm of mind, and cries, with Fénelon's master, Clement of Alexandria, that philosophy is a burning-glass kindled by His Light.[1] Or else it holds with Fénelon himself, that there is no explaining the contradictions in human reason, its alternations of strength and weakness, of intuitive certainty and helpless error—there is no giving account of a faculty that continually sees the Infinite, and in the Infinite all finite things, yet knows not what it is, nor what it thinks, nor what it wills—unless we believe that underneath an outward pall of hasty blindness, of daring hesitancy, there dwells the One Eternal Verity, revealing to us such chance beams of Truth as we can grasp and understand.[2] Yet, truly mystical as these ideas may seem to-day, it was not through them that Fénelon claimed a place among the theorists of mysticism; that word betokened in his age and Church no vague congeries of feelings, but a definite science of spiritual perfection, a means of supernatural approach to God. Based on a recognition of the boundless gulf that separates the finite from the Infinite, the realm of Nature from the realm of Grace, it was an attempt to bridge that gulf by transformation of the soul in God; the Elect, abandoning all mortal powers, were to be raised up to a state of Ecstasy, where they could contemplate their God in peace, endowed with faculties of perception in a higher Light, with faculties of action under a higher Freedom, than falls to the common lot of man.

The need of some such royal road to God began in a conception of His infinite remoteness, first taught to the early Church by the pagan schools of Alexandria. There Clement, the founder of Christian Mysticism, learnt to graft upon the Heavenly Father of the Gospels the Neoplatonic

---

[1] See de Faye's Clément d'Alexandrie (Paris, 1898), p. 175.
[2] Fén. Wks., i. pp. 25, 63, etc.

Absolute God, a spectral Frankenstein of Dialectics, far above our world of nature, and no nearer to our world of thought, to be sought for, after the manner of the Greeks, by endless distillation of abstractions, to be conceived of as the metaphysical pre-requisite of all things, a nameless, kindless, One unthinkable, not in space or time, not thought, nor goodness, nor existence, because before all of them and their hidden root—a God whom we call Lord and Father, only because our starveling speech can call Him by no worthier name.[1] And the second founder of Christian Mysticism, the so-called Dionysius the Areopagite, takes up the tale with more impassioned rhetoric, and shows God revealed, indeed, to sensuous souls in allegories and figures, but by the Initiated to be thought of only in negations, as existing absolutely and infinitely, not in any definable way, embracing and anticipating in Himself the whole of Being, and therefore rightly called the Lord of Ages, Providence because the cause of all things, although to be recognised in none, the Fount of Life, though Himself beyond all action, all conception, all existence, the spaceless, indistinguishable Centre, whence dart all rays of light.[2]

To reach a deity so exalted no mortal faculty could avail. Reason, said the Areopagite, can scarcely tell us what He is not, and it followed that only a Divine enlightenment could tell man what He was: the doctrine of the Absolute Godhead called for its logical correlative of Ecstasy, and Ecstasy, in its turn, for abdication of all finite powers.

Clement, indeed, had shrunk from his own conclusions, and made God the Son our object of knowledge, and the disciplined reason our means of advancement;[3] but the passionate Areopagite was bolder, and from an utter disbelief in human intellect passed quickly to conviction of its mischievous obstructiveness. Henceforward reasoning and

---

[1] Bigg, Christian Platonists of Alexandria, pp. 62 and *ff*. De Faye, pp. 218 and *ff*.
[2] See Inge, Christian Mysticism, pp. 104 and *ff*, and the fine chapter of Görres, i. p. 221.
[3] Bigg, p. 63.

perception were but delusive witch-lights in the Dark Night of Faith; the soul must set out on its mystical journey along the path-way of Renouncement. "Do thou, beloved Timotheus," the master wrote to his disciple, "leave behind thee sense, and all the senses can perceive, and all that reason can bring forth, and all things created and uncreated, that thou mayest be caught up to the beams of Heavenly Darkness, to Him who is above all knowledge and all existence."[1] Only thus could man rise to the state of thrice-holy Contemplation, wherein, as every mystic believed, the Heavens were opened, as once to Monica and Augustine in the garden, when the tumult of the flesh, and the phantoms of the earth and air were still, vanished was every dream and image from the mind, no mortal voice disturbed the silence of the soul, but for a moment it attained upwards to the wisdom that abides above all things, and heard Him speaking, not by tongue of flesh or voice of angel, not by parable or sigh, but speaking as He Is.[2]

First introduced into the western world by our own countryman, Erigena, the writings of the Areopagite were held in high honour through the Middle Ages; and it is round his characteristic doctrines of Absolute Godhead and Renouncement, of Ecstasy and Contemplation, that all the later mysticisms revolve. Yet, often as his theories reappear, the spirit that altered them was not the same; mysticism, when it began to speak by the mouth of St Bernard, entered on a new era in its history. The Areopagite's system had been essentially speculative, the child of an age when doctrine was fluid and thought was free, an attempt to dress religion in the clothes of metaphysics—nay, he often enough lies open to the charge brought against his Neoplatonist masters, of philosophizing less in the real spiritual interests of man, whose God they destroyed, than in the fancied honour of their Deity.[3] But the new

---

[1] De Myst. Theol., i. § 1. Heaven is, of course, "dark with excess of light."
[2] St Augustine, Conf., bk. ix. ch. 10. [3] See Bigg, p. 9, *note*.

Western mysticism was, above all things, devotional, entered upon wholly for the sake of man, and called, not to create new theories, but to make alive the old, to interpret hard dogmas to the heart and conscience, and clothe dry bones with flesh and blood. Through the veins of its leaders surged the fierce theology of the Middle Ages, with all its tender, boiling, passion, with all its deepened sense of sin ; poets, rather than philosophers, they could not rest in bare abstractions ; the metaphysical prerogatives of Sovereign Being became in their hands the apanage of a Godhead at once Absolute and Personal, of a Heavenly Father, who was also the Supreme Ineffable Name. Yet the savour of Neoplatonism still remained ; it was still on God's infinite perfections, on His inaccessible grandeur, that the mystics chiefly fixed their gaze ; if it was good to be mindful of His benefits, and better still to meditate His judgments, St Bernard held it best of all to contemplate His majesty, with souls lost for a while in ecstasy and stupor.[1] And the voice of the Areopagite echoes on in the unwillingness of many of the mystical saints to " beg from the creature a knowledge of the Creator "[2] by tracking His footsteps in the world ; they would have no other guide to God than God Himself, teaching the soul " without the sound of words, or the intervention of any bodily or spiritual sense, as it were in silence and repose, in the darkness of sense and nature, in a most secret and wonderful way."[3] Or we may find some traces of the old among the most personal mystics of the new, in the chill visions of St Teresa, where the soul dwells, anguished and lonely, in the midst of an inexorable desert of Silence,[4] in the grand austerity of feeling that made many a mystic keep for the Father the place usurped in popular language by the Son, and sink all metaphysical distinction of the attributes of God in the brighter conception of His unity. Nevertheless, the two chief mystical

---

[1] St Bernard, de Consideratione, v. § 32.   [2] *Ibid.* § 1.
[3] St John of the Cross, Spiritual Canticle xxxix. § 15. (E. T. Lewis, ii. p. 400).
[4] St Teresa, Autob., ch. xx.

conceptions have changed place; by Alexandria Ecstasy had been brought in simply as a correlative to the Absolute God; by the new Latin mysticism the Absolute Godhead is only retained for the sake of its machinery of Ecstasy.

For the new mystics, like the old, held that the best and truest knowledge of God was reached in a state of supernatural enlightenment, where the soul was well assured of the Presence of its Lord, though Reason had grown dim, and Feeling died away.[1] Nay, a vocation to this state was the mark that set apart the mystic from among the generality of men; they, when they prayed, could only meditate, passing slowly and with difficulty from one thought to another, holding converse with their Maker in words borrowed from some human tongue. But mystics had no need of speech or language; they fled to their higher prayer of Contemplation, where, as even unecstatic Bossuet allows, the soul spoke in a voice heard of God alone; only through Himself did they approach Him; only in loving did they tell Him of their love.[2] And therefore in its higher stages Contemplation was still and silent, 'passive' rather than 'active,' reposeful, like a living statue in its niche, the soul's loving, simple, and lasting attention to heavenly things, its absorption in the exceeding sweetness of the Beloved.[3]

And yet there is a vital difference between the old and new ideas of Ecstasy. With the Areopagite the difficulty of reaching God had been so great that he had little thought for other things beyond; the soul attained to super-sensuous knowledge of Him and rested there, feeling no need to turn that knowledge into virtue—was not one moment's Contemplation worth a thousand years' good works? But Western mystics, even when they echoed his language, understood it in a different spirit; their Contem-

---

[1] St Teresa, Autob., ch. x.
[2] Bossuet Wks., xiv. pp. 97, 98.
[3] St Francis of Sales, Traité de l'amour de Dieu, vi. ch. iii.

THE MAXIMS OF THE SAINTS 93

plation was not synonymous with Ecstacy—it was only one of God's means of moulding the soul, and should be deserted, says St Teresa, for more pressing duties, such as the nursing of the sick and poor.[1] And still less was Ecstasy made up of the sensuous visions and revelations, on which the greater mystics set but little store, even if they did not wholly disregard them, as did St John of the Cross;[2] they had none but hard words for the spiritual covetousness, that "gluttony of the soul," which delights in tears and trance and dreamy reverie, and forgets to show its love in doing justice, in serving God with courage and humility. Their notion of the Interior Life bore essentially a moral stamp; their Ecstasy was a state, not so much of wisdom as of holiness, of moral freedom, the Practical Reason clothed in supernatural dress, and delivered from 'God's only foe, the Evil Will.' It was a new supernatural life in Him, with fresh springs of action, fresh necessities, fresh ideals, "passive," in that it meant a glad, resigned, acceptance of all His workings in the soul, "active," in that the old human faculties were still alive, although transformed and purified, shackled no longer by the cramping chains of sin.

With such a spiritual aim before them, the new mystics, like the old, were plunged into deadly war with the natural man, and eagerly turned to the old Areopagitic gospel of Renouncement, reading into it a new and terrible moral intensity. Renouncement was not now a simple blotting out of forms and images and concepts from the mind, its cleansing from all that dimmed the radiance of the Nameless One; it was become a Detachment from all earthly ties, a breaking of Creation's bonds, whether these were worldly pleasures, or health, or friendships, or independent thinking, or even the consolations of religion: it was that Perfect Poverty which, in the bold words of Tauler, made man the

---

[1] See the quotations collected by Rousselot, Mystiques Espagnols, p. 368.
[2] Fénelon has stated the Saint's principle with great succinctness in Maximes des Saints (ed. Paris, 1697), p. 64.

equal of God. As the body draws gradually nearer to death, losing every day certain tissues till at length the wall of separation is broken down, so the soul must die to itself, not in any spirit of aimless hysterical sacrifice, not in any sensual lust of suffering for suffering's sake, but that it might be raised again a spiritual body, that its death might, even in this life, be swallowed up in victory. "Just as we know God rather by what He is not than by what He is," says St John of the Cross, borrowing the language of the old to express the meaning of the newer mysticism, "so it follows of necessity that, if we are to draw near to Him, it must be by renouncing and denying to the uttermost all that may be renounced or denied of our natural powers and faculties, in order that He may enter in and possess the soul. For, as the rays of the sun cannot shine through a window that is soiled or unclean, so the Spirit of God cannot light up, or transform into seeming identity with Itself the soul that is still tainted with the spot and stain of the creature. Then only is the mystical union accomplished, when the soul seems to have become God rather than itself, when, indeed, it *is* God, by participation in the Divine Nature."[1]

And from this ruthless immolation no human faculty was safe. The intellect must be purged by Faith, by Hope the memory, and by Charity the will, though the chief of the sacrifice fell on this last, as being, in mystical parlance, queen in the kingdom of the soul, worthy, alone of our faculties, to be the free mother of a free child, and give birth to that Love, which is the true bond of union between God and man.

For St Teresa and St John of the Cross were not all asceticism; above their mystical doctrine of Renouncement comes their mystical doctrine of Love. The school Theology had made much of knowledge—but what, they ask, is knowledge in comparison with Love? And answer that

[1] St John of the Cross, Ascent of Mount Carmel, ii. § 5 and iii. § 1. E. T Lewis, i. pp. 77, 242.

our understanding is dissipated on many things: not so our love. Knowledge is mortal, but Charity will never die. Love rushes in where thought shrinks back aghast; it fills with meaning and reality that infinite bond where speculation is helpless to affirm or to deny. The philosopher of old was right when he said that to meditate the things of God was to purify the soul, but to love them was to deify it, for the understanding must drag them down within the range of its eyes, but love raises itself on its own wings to the level of the Beloved.[1] "As a woman at marriage," says St Francis of Sales, "takes the name and rank of her husband, becoming noble, if he is noble, a queen, if he is a king, so the will changes its state according to the character of the love it has espoused, becoming carnal, if it is carnal, spiritual, if it is spiritual; nay, the very affections and passions, like children born of such a marriage, inherit also their own quality of love."[2]

Thus, even here, the peculiar moral character of Western mysticism pursues it. Its love might be passionate and inebriating, like the Areopagites, $ἔρως\ ἐκστατικὸς\ καὶ\ ζηλωτικὸς$,[3] but it was a love that showed itself not so much in outward works or sentiments as in the hidden roots of character—a vital indwelling principle, the mainspring of man's nature, the leaven of its lump; it was that truly Christian Freedom, which had, which could have, no other desire, no other glory, than always and everywhere to bear the yoke of God. "By Love," says St Bernard, "the soul moulds its will in the likeness of God, and loves Him as it would be loved."[4] "By love," says St Teresa, "I learned, a girl of nineteen, to tread the whole universe under my feet."[5]

With the seventeenth century the fiery heroic element in Latin Mysticism disappears. Its earlier leaders had

---

[1] Rousselot op. cit., p. 194, 451, etc.
[2] St Francis of Sales, Traité i. ch. iv.
[3] De Div. Nom., iv. § 13.
[4] See Helfferich, Christliche Mystik, i. p. 314.
[5] Autob. ch. iv.

written only for the cloister; but, by the time of St Francis of Sales, it had become 'an error, even a heresy,' to banish the higher devotion from the haunts of men. And, in adapting itself to this new environment, the whole theory takes a milder form. God dwelt no more apart in majesty immeasurable, but was to be seen and loved of all men, as the Heavenly Beauty;[1] the boundless asceticism of St Bernard must be translated into more modern language by one who was both a Christian and a man of the world. The old principle of Renouncement remained as before; man must still crucify the world in his soul, and make of piety a surgeon's knife, that cut between the sinew and the nerve; nevertheless, St Francis, the friend of unconverted man, the respecter of human powers and human possibilities, preferred the humble to the splendid virtues, the more useful to the more esteemed. 'It is enough,' he said, 'if we are good and faithful, pious and honourable men and women; it is for God to raise us higher, to choose whether we shall be His privy councillors or the scullions of His kitchen.'[2]

And Fénelon, the Fénelon of the Spiritual Letters, follows in his footsteps; in piety, as in literature, he would have a sublime so simple and familiar that all might understand it. His model in the Interior Life was Mary, the Mother of Jesus, of whose later days, he said, Scripture recorded nothing marvellous or striking, no stories or miracles, no prophecies or teachings of the people; she continued in prayer with the other women, not even outwardly distinguished from them. And how much greater was she thereby! Without all was simple and homely and hidden; within all was abandonment and silent love, endurance of the world for the sake of God alone, complete surrender of the heart and will, that He might the more abundantly love Himself within her—this was an adoration in spirit and in truth.[3]

---
[1] See Strowski's Saint Francois de Sales (Paris 1898), pp. 295, 334.
[2] St Francis Vie Dévote III., i. ii.   [3] Fén. Wks., vi. p. 69

And thus it was that Fénelon's teaching called for no retirement into a solitude, no theatrical process of 'conversion,' not even for any great change in worldly habits. Piety, he told his penitents, was not like worldly business; it needed no long stretch of uninterrupted attention, but much might be accomplished in a short space of time, even in those spare moments of their daily life, which most men were content to waste. The devout soul would still appear at Court, would live sociably and easily, without appearance of austerity, yet in continual subjection to its duties, in cheerful and hourly obedience to the will of God. Life would thus become a perpetual prayer, that spread itself over all the actions of the day, needing neither knowledge nor preparation, but able to be offered up in the midst of other occupations, for it meant no more than going about the duties of the day with the sole intention of pleasing God. The Saint would join in all that others did, except sin, yet by him all would be far better done, because entered upon in God's Presence, and for His sake, and not for the pleasure of the self.[1]

Yet, simple as was the state of sanctity, it could not be attained to without grave sacrifice and loss. Bitter enough, cries Fénelon, will be the deathbed of the natural man, for God is a jealous suitor, and, rather than suffer the continuance of self-love, he will tear the soul up at the roots. He afflicts it with spiritual trials and vertigo, till it does not know where it stands, or what is the reason of its pains; it cannot endure itself; it is full of languors and dryness; like a sick man, it is faint for lack of food, yet cannot bear the sight of the most tempting dainties. Slowly it begins to know itself, and be appalled at the sight; it loses all belief in its wisdom and virtue; self-love is driven from its hiding-place; it utters loud cries; it is made to unmask, and show itself in all its hideous deformity. The soul surrenders to the Will of God; it becomes like clay in the hands of the potter, like a

---

[1] See the 1st and the 231st Sp. Letters (Wks., viii. pp. 440, 595) and Wks., vi. p. 74.

weather-cock blown around by every breath of the Spirit ; with equal loving obedience it accepts pain or pleasure, health or sickness, death or life.[1]

After the winter has come the spring. Our old affections are withered and dead, and God is planting new supernatural affections in their place. For the soul cannot remain long in this state of nakedness, unprovided with any sort of affections ; it must put on the garments of the New Man, so soon as it has cast off those of the Old. Often we clothe ourselves again in the same virtues and affections as in our former state; taste and sensibility are with us again, but purified and chastened into conformity with God's Will ; our old affection for our friends returns, yet now we love them only in and for God. And how great is this friendship ! Our heart is boundlessly large, for it has taken on the immensity of Him Who professes it ; our love is infinite, generous, perfect, like His Own. Those who enter upon these ways of Pure Love become daily more enlarged, till at last God gives them a heart fashioned like His own, and a mother's tenderness for all that unites them to Him.[2]

Thus the Saint would have solved the problem of the Interior Life, and reconciled Liberty with Obedience. The just man did the Will of God, but the Saint's was a loving allegiance; he made an end to anxious quibbling with the Law—for the Law was hard and a stumbling-block ; it was a menace and a bondage—but the Children of God had passed beyond its grasp : he who had charity might do whatsoever he would.[3]

"Love is an excellent casuist, and will quickly set your doubts at rest," was Fénelon's best answer to the scrupulists, the evil outcome of an age of moralizing and literary portraiture of La Rochefoucaulds and La Bruyères and great Directors of Consciences, which had already sent forth many a bold explorer into that trackless land of selfishness, whose

[1] Wks., vi. p. 126 and see the 368th Sp. Let.   Wks., viii. p. 660.
[2] 40th Sp. Let.   Wks., viii. p. 486.   [3] 128th Sp. Let., p. 543.

boundaries ever stretch beyond our ken. No man knew better than Fénelon the dangers of that devouring preoccupation with self, that was always looking over its shoulder to judge the distance covered, or straining its eyesight forwards to count its future steps, that fled in prudish terror from little harmless indulgences, even from Divinely-sent consolations, yet was itself a vanity diseased. At its bidding imaginations were 'hung in black'; souls were tormented by vague, unreasoning, terrors, were troubled by the fear that they might some day be troubled, at the thought of sins past and sins to come. The loving, tender Father sank into a spy on the watch for man's transgressions, into a fowler who caught his feet in snares; he was a torturer who delighted in the sufferings of His creatures, so that many ruined name and health and fortune by their self-imposed austerities, and buried all the good they might have done under this hideous pyramid to pride. Others took a passionate interest in their own condition, grew tender to their trials, and maudlin over their faults; they felt their pulses twenty times a day, and sent continually to the Director, to beg new drugs and promises of quick recovery. But Fénelon could tell them of a better medicine—the simplicity that was at ease with God and men, for it turned away its eyes from self, content to see its own follies and vices only when they showed black against His light.[1]

And, as he preached self-forgetfulness to the scrupulists, so to the Pharisees Fénelon taught Humility, the second cardinal virtue of the Interior Life. True humility, he said, was the child of love, and not of despair; it saw and acknowledged its wretchedness, hoped nothing from its own strength, but all things from God's grace. It did not grovel in abject, false, abasement; nor was it as those hard, cold, proud, scornful, Christians, who were content to be guided by their own reason, and scoffed at the constant, inward Monitor as a chimera of the fanatics. The life of such men

[1] Wks., vi. pp. 133, etc.

was regular, and full of all the virtues; admirable moralists, they had meditated much about miracles and Providential interferences with history; cautious and self-possessed, they were always in the hands of their own good counsels. Yet they had feared to bow down and become as little children, and God treated them with a distant ceremoniousness becoming to their gravity; He endowed them with magnificent talents, and made them heroes in the eyes of the world.

Nay, such was his horror of self-righteous gravity, that Fénelon fled to the other extreme, and let his voice rise into a falsetto affectation of the nursery, crying to the immaculate wise that God's caresses and familiarities were not for them; He never called them to play upon His knee, but left them to grow old in their own enlightenment, often knowing less of His Love than many a converted sinner.

All their disdainful reasonings, the voice of the priest, the words of Scripture, could profit nothing; the Gospel itself was but a vain sound in their ears, unless the Inner Voice were there, to lend it strength and efficacy. This stirred up no discord, led into no pitfalls, preached no new doctrines; the soul abode in God's Hand, its presumption unincreased, its freedom undiminished, knowing only that God is all, does all, and demands all, that no good thing comes about but by His Grace.[1]

But the whole of Fénelon's spirituality could not be summed up in this desire to live by Faith alone. Like all mysticisms it was a compound of two separate elements, the one of permanent universal value, the other always a danger, often a curse. This higher longing to make religion commensurate with the whole of life, *esse et dissolvi in Christo*, never altogether absent, was chiefly characteristic of his later days at Cambrai; during the middle period of his life it was heavily weighted by a second factor, the spirit of his

[1] Wks., vi. pp. 119 and *ff.*

formal mysticism, of the Maxims of the Saints. And this differed from the first as the artificial differs from the natural, as a laboured contrivance from the freeborn gift of genius ; it was not an inspiration but a measure of policy, not an enjoyment but a stratagem, an attempt, as it were, to take the kingdom of heaven by force, to slip quickly and easily past all obstacles, whether humanly or divinely planted, and pack the whole of religion within a single formula of Pure Love, which, pale and faint and ordered as it was, recalls the Justification by Faith of greater Reformers.

Some pressure from outside there must always be, for mysticism whether preached in a grand or a debasing form, whether its prophet be St Teresa or some sensual and ignoble impostor, has never thriven except at periods of general restlessness and misery, when it could teach the gentler spirits to find refuge from surrounding evils within the castle of their own souls, or, as often in the Middle Ages, find voice for the Italian patriot's denunciations of his tyrant or the Flemish workman's discontent with a rotten social system. Wrong as it would be to place the whole strength of mysticism in the vehemence with which men recoiled from the known evils of this world to the shadowy glories of a world to come, it may be doubted whether even the flame of St Teresa would have burned so brightly, had not sixteenth-century Spain been crushed under a pall of such heart-rending wretchedness as to call forth from one of her contemporaries the saying that what chiefly kept men back from God was the belief that He had reserved all happiness for a future life.[1]

Yet it was at his peril that the mystic yielded to an easy temptation and turned the gift of God into a scourge for the drowsy gloom or the base spiritual covetousness of the many, into an engine for raising their common-place devotion to a higher power. For mysticism was in itself no commission to preach, though many mystics have been preachers, no fourth Counsel of Perfection, though in Latin countries it

[1] Louis of Grenada, qu. Rousselot, p. 68.

became the soul, the very conversation, of asceticism; it was a desire 'not to encompass but to be encompassed by its happiness,'[1] a dialogue of the soul with God, entered upon for love of Him, not in mere horror at the world. It was an incommunicable Grace, the outcome of a wholly personal experience, akin to the genius of the poet or the painter—nay, the mystic was himself an artist, enraptured by the moral grace and loveliness of One 'who had made all things good and beautiful, had brought their multiplicity and diversity into a perfect unity, so ordering and disposing of them that every part kept harmony one with another, and all were fitly ranged round Him who was the Sovereign Lord of All.' Catholic Saint and Protestant poet had but one prayer—

> Cease then my tongue and lend unto my mind
> Leave to bethink how great that beauty is
> Whose utmost parts so beautiful I find;
> How much more those essential parts of His—
> His Truth, His Love, His Wisdom and His Bliss,
> His Grace, His Doom, His Mercy and His Might,
> By which He lends us of Himself a sight?

And mysticism, like other arts, has also its paradox. The most self-centred of all studies, it must be pursued unconsciously by those who would not have to say with Fénelon, that, 'my love of God reaches madness whenever I do not seek it, but when I search I cannot find it. That which was truly in my mind at first becomes a lie so soon as I wish to put it into words.'[2] For with Fenelon the mystic was often lost in the Director of Consciences; he could not abandon himself to an inspiration so profoundly personal or forget his penitents, to find himself *solus cum solo*, alone with God, but moved heavily encumbered by the wants of others, like a poet who, being compelled to teach as well as feel, should spend his best efforts on a *Gradus ad Parnassum* for the use of those who would write

---

[1] Fén. Works, vi. p. 124. [2] 315th Spir. Letter, Works, viii. p. 640.

none but schoolboy verses. Too often his spirituality lived, as it were, from hand to mouth, hurriedly minting each interior sentiment into the current coin of language, that it might snatch for commoner souls some little profit from the 'Interior Ways,' even at the risk of vulgarising the whole, of distorting details into principles, ends into means, at the call of a momentary convenience. His conception of the Spiritual Life is marred, like the Ideal State in Télémaque, by a strain of nervous, reforming short-sightedness, a love of sweeping principles carried to their *reductio ad absurdum* in a trifle, an intemperate temperance that would proscribe each harmless luxury, because of its occasional misuse.

Thus, in contrast to the earlier mystics, he affects an almost Puritan rigidity in dealing with the lawfulness of Feeling. They, although no undiscriminating friends to passion, had not feared to glory in the joy and courage that pierced the dark clouds of earthly sorrow with the bright rays of victory to come; St Teresa marched to eager conquest under her banner of humility; even that more tremendous countryman of Cortes, St John of the Cross, had voyaged through strange seas of thought to islands that never mariner saw. But Fénelon was obsessed by the fear that his penitents would make even their religion the servant of their pleasures—"we show a strange ingenuity," he said, "in discovering means of self-gratification everywhere, even in our trials and adversities"—souls would tell over their own triumphant victories over temptation, or dwell with delight on their outbursts of emotion, till they came to lean on these alone, and think that there was no true piety without a transport of the imagination.[1] And so he excommunicated courage, as a remnant of the natural man, and declared that the soul which prayed with joy and fervour was a hireling, serving its Creator for a wage, but he who persevered through darkness and despondency was a loyal vassal, fighting for his Master at his own expense.[2] For the Interior Life was no battle-field, no bursting into

---

[1] 352nd Spir. Let. Wks., viii. p. 656.   [2] Wks., vii. p. 479.

unknown hemispheres, but the purgatory of a dark and languishing will; the soul was never better than when stretched, naked and thirsting, on the Cross, after all emotional solace was withdrawn.[1]

And this dismal conception of the Interior Life extends to other things than Feeling. The earlier mystics, although preferring the 'passive' to the 'active' life, had held that the best of all lives was a mingling of the two; Mary and Martha must join their labours, if the Guest were to be received with perfect hospitality.[2] But Fénelon circumscribes 'activity' within the narrowest possible bounds, out of dread lest every good deed we choose for ourselves should prove a pasture ground of vanity and self-love. We hear no more of works of mercy, or of St Teresa's maxim that the love of our neighbour is our best preparative to love of God;[3] Fénelon has little to say of active Charity except that its fussy practitioners are commonly the only persons who do not profit by their own enthusiasm.[4] Religion, indeed, would smooth and sweeten the course of daily life, and make us more tolerant of our neighbours; but there must be no romantic pretence of philanthropy—that teeming source of spiritual pride.[5]

And, in a larger sense, the older mystics, beginning with the same Renouncement, had "risen from the love of crosses to the love of souls," but Fénelon presses his penitent downwards into a poor, faint-hearted inaction. The Detachment that, in St Bernard or à Kempis, had been a mere condition, the self-forgetfulness everywhere begotten of a hotly-pursued ideal, becomes with him almost a sacrament, itself a goal, itself a resting-place in that age of scruples, because it raised men into a larger area than the gratification of their passions, because it freed them from all return upon themselves, from all the tenter-hooks of Hope and Fear. "We

---

[1] 156th S.L. Wks., viii. p. 557.
[2] St Teresa, in the closing words of the Castle of the Soul.
[3] Rousselot, pp. 366 and 436.   [4] Wks., v. p. 667.
[5] 352nd S.L. Wks., viii. p. 656.

THE MAXIMS OF THE SAINTS 105

must strive," he said, "to become always and everywhere a mere nothing, since all our miseries come from self-love, and only on nothingness has self-love no hold."[1]

Bossuet might cry out against this degradation of our race, little enough when it stood by itself, but capable of all things with God's help; but Fénelon could not stay to listen to his reproaches. His philosophy of life had darkened since the famous *L'homme s'agite, mais Dieu le mène* of his youth; man was no longer even Pascal's "thinking reed," but a reed which broke, and pierced the hand of him who leaned upon it.[2]

For indeed "it is only too often that our piety is coloured by our character." This author of Télémaque had all the dreamer's scorn for man in his mean and base reality, in his utter actual helplessness for good; this trembling, melancholy Christian, afraid to live, yet more afraid to die, shrank from the Destroying Spirit, so hard in His counsels to the children of men, so jealous of the glory of His Work, that He made nothing of man's merits, but bored down to the foundation of nothingness in the hearts of His Elect, as the builder of a castle bores down till he comes to the solid rock.[3] 'As the sacristan, at the end of the service, snuffs out the altar-candles one after another, so must Grace put out our natural life, and as his extinguisher, ill-applied, leaves behind it a guttering spark that melts the wax, so will it be with us, if one single spark of natural life remains.'[4]

Nor did the uttermost self-surrender, the sacrifice of all his thoughts and all his feelings, seem too heavy a price to pay for inward quietude to this Apostle of Simplicity, of whom an enemy said that he never could be simple for a single moment, but felt his own nature slipping away from him, his own words becoming false before they had passed his mouth, who could never be wholly mastered by a single emotion, but must watch and test and analyze while he felt,

[1] 190th S.L., p. 572.   [2] 240th S.L., p. 601.
[3] Wks., vi. p. 54.   [4] 203rd S.L. Wks., viii. p. 580.

must weep for himself while he was weeping for the death of a dearly loved friend, and find his only consolation in the exhaustion caused by grief.[1] Others might struggle; he wrapped himself in a dry and bitter peace, without pleasure or weariness, without great suffering, as without consolation, took no thought for the Future, but lived in a dry and thorny Present, letting his crosses come and go, as one sees a servant enter and leave a room again without speaking, and looked upon life as a third-rate comedy, on which the curtain soon would fall.[2] For he had plucked a Dead Sea apple from the coming century; we have not far to travel to the melancholy voluptuousness of Rousseau, or the "drowsy, stifled, unimpassioned grief" of later poets, whose rule it was—

> not to think of what I needs must feel
> But to be still and patient, all I can;
> And haply by abstruse research to steal
> From my own nature all the natural man:
> Till that which suits a part infects the whole,
> And now is almost grown the habit of my soul.

It was under stress of moods like these that Fénelon wrote the Maxims of the Saints, the book in which the weak, unworthier element in his mysticism gathered head, and brought him near the extravagances of Quietism.

For Quietism was a form of Stoicism run mad, of moral suicide, at once the gravest symptom and an attempted remedy for the disease characteristic of that age. It was the penalty of its willingness, both in politics and theology, to immolate the rights of the many before the glories of the One, of the encouragement it had given to literary hyper-analysis of motive and subtle spiritual pathology, of the determination—more than once rebuked in Fénelon's wiser moments—to pry into those secrets of our nature, over which God's mercy had thrown a veil. Morbid self-consciousness had passed from literature to life, and from life back again to literature; body and soul were sick

[1] See the 20th S.L., p. 457.   [2] 281st S.L., p. 625.

with it, and could not move without a dully smarting pain;
for it swelled and swelled, till the whole earth seemed full
of it, till it was: "Woe to him who is alone! For such a
one there is no silence! Even the desert is peopled with
Self."[1] As the sages of the fable grew mad through
knowing their own wisdom, so souls were poisoned by a
feeling of their own existence; the itch of personality
became at last intolerable, and the soul, tearing out its
own vitals, threw itself, a shell, a nothing, into the arms
of God.

To justify this murder of the Self the Quietist theory
was invented; where their predecessors had been satisfied to purify and transform, its leaders were resolute to
annihilate. Henceforward there were to be 'only two truths
in the world, the Allness of God and the Nothingness of all
else; and man could not honour the Allness of God except
by his own destruction. He must empty himself of all
content, just as in the Sacrament of the Altar, the true
type of the mystical life, bread, yielded up its substance to
the Body of Jesus Christ, and became but an accident of
itself.'[2]

An unacknowledged offspring of the mysticism of St
Teresa, Quietism spread rapidly, both in France and Italy,
during the seventeenth century, though without attracting
any general notice. Its first father, the Spanish monk,
Falconi, died quite unremarked (in A.D. 1632); nor did
authority meddle with the more striking figures of Mme.
Guyon (A.D. 1648-1717), or Francis Malaval, the blind seer
of Marseilles (A.D. 1627-1719), till, in 1687, a European
notoriety was given to Quietism by the trial of Michael de
Molinos. This enigmatical personage, by birth a Spaniard,
but by office a Director of fashionable consciences in Rome,
was, after enjoying many years' popularity, convicted by
the Inquisition of grave transgressions both in doctrine and
morals, and sentenced to lifelong imprisonment. Sixty-

---

[1] 165th S. L., p. 562.
[2] Mme. Guyon, Opuscules Spirituels (ed. 1791), p. 42.

eight Propositions, purporting to be extracts from his writings, were condemned by the Pope, and these have ranked thenceforward as the official definition of the Quietist heresy.

Not that Molinos and his brethren were deliberate innovators. They believed themselves to be carrying on the tradition of the great Spanish mystics, whose authority they quoted, whose expressions they freely used, till there often remains no more than a "dry, but true distinction" between St Teresa's language and their own.[1] Nevertheless, the ultimate difference was not small. Orthodox mysticism claimed to be only one of several roads to perfection, more excellent, indeed, than any other, but also more dangerous, and therefore accessible only to few. But Quietism was far from this exclusiveness; no product of the Universities, like Jansenism, nor, like the older mysticism, of any Religious Order—for Molinos was a secular priest, and Malaval "a layman without theology"—it was a movement of the spiritual democracy, of ignorance against learning, of personal experience against the dogmas of the Church, that longed to sweep away the barriers of Scholasticism, and install itself a truth for all men, and the only truth. Few could meditate, said $M^{me\cdot}$ Guyon, but all could rise to contemplation through the ecstatic prayer of the heart. Without this, said Molinos, there was no perfection; Meditation was for boys and weaklings, but Contemplation for strong men; the two forms of devotion stood to one another as a few drops of water to the fulness of the sea.[2]

The extravagance of the movement soon robbed it of all possible effectiveness; all Fénelon's intemperance is there, but raised to the superlative degree. Under the heading of 'Activity,' he had denounced only actions planned by us (as distinct from 'passive' actions planned by God, and simply accepted by our will); but Quietism included under

---

[1] Une sèche, mais véritable distinction, Bossuet, Wks., xiv. p. 143.
[2] $M^{me\cdot}$ Guyon, O. S., pp. 10, 142. Molinos, Spiritual Guide, i. §§ 25, 163; iii. §§ 177, 178.

THE MAXIMS OF THE SAINTS 109

that hateful name all conscious action whatsoever. For it held that spiritual covetousness and pride were so inseparably connected with every thought and action of the conscious Self as to make the only safe road to Detachment lie in entire cessation of self-consciousness: Often, said Molinos, the one thing that keeps men back from God is their soul's knowledge of its own operations.[1]

The means to this end was dictated by psychology. Like all the mystics, Molinos divided the soul into two separate portions, an upper realm of thought and will and memory, a lower of imagination and appetites and feelings. In this lower realm he placed self-consciousness; the upper nobler region of the soul was 'pure spirit,' and, as such, will and intelligence moved unconsciously, knowing scarcely what they did, leaving no trace of their actions on the Self.[2] Only when there was communication with the lower self of feeling could the soul take count of its own operations; and this door of communication it was the business of the Interior Life to close by means of trials and purgations. Self-knowledge would then cease, and feeling die, except it were a simple, dumb, capacity for suffering, or the soul's 'deadly, but still and tranquil hatred for itself.'[3] Lastly, having thus sold or killed that cruel beast, self-conscious will,[4] the soul would give itself over to God in one solemn act of unreserved surrender, and 'continue in that holy indolence and nothingness for a whole day, for a whole year, for its whole life.'[5]

Nor need this quiet be disturbed by the speculative vagaries of the intellect. To save the soul the trouble of thinking, Molinos borrows a formula from the Areopagite, and bids it rise above pictures and attributes and dogmas, beyond the Trinity and the Incarnation, to a view, wholly obscure and indistinct and general, of the Divine Essence as It was.[6] "If Christ be the Way," said Malaval, not without a touch of sublimity, "let us certainly pass by Him to God;

[1] S. G., i. § 29. [2] *Ibid.* § 35. [3] iii. § 108.
[4] ii. § 67. [5] i. § 86. [6] i. § 9.

but he who is always passing never arrives at his journey's end."[1] Mme. Guyon's "carnal perversions of spirituality" are more redolent of earth, notably when she separated God's Being from His attributes, and called these last the three-score valiant warriors, who stand round the bed of the true royal Solomon, to ward off such as have not been wholly annihilated.[2] But Molinos wastes few words on this, and hurries on to describe the state where the soul is dead and buried to itself, after all thought and action, all life and feeling, are laid aside, where, dying and not dying, resigned and not resigned, suffering and not suffering, it is encompassed by the spouse with the soft and savoury sleep of nothingness, wherein it receives in silence, and enjoys it knows not what.[3]

Of outward matters such a true Christian need not think at all, for he had made a submission, at once free and interior, blind and persevering, to God's earthly vicegerent, the Director of Consciences[4]—a rule of life unhappily not peculiar to the Quietists, but common, in greater or less degree, to the whole Catholic Church, ever since Ignatius Loyola had crystalized the mystical doctrine of self-surrender into his precept of Obedience.[5] But it was reserved for Molinos to outdo all previous extravagances, and claim for the Director's words a miraculously granted infallibility.[6]

Thus guided, the Saint would plod along with bandaged eyes, like an ox at the mill, assailed every moment by horrible thoughts and temptations, till he seemed to be enduring all the tortures of the damned. Yet in the midst of this darkness grew wisdom and valiant love; only through its trials did the soul come to a knowledge of its own unworthiness; the worst of all temptations was to be without temptation.[7]

[1] qu. Bossuet, Wks., xiv. p. 48. [2] *Ib.* p. 50.
[3] S. G., iii. §§ 69, 102, 127. [4] *Ibid.* ii. §§ 68, 76.
[5] See the remarkable chapter on the Constitution of the Jesuits in Gotheim's Ignatius von Loyola, pp. 402 and *ff*.
[6] S.G., ii. § 72. [7] i. § 62.

Nor might holiness dare offer any active resistance to the Enemy; it received his onslaught with 'tranquil dissimulation and quiet contempt,' flying, in its helplessness, to God, as a little child, terrified at the sight of a monster, hides its face in its mother's bosom.

The Christianity that strove to fight its faults was exterior and fragmentary indeed: God's gifts of strength and perseverance were for beginners, not for the Perfect; the true soul cast away this garish raiment, and hid its shameful nakedness in him.[1] Now it would not be perturbed or sorrowful, though it fell even for the thousandth time, but would continue in the same serenity and confidence, not even asking whether pardon had been granted or no.[2] For, although the virtues, as virtues, had been lost, it had recovered them again in Jesus Christ; now it exercised them all without knowing that it did so, without power of distinguishing one action from another.[3] Now its only occupation was a general love, without motive or reason for loving; prayer was become action, and action prayer; and all things were indifferent to this holy soul, for all were one, and all were God.[4]

To forswear the evil and save the good which he believed to be latent under this mass of mischievous extravagances, was Fénelon's aim in writing the Maxims of the Saints. As it stood, the Quietist doctrine was clearly indefensible; by their perpetual Sleep of Nothingness, their abiding surrender of their will, by bidding the upper and lower souls live together 'as next-door neighbours that had no acquaintance,'[5] Molinos and Mme. Guyon seemed, even to their more dispassionate judges, to be ruining the foundations of moral responsibility, and laying the axe to the root of Repentance.[6]

And Fénelon had no wish to pose as their defender.

---

[1] Mme. Guyon O.S., pp. 198-203.   [2] Mol. S.G., ii. § 124.
[3] Mme. Guyon O.S., p. 247.   [4] *Ibid.* pp. 169, 231.   [5] *Ibid.* p. 254.
[6] For the opinions of Leibnitz and Jurieu see Scharling, pp. 93, 115.

Molinos' book he had never read, and was full of reprobation of its author; Mme. Guyon, though an excellent person and speaking 'quite correctly enough for a woman,' he found grossly ignorant of the first principles of theology.[1]

Nevertheless, he believed that, by transposing the question on to a different ground, it might be possible to conciliate an unbounded 'passivity' with the tradition of the mystical saints, and their reverence for the freedom of the will and the lawful ordinances of the Church. Scrupulosity would now receive its death-blow in a state habitual, yet not invariable, of tranquil co-operation with Grace, that willed nothing for itself, but bent all its forces towards the accomplishment of the divine good-pleasure, swallowing up the separate virtues in an all-embracing love, and yet in a tissue of acts so simple, so peaceable, so uniform, that they could hardly be distinguished from one another, fulfilling every daily duty of the Christian life.[2]

Mme. Guyon and Molinos had resolved the whole Interior Life into the trance of Passive Contemplation, but Fénelon tries to keep the two apart; his Passivity was as little as possible ecstatic; it was an inspiration in no way different from that of all the Just, except that it was stronger and more special, inasmuch as God showed Himself most clearly to those who were nearest to Him.[3] His Elect would dwell in no slothful Buddhist *Nirvâna*, but in a state of peaceful, otherworld serenity, far different to the jading Activity of commoner souls, always eager to run before Grace, to recall its past impressions, to co-operate with

[1] See Wks., ix. pp. 363, 570.

[2] Maxims, pp. 201, 238. The Maxims, being a condemned book, is excluded from the standard edition of Fénelon's works. I therefore quote from the original edition of 1697.

[3] pp. 67, 179, 199, etc., but the matter is put more clearly in the later controversy with Bossuet. Tous les Chrétiens sont appelés à la passivité, mais ils ne seront pas tous appelés à la contemplation passive. On peut être passif sans contempler, et on peut contempler sans être passif: être passif n'est autre chose que retrancher l'activité, c'est-à-dire, les actes inquiets et empressés de 'intérêt propre. Wks., ii. p. 365.

THE MAXIMS OF THE SAINTS 113

it more violently than they need.¹ Never more truly active than when it was wholly passive in God's Hand, the soul became a feather blown about by all the winds of Grace; like a ball on a plane, it had no natural resting-place or movement of its own, but ran with equal readiness to every side, obedient to the lightest whisper of God's Voice, for love of Him was now its life, its substance and its soul, the one determinant of all its acts.²

Such was the state which Bossuet was to call an unscriptural indolence, a disguised apology for Molinos, a flat defiance of the first principle of Grace: "God only helps him who strives himself."³ And certainly there are moments—not only in the Maxims—when Fénelon seems to speak the true language of Quietist aberration, as when he dwells on his tissue of acts almost imperceptible, or on an abandonment of self so perfect that it abandons the abandonment itself,⁴ or bids the sinner endure the sight of his defects with patience, and hate them because they are faults, not because they are his own.⁵

Nevertheless, Fénelon tried, although not very successfully, to stop short of the worst moral danger of Quietism. Molinos and M$^{me.}$ Guyon might keep the soul in ignorance of its own operations, but for Fénelon the will and intelligence were conscious agents, responsible, not only for themselves, but also for the imagination and the feelings.⁶ The sacrifice of consciousness was, in his view, not only dangerous, but unnecessary, since, the real enemy of Detachment being, not man's simple knowledge of his actions, but the selfishness which that knowledge called forth, it was enough to kill that selfishness, and install in its place the love of God.

The keynote, therefore of the Maxims is Disinterestedness in its widest sense, complete indifference to ourselves;

---

[1] p. 100. [2] p. 231.
[3] Nec adjuvari potest nisi qui aliquid sponte conatur. Wks., xiv. p. 422.
[4] 199th S.L. Wks., viii. p. 578.   [5] 288th S.L., p. 628.
[6] Maxims, p. 121. Fénelon's language, however, was thought unsatisfactory by the Pope, and is condemned in the 14th Proposition of the Roman judgment.

for between the two loves there is no peace, both cannot govern in one soul—

> Our hearts, their scantiness is such,
> Bear not the conflict of two rival tides.

Yet it is when he passes from the negative to the positive, from the perfect soul's neglect of self to its all-absorbing love of God, that the old dread of spiritual avarice and pride drives Fénelon to the farthest lengths, and makes him stretch acknowledged principles, until they snap beneath his hand. It was a common doctrine of the mystics that, the stronger the love, the less it held by love's accompanying benefits, the 'sensuous relish' of piety in this present world and hopes of Paradise in the world to come ; and many of them had played with the mystical paradox, which offers to forego all claim on Heaven, if it can better do God's Will in Hell—though none more trenchantly than Tauler, who said that, if sentenced to Hell, he would certainly go, and drag his Maker with him. But for Fénelon such mere conditional sacrifice of Heaven was not enough ; perfect Disinterestedness was only reached when the impossible case was become a reality, and the will still clung to God, though the disordered imagination saw itself actually predestined to eternal fire—[1]

> My soul is a forgotten thing ; she sinks—
> Sinks and is lost, without a wish to rise ;
> Feels an indifference she abhors, and thinks
> Her name erased for ever from the skies.

The Many, indeed, might struggle on, buoyed up with present Graces and hopes of future Paradise, but the perfect soul disdained these hireling Righteous, these mercenary Just, and loved the Heavenly Beauty for itself alone, tearing out from its heart all feeling of pleasure or complacency, nay, of all reflection on God's love.[2] Nor was the sacrifice of self completed if the soul still loved Him as its Benefactor ;

[1] Max, pp. 87 and *ff*.   [2] p. 226.

gratitude and friendship and desire of Union must go the way of Hope and Fear, for the Perfect must love Him as He loved Himself, by passionless, high abstraction, as the Divine Goodness self-subsisting, not as *their* Maker, *their* Redeemer, not as the eternal reward of man.[1]

Such was the system of Pure, Disinterested, Love, which Fénelon preached, not as the occasional luxury of a sensitive conscience, but as the highest expression of Christian Truth, as the goal to which all faithful souls must tend. And certainly the doctrine has its barren grandeur, even on Mme· Guyon's fervid lips, though it is difficult not to convict it of unreality, not to feel that it mistakes the nature as well of God and man as love. In it speaks first the anxious Director, wishful by one bold stroke of nervous tactics to cut off scrupulosity's last retreat, to rout the gross and sensual piety that lusted after a Paradise crammed full of all the gifts of God, whence only God Himself was absent. And its best apology is its utterance in an age when Jesuit cheap-jacks were accustomed to haggle with God for the price of a soul, to discuss whether it was necessary to love Him once in the week or once in the year, or whether salvation might more cheaply be purchased at the price of one act of love in a lifetime.[2]

But there was more in Fénelon than the apostle of Passivity—even in devotion he had much of the intellectual epicure, in love with that idea of the Good for the sake of the Good which has never wanted for champions from the days of Plato till the time when Goethe confessed himself " haunted by Spinoza's wonderful saying : ' He who would love God aright must not seek to be loved in return.' To be disinterested in all things, but especially in love and friendship, became my rule, my joy, my exercise, so that

[1] p. 10. The idea is developed in the later controversy, see esp. Wks., iii. pp. 360, 361, and see the excellent summary in Deharbe's Volkommene Liebe Gottes, ch. ii.

[2] See the Propositions condemned by Alexander VII. and Innocent XI. in Denzinger, Enchiridion, pp. 254, 258.

the froward words I later wrote—*Wenn ich Dich liebe, was geht es Dich an?*—came from my very heart."[1]

And Fénelon was the child of a delicate graceful fastidious age that could never lay by its pretty romantic tendernesses, its love of beautiful sentiments finely analyzed, to follow the ruder counsel of St Bernard and 'love without a way.' The model suitor of its earthly courtships often found his own raptures more engrossing than the charms of her who called them forth; and, even in religion, St Francis must distinguish between a love of holy Resignation and a love of thrice holy Indifference, between a love for the sake of the benefits and a love arising out of the benefits, between a love that was really of God and a love for the pleasure of loving.

And the influence of his age was strong on Fénelon in determining the form in which he should cast his images of the love of God. For the mystic, driven to express the inexpressible, must of necessity speak in parables and metaphors, must inflict on the Lord the shame of man's words, and limit and accommodate His Love to the cramped vocabulary of some human passion. Just as the East had turned to the Spirit, so Western Mystics found their symbolism in the Flesh; they took the Song of Solomon as the charter of their faith, and made the love of man for women the pattern and initiation into the love of man for God.[2]

But Fénelon would hear nothing of this bridal love; his age thought more of friendship, as a union rarer and better, more reasonable, more stable, more within man's own control. Marriage was at best, a state of very toilsome bondage, to be entered into in a spirit of penance, and only made tolerable by God's Grace; but friendship was the chief of earthly blessings or curses, the world's worst embassy to our soul if it were only natural, an almost sacramental union, if it were ordained for us by God. And therefore it was

[1] qu. Baumgartner's Goethe, i. p. 156.
[2] See Mr Coventry Patmore's Rod, Root, and Flower, p. 136.

the worthier type of man's relation to his Maker : " Be with him," Fénelon cried, " as though you were in the company of a dear friend with whom you feel at ease. You meet, you listen, you speak, or else "—adds this true Quietist— "you say no word ; you are as happy in your silence as though you had talked the whole of the time." [1]

Nor did Fénelon always conceive of this friendship as reciprocal ; often it was modelled on that romantic devotion of man to woman, which was known to his age as Gallantry and pronounced to have nothing in common with Love. Indeed the two feelings were as the poles asunder, for the one was an affection of disinterested benevolence, but the other an imperative desire for union—Friendship, said La Bruyère, lives on sacrifices and services rendered, while love lives on itself. And Gallantry—if by the word he understood no flimsy drawing-room devotion, but the very noble and chivalrous Stoicism of Corneille—was of all friendships the most unselfish ; it asked for no payment, no return of affection, its best requital was acceptance of its service. And so, thought Fénelon, should it be with the Love of God ; the perfect soul's devotion would be no whit the feebler though God knew nothing of its Love.[2]

And the same thought pursues him even into that Ode on Christian Childhood, wherein, far better than the Maxims, his theory finds its true expression. There Pure Love is painted as a night of endless darkness, of holy quietude unspeakable, a martyrdom of sighs without desire, where—

> Loin de toute espérance
> Je vis en pleine paix
> Je n'ai ni confiance
> Ni défiance
> Mais l'intime assurance
> Ne meurt jamais.

---

[1] 141st Spir. Letter. Wks., viii. p. 550.
[2] Ou aimerait Dieu autant, quand même par supposition impossible, il devrait ignorer qu'on l'aime ou qu'il voudrait rendre éternellement malheureux ceux qui l'auraient aimé. Maxims, p. 11.

> Content dans cet abîme
> Où l'amour m'a jeté,
> Je n'en vois plus la cime,
>   Et Dieu m'opprime ;
> Mais je suis la victime
>   De vérité.[1]

But theologians will tell us it is right that the voice of Bossuet should break in on this solemn silence, proclaiming that the Maxims and all that appertained to it was no victim of truth, but fell itself under the very condemnation hurled by its author against Molinos, of destroying Christianity under pretence of making it more pure. Like many before him, Fénelon would not recognize that Christian Mysticism is no single tendency, but a nice adjustment of two opposite forces, where the Particular must qualify the General and the centripetal hold its contrary in equipoise; as, in its first principle, belief in a limited Personal God must check the doctrine of Absolute Godhead from expansion into a Pantheistic *Alles ist Gott und Gott ist Alles*, so, in its practice, Contemplation of the far-off abstract Essence of Divinity must be balanced by the remembrance of an ever-present Crucified Saviour, God made Man. Forgetfulness of this last condition was the great blot on Fénelon's system, nor could the stain be washed away by many half-hearted correctives; it was of little use to style neglect of Christ's Humanity ' a damnable error,'[2] when traces of that very error were discoverable in the Maxims, or to bid the Disinterested still view God as a Person, yet love Him chiefly as an abstraction of the Schools, as the Idea of His own Goodness, separated from Himself.

" Christ's Church," said one of Fénelon's opponents, " is not a school of metaphysics," and more than once the author of the Maxims stood in sore need of this reminder. For he had broken away from the tradition of the Latin

---

[1] Wks., vi. p. 660.   [2] Maxims, p. 197.

THE MAXIMS OF THE SAINTS 119

Mystics to follow Clement of Alexandria,[1] the most metaphysical of all the Fathers, and, though at heart a Christian, a Greek philosopher in tongue, nor ever so more openly than in his teaching of Disinterestedness, the doctrine for which Fénelon chiefly valued his authority. Their ends in view, indeed, were not the same ; Fénelon's was a purely spiritual, Clement's an also philosophic Detachment, Fénelon's Saint a puppet in the hands of God, Clement's Gnostic himself already, ' a god that walked abroad in flesh,' a sage, half Christian half Platonic ; his fulness of perfection was a state of holy ' apathy,' rough-hewn, it may be, by the precepts of the Gospel but shaped in the Stoic mould of Epictetus.[2]

But Fenelon, with his master's language, adopted not a little of his master's spirit. Both dreamed the same ideas of sunny passionless serenity, unaided by feeling, untainted by desire, that touched earth lightly with one foot ; both made its mainspring Love, yet a love far different from the tumultuous cravings of St Bernard, an ordered calm affection of the Reason, worthy of men to whom ideas stood nearer than realities. ' In St Clement,' said Bossuet, ' we should look in vain for tender communings of the soul with God, for the delights of Spiritual Marriage, the chaste embraces of the Song of Songs.[3] For Clement's Platonism raised him high above the gross emotions of a carnal world : " he could not bear that the rose of Sharon should blossom on this common soil, and he paid the price of his transcendental theology in that his love was not for Jesus but for the Logos, the Ideal." [4]

And Clement's disciple also put an Idea in place of a

---

[1] Clement (fl. circa A.D. 150-213) was treated as a Saint by Fénelon and Bossuet, though his name had been omitted from the Roman Calendar by Clement VIII. See Bigg, Christian Platonists, p. 272.

[2] Dr Harnack (Dogmengesch, i. p. 557) declines to fix the respective limits of Clement's Christianity and Greek philosophy. The interaction on his doctrine of Gnosis (or Perfection) of Christianity, Stoicism and Platonism is well brought out in Eugène de Faye's Clement d'Alexandrie, pp. 256 and *ff*.

[3] Wks., xiv. p. 395.   [4] Bigg, Christian Platonists, p. 93.

Being, and also paid the price, in that, by his doctrine of Disinterestedness, he choked with the sand of over-subtle distinction the simplest spring of Christian motive, and threw the chill reproach of selfishness over the most natural of Christian aspirations. For, when love is of a Person, selfishness and unselfishness have no meaning; the poet who wrote that 'Love seeketh not itself to please' added immediately 'Love seeketh *only* self to please,' and the one maxim is as true as the other; in heavenly as in earthly love there is no answer to the eternal dualism save that of the wisest of theologians: 'Duplex est dilectio, une concupiscentiæ, alia amicitiæ, utraque diliges Dominum Deum tuum.'[1]

Nor does the true lover wish a nearer solution. 'He loves,' says St Bernard, 'and asks not how or why. He loves because the Beloved is worthy of his love; he loves that he may love the more, seeking no reward yet earning, it, for his Reward is the Beloved Himself.'

[1] St Thomas Aquinas quoted Deharbe, p. 191.

MME. GUYON

FROM AN ENGRAVING

CHAPTER VII

MME. GUYON

> Ce style inusité ne peut s'autoriser
> Et, croyez-moi, madame, on peut en abuser.
> Par l'époux quelquefois une jeune mystique
> Entend un autre époux que celui du Cantique.
> —Bishop Fléchier.

A FEW months before he went to the Court, Fénelon became acquainted with the woman who was destined to be the evil genius of his life. Jeanne Marie de la Motte Guyon was the daughter of a gentleman of Montargis of considerable wealth and position, and ardently devoted, like all his family, to the interests of the Church. Born in 1648, three years before Fénelon, she was married very young to an invalid twice her age, and left a widow before she was thirty, with three small children and a large fortune. From her youth up, she had been a victim to the religious 'experiences' common to hysterical women, and these were turned in a definitely mystical direction by the Duchesse de Béthune, daughter of the disgraced Minister Fouquet, who spent some years at Montargis after her father's fall.

But the lode-star of Mme. Guyon's mystical career was a certain Father Lacombe, a Barnabite monk of ready wit and attractive presence, though at bottom a poor creature, eaten up with vanity, unable to exist outside of a circle of feminine admirers, though willing enough to sit at the rich widow's feet. Not that he was a mere rascal, trading on her credulity; in his small way he was sincere enough, a dupe rather than a swindler, a hanger-on of the bounties, spiritual and material, of the 'mother of the little Church,' the contented son in Grace of a patroness who was also his penitent, and some years his junior in age.[1]

Their close friendship did not begin till after the husband's death. During the earlier years of her widowhood, the mystical attraction grew steadily in violence; M$^{me.}$ Guyon fell from one nervous crisis into another, she could no longer pray, she could not withstand temptation, she had fallen from Grace, Hell was opening its mouth to receive her. In her earlier troubles light had alternated with shadow, but now all was dark; she fell at last into a state of utter insensibility, that seemed the consummation of all her woes.

From this she was awakened by the voice of Lacombe. A single Mass freed her from her pains; her soul awoke, and conceived a violent desire to join Lacombe in Geneva, there to renew, on the same spot, the famous spiritual friendship which had bound her patron saint, M$^{me.}$ de Chantal, to St Francis of Sales.[2]

Justifications for this craving were easy to find. Like M$^{me.}$ de Chantal, she must have been called to forsake home and family for God; her late despondencies were the Mystical Death, the last stage in the purgatory of the soul. By the time she set out for Geneva (July 1681) she was already Perfect; she now practised all the virtues without knowing that she did so; she could not mortify herself, because she was beyond the reach of mortification; virtually she could not sin, because the sin is in the Self, and the Self had been stripped off; all she now did was done in God, and done divinely.[3]

Yet it was not enough to enjoy "all the happiness of the Blessed in Heaven, except participation in the Beatific Vision"; after the Resurrection came the Apostolic State, in which assistance must be given to others.[4] Now she could teach and preach with marvellous ease, because her

---

[1] Autobiography of M$^{me.}$ Guyon (ed. of 1791), ii. p. 70, and see Lacombe's letters to her in Bossuet Wrks., xviii. pp. 467 and *ff*.
[2] Aut., i. p. 263.   [3] Opusc. Spir., p. 246.   [4] Aut., iii. p. 103.

words were given her from Above; she could write without thinking what she was saying, because an excellent Penman held her hand; she could perform miracles, knew what was passing in the minds of others, had absolute power over their souls and bodies.[1] And at her first meeting with Lacombe she developed a new mastery over Graces physically bestowed—the Plenitudes and Spiritual Maternity and Fecundity that an indignant Bossuet was one day to declare unexampled in the Church—and later defined as an influence so pure that there was nothing of human sentiment in it, a mere flux and reflux, that went from her to Lacombe, and back again, to lose itself in the Divine and Invisible Unity.[2] And in her later career these Graces came upon her in such numbers that she must take to her bed till she could discharge them on someone; it was only after long practice that she learned how to bestow them in silence and from a distance.[3]

For five years (1681-1686) she rambled about Savoy and the south-east of France, sometimes with Lacombe, sometimes at his heels. Everywhere it was the same story, first, a rain of spiritual blessings, conversions, miracles, devils cast out, exclaiming, as they went, that Mme. Guyon was one of their deadliest enemies;[4] later, the affrighted Satan stirred up wicked men to accuse her of heresy or sorcery or impure relations with her friend. One bishop after another esteemed and admired her more than words could say, but begged her to leave his diocese, either because its air was dangerous to her health, or because he could not approve her fashion of introducing her peculiar opinions everywhere, to the destruction of all peace, even in the holiest religious communities.[5] Eventually Lacombe was recalled to Paris, and Mme. Guyon went with him, little thinking that both of them were marching to their doom. Fifteen months later, he was arrested, convicted of teaching Quietist heresy, and imprisoned for life in the castle of Lourdes; Mme. Guyon

[1] ii. pp. 133, 187. [2] ii. p. 10. [3] p. 233.
[4] p. 103. [5] See Fén. Wks., iii. p. 7.

was shut up in a convent and examined, but discharged a few months later through the influence of some devout ladies of the Court, who had become interested in her case. (September 1688).

A very notable change now took place in her state. Her old friend, the Duchess de Béthune, had returned to Court, to become a chief figure in the devout Beauvilliers' circle, and through her, M$^{me.}$ Guyon made her way into the confidence of the whole society. They were none of them critical: besides, the Duchess was a masterful woman, before whom Fénelon himself bent in reverence, and she had lately married her younger brother to M$^{me.}$ Guyon's rich little daughter.

Moreover, that lady bore about her none of the marks of the shady religious adventuress. Though past forty, she was still striking and attractive in appearance, never at a loss for a word, but able to speak with great force and eloquence on matters of devotion.[1] And her peculiar mystic 'inwardness' was of a kind to commend itself specially to these pious courtiers who had long made religion the chief business of their life, their one screen from the intolerable glare of publicity which beat about the comfortless splendours of Versailles.

Devotion, indeed, *le spleen moral de la spiritualité*, had become a general refuge of the Court, now that its glories were departed, leaving behind them nothing but forms, whose substance had long withered away. The solemn melancholy chess-game still went on; men still went to sleep on self-interest and rose up to self-interest in the morning, still wooed the good opinion of a world they despised, and sought the company of those they loathed, rather than suffer the disgrace of being alone. But there was now no need of a preacher to tell them all was Vanity; a chill of utter gloom and lassitude had settled on Versailles, and men grew old there quickly, having nothing that they wanted, and all they did not want. There was no glamour

---

[1] Phélippeaux. *Relation du Quietisme*, p. 4.

left, and no illusions; 'the king of the gods was aweary,' the old light-hearted gaiety was gone, and in its stead, the ante-chambers were haunted by 'a swarm of little teasing elves, that fluttered from one ear to another,' each with its whispered tale of envy, wounded pride or disappointment.[1]

Hitherto the devout had found a medicine for their evils in Fénelon, and precepts of self-sacrifice and life in God, that had not yet become the Maxims of the Saints, but were a kind of Categorical Imperative, translated into the terms of mystical theology. It was this that won for him the favour of Mme. de Maintenon, the victim of unendurable *ennui* in the midst of unimaginable greatness, who wore on her shoulders the whole weight of the Court, of the King's inconsiderateness, his unending desire for company and amusement, his passion for tyrannically interfering with the affairs of others. 'Read M. de Fénelon's exhortations of surrender to the will of God, and willing acceptance of all sorts of duties,' she wrote soon after making his acquaintance : 'I have never seen anything more tender, more sterling, more free; his spirit of devotion is indeed the right one.'[2] She would have taken him as her Director, had he been a little less clever, a little less exacting of undivided allegiance; as it was, she made him a chief power in the little company, that held the Court at its feet, though it rarely appeared there, but met together, shrouded in mystery, at the house of Chevreuse or Beauvilliers.[3]

Into this inner sanctuary Mme. Guyon was presently introduced. With all her prudence, Mme. de Maintenon's judgment was not seldom at fault; she looked out at the world through a key-hole, says St Simon, and was easily duped by those who took her fancy.[4] She had all Fénelon's contempt for the opinion of the vulgar in such matters

---

[1] See Fén. 264th Spir. Let., Wks., viii. p. 614. See also La Bruyère's chapter on the Court, and various utterances of Mme. de Maintenon, esp. Geffroy, ii. p. 188.

[2] Geffroy, i. 200.   [3] St Simon, i. p. 274.   [4] *Ibid.* x. p. 20.

as did not touch on her own reputation ; she had his love of novelty, as well as a readiness, all her own, suddenly to adopt, and as suddenly to discard, any idea that struck her fancy as noble or sublime. Neither she nor Fénelon could have been led captive by Spiritual Maternity or the Apostolic State, but they were charmed by Mme. Guyon's ecstatic zeal and singularity, by language about Disinterestedness and absolute surrender to the will of God such as might often pass for Fénelon's own, shorn of a few theological niceties and correctives. The prophetess well knew the temper of her disciples, for Fénelon she had his own favourite ideas, dressed up in all the heady eloquence of which she was a mistress; for the superstitious many—among whom it is to be feared that she numbered Chevreuse—there were the Plenitudes and all the nauseous thaumaturgy of her voyages with Lacombe.[1]

But her exact relation to Fénelon is a secret that lies buried in their lost correspondence, hidden or destroyed at the outbreak of trouble. All the world knows the traditional story, how Fénelon was led away by the voice of a woman, not into a pitfall of the senses, but into an illusion of the intellect, into fancying himself a theologian and a philosopher, when he was no more than a master of eloquence.[2] And, in a certain sense, the traditional judgment is right. Posterity can only echo the amazement of Bossuet, when it sees one of Fénelon's transcendent ability and insight duped by a visionary so ignorant, so puffed up by spiritual pride, so palpably herself in error. Yet it is easy to over-rate her hold both on his heart and his affections. Mme. Guyon was his friend, but it was according to the laws of "that hieropathic affection, of which the female bosom is the seat, and the ministers of religion the objects"; she had all the "feelings of extraordinary force and sweetness" that come natural to an enthusiast full of belief in her own irresistible charm, when she wishes to capture a priest who is 'kept

---

[1] Phélippeaux, p. 88. See Bossuet, Wks., xv. p. 223.
[2] d'Aguesseau's Memoirs, xiii. p. 167.

like a relic' by the greatest ladies of the land. Before she ever set eyes on Fénelon, Christ had united her to him more closely than to any other human being: after a week's acquaintance, her soul was knit to his as the soul of David to the soul of Jonathan.[1]

But Fénelon was not one of those who feel so keenly—his friendships were 'subject to the law of charity: they were sober and discreet.' His admirable tenderness has turned stronger brains than poor Guyon's, but it was of a kind that would not readily be bound down to individuals; it found a fitter outlet in the vague philanthropy of Télémaque, or in a passion for pleasing—"coquetry," says St Simon, "worse than any woman's"—which embraced the servant no less than his master, small folk as well as great.[2] For M$^{me.}$ Guyon he had sympathy and esteem in plenty, but 'no special attraction, either natural or supernatural;'[3] she was a very excellent, even a holy, woman, and a persecuted saint, whom he had never scrupled to admire himself, or to recommend to others as very experienced in the ways of prayer. But he never introduced her to anyone, he never put her books into any man's hand; he well knew how shocking to many would be her ignorance of theology, her extravagant incautiousness of language, how hard she was to understand, except by the few who knew her well and had her confidence.[4]

Nor was Fénelon even secretly her disciple—self-confidence like his swears allegiance to no master, much less a mistress; his doctrine was his own, though for a while it ran parallel with hers. The true link between them was a strong community of sentiment: "they met," said an enemy, "they pleased each other, and their sublimity amalgamated."[5] Such alliances are not uncommon in the history of mysticism, a region where women can prompt when they cannot lead, can inspire though they may not teach; we

---

[1] Aut., iii. p. 101.
[2] St. Simon, viii. p. 419.
[3] Wks., ix. p. 81.
[4] *Ibid.* pp. 100, 264, etc.
[5] St Simon, i. p. 273.

do not think of St John of the Cross without St Teresa, nor deny to Mme. de Chantal her influence on St Francis of Sales; beside a greater Francis had stood St Clare.

But in these unions there was danger for the wisest, and Fénelon was no saint, but a man of unstable equilibrium, greedy of sympathy yet profoundly self-centred, immovable by authority yet often a prey to the flatterer. Mme. Guyon's gentle yielding pressure could tempt him to carry his own principles of sacrifice and renouncement to lengths whence his genius would otherwise have shrunk; she could entice one who was always on the quest of spiritual beauty into giving solid theological form and substance to the thoughts that were racking through her brain, into finding, it may be, some dim reflexion, some Brocken phantom of his own ideas thrown out, all garbled and distorted, upon this whirling cloudbank of confusion. Fénelon's insight was keen, but it was not the supreme impersonal faculty of the greatest masters; it was sympathetic not dispassionate, a power of conjuring up marvellously drawn pictures, not of coming face to face with truth in all its naked reality. He saw others as he wished to see them, as they corresponded with himself, fastening closely on all the points of agreement and blind or careless of the rest. Mme. Guyon's vagaries were nothing to him; it was enough if he could find behind her frothy unrealities of doctrine, behind the boldness that was not force, the unworldliness that was not spiritual, the chastity that was not pure, some ray of humble loving pathos, some gleam of a grey spiritual grandeur like his own.

And had she never put pen to paper, his purpose might have been achieved; her enemies would have had no ground to attack her, and Fénelon might have peacefully gathered up her scattered intuitions and welded them into his own scheme of thought.[1] But she had written much,

---

[1] On peut apprendre tous les jours en étudiant les voies de Dieu sur les ignorants expérimentés. (Works, iii. p. 10.) This relation will become more intelligible if read in the light of M. Renan's remarks on the 'sublime' porter of the Issy Seminary.—Souvenirs, ch. iv.

and that with utter recklessness and want of caution on matters where a fault of language was a serious crime; turn and twist facts as he would, he could not separate the person from the doctrine or the doctrine from the books. All he could do was to pronounce these sound in intention but very faulty in their terms and to avoid knowing more about them than he could help, so as to be unable to speak either well or ill of them to those who tried maliciously to wring an opinion from him.[1]

But far worse than the printed works, which contained only Mme. Guyon's 'doctrine,' were the Autobiography and other records of her spiritual experiences, her miracles and plenitudes and revelations, which circulated only in manuscript copies among the inmost band of true believers.[2] These Fénelon always denied that he had ever read, though he had had the Autobiography in his hands; he believed it to be no more than a spiritual diary, a 'temperature-chart' of her mind, kept, as was then not unusual, by order of her Spiritual Director and only for his use. Moreover, she had assured him that she believed no more in the reality of her visions than he did himself—they were simply fancies straying through her mind, without significance either for good or evil. 'Had she thought otherwise about them,' he wrote to Mme. de Maintenon, 'my opinion of her would have been poor indeed.'[3]

A certain misunderstanding, however, was made easy not only by Fénelon's dexterous blindness but by the conditions of their intercourse. They rarely met, for he came seldom to Paris and she not often to Versailles,[4] but for four years (1689-1693) they corresponded, probably with a freedom that Fénelon had afterwards cause to regret—there is real alarm when, in the thick of the Quietist controversy he

---

[1] Works, ix. p. 78.
[2] Mme. Guyon declared that the Autobiography (not the book that now passes under that title, but an earlier work) had been given to Bossuet in the secret of the confessional, and the charge is repeated by Fénelon in Works, ix. p. 81. But the expression must not be taken literally, see Bossuet, Wks., xviii. pp. 411, 493.
[3] Works, ix. p. 81. [4] *Ibid.* p. 441.

feared that one of his 'letters of particular confidence' had fallen into the hands of the enemy.'[1]

But so soon as ugly reports about Mme. Guyon got abroad, Fénelon broke off the correspondence, and promised his family to let the zeal of the zealous take its course; he would defend neither the woman nor her book, but observe the silence of a profound repose.[2] Thence he was roused by no feeling of sympathy, no knightly devotion to the cause of an innocent woman unjustly oppressed; as he afterwards reminded Mme. de Maintenon, he saw his friend imprisoned and tormented without pity; he would have let her die in prison, if only the doctrine of the Saints was secure.[3] Had not chance bound up the future of his theories with the fate of this woman and her books, had he not thought the whole of Christianity involved in the fall or triumph of his views, we should have heard no more of Mme. Guyon; she would have found her natural level in a country convent or an asylum, and one of the most eloquent tongues in Europe would never have bestirred itself to sing her praise.

The first act in the drama was played out at Mme. de Maintenon's college of St Cyr. Thither had come, as a supernumerary governess, a certain Mlle. de la Maisonfort, a cousin of Mme. Guyon, whose wit and attractions soon gained the special favour of the foundress, and marked her out as a future Superior of the house. But St Cyr, from the first, was more than half a convent, and Maisonfort's anxiety was to find a husband, not to take the vows.[4] To Mme. de Maintenon's plans, however, a flighty girl's will was no great obstacle; if Maisonfort was not naturally drawn to Religion, an unnatural vocation must be found for her, and Fénelon, the most persuasive of men, should find it. In December, 1690, a committee of ecclesiastics sat on her case, decided that she ought to take the veil, and handed

[1] Works, ix. p. 544.
[2] Ibid. vii. p. 407.
[3] Ibid. ix. p. 103.
[4] Phélippeaux, p. 27.

her over to Fénelon, with an admonition to tie a bandage over her eyes, and prepare herself for the sacrifice.[1]

Fénelon showed himself more than worthy of their confidence. 'Vocations,' he told his victim, 'shew themselves in the will of others, as clearly as in our own heart; when the Spirit does not call us from within, He sends an outward authority to decide.'[2] This frightful and truly Quietist maxim brought her to her knees; fifteen months later (March, 1692), in an agony of grief and terror, she received the veil.

Hardly was the crime committed, when punishment began to follow in its wake. Once fettered to the Church, Maisonfort threw herself with enthusiasm into her cousin's system of devotion, rushed with irresponsible and flighty logic to the farthest extreme, and forced her Director to sustain his own abominable beginnings by a series of more and more dangerous arguments. With M$^{me.}$ Guyon at her side, the task was easy; Fénelon's letters to Maisonfort are the milestones on his journey to the Maxims of the Saints.[3]

And the victim also worked a more immediate revenge. Even before her Profession, she had plunged wildly into propagandism, begun to make public property of Fénelon's most private letters, and gathered round her a little coterie of ladies, who looked to M$^{me.}$ Guyon as their common Directress. The new doctrines quickly made their way all over St Cyr; the house resounded with talk of Disinterestedness and Self-abandonment; the very housemaids and lay sisters bought M$^{me.}$ Guyon's books, and fancied they could understand them.[4]

For a long time M$^{me.}$ de Maintenon took no notice, though the Superior was complaining, and Fénelon warned her that his maxims of high spirituality were not food for every palate.[5] Only when responsible persons began to

---

[1] Phélippeaux, pp. 37 and *ff.*   [2] Wks., ix. p. 5.
[3] See these letters in Fén. Wks., ix. pp. 1, etc., and the excellent analysis in Bonnel, Controverse du Quiétisme, pp. 14, etc.
[4] Geffroy, i. p. 224.   [5] Wks., ix. p. 16.

revive old stories about Lacombe, did the prudent lady take alarm, and beg Mme. Guyon to go no more to St Cyr (May, 1693).

Her agitation was shared by Fénelon. At once he broke off all direct relations with the prophetess, yet, feeling sure of her perfect innocence, urged her through Chevreuse to take a bold step and appeal from all her critics to the supreme authority of Bossuet.[1] The Bishop of Meaux was no friend to ecstatic devotion, but Fénelon believed that his prejudice was grounded on an ignorance, which it might now be possible to dispel; perhaps, too, he had seen that a conflict was one day imminent, and was glad of this chance to cross his first sword with Achilles on behalf of a doctrine not precisely his own.

Bossuet, on his side, welcomed this opportunity of coming to an explanation with his former disciple, of freeing him and others from what might prove to be a dangerous illusion. As high-priest of Authority and common-sense, he had little sympathy with a preaching woman; as one of the old generation, to whom Versailles was the centre of the universe, yet himself no courtier, no expert reader of the fickle tides of Fashion, he had watched the rise of Mme. Guyon with a concern scarcely warranted by her importance. He readily consented to examine her books, on condition that she offered no commentary, ceased in the meantime from writing or 'dogmatizing,' and submitted absolutely to his judgment once it was pronounced. It was hard for Mme. Guyon to desert, even for a few months, the spiritual children who cried so piteously for food;[2] nevertheless there was no alternative—she accepted Bossuet's terms (September, 1693).

By the end of the following January the examination was over. Bossuet found in the books 'much that was intolerable as well in matter as in form,' and one positive heresy, namely, the doctrine that the Perfect should never pray for Graces for themselves, because, being wholly in

[1] Bos., Wks., xv. p. 222.　　　　　[2] *Ibid.* xviii. p. 405.

God's Hand, their state is His concern rather than their own.[1] At first Mme. Guyon raised objections; she said that she could no more say the Lord's Prayer on her own behalf than a paralyzed man could move his limbs,[2] but in the end Bossuet's firmness and her friends' wiser counsels carried the day; she submitted 'without reasoning' to his condemnation of her errors, promised to write and preach no more, and retired to the country (April, 1694).

Bossuet then confronted Fénelon with some of the more extravagant passages from her manuscripts, wherein she claimed precedence over the Madonna or compared herself with the Woman of the Apocalypse.[3] But Fénelon only replied in great amazement that he had never heard anything of the kind from her lips; it was clear that Bossuet had failed to understand her.[4]

This answer increased the uneasiness of Fénelon's friends; they began to suspect that this deplorable friendship was leading him into serious errors of doctrine. For some years he had been in regular correspondence on spiritual matters with Mme. de Maintenon, but the tone of his letters was becoming less and less pleasing to the cold and circumspect lady, till at last she sent one of them for examination to her Director, the Bishop of Chartres. Paul Godet des Marais was a heavy, learned prelate, of high character and ability, cautious but not suspicious, and a great enemy of Mme. Guyon. But he was a just man and one of Fénelon's oldest friends, and answered that, though the language was certainly curious and often unintelligible, he was sure that the writer's doctrine was, at bottom, the same as his own[5] (May, 1694). Yet Mme. de Maintenon was not wholly reassured. There had lately been a plentiful crop of troubles at St Cyr, where the irrepressible Maisonfort had broken out into open rebellion against the discipline of the house and the 'petty

---

[1] Works, xviii. p. 414.
[2] Ibid. xviii. p. 410, and cf. Works, xv. p. 229.
[3] Ibid. xv. p. 230.   [4] Fénelon, Works, iii. p. 12.
[5] Ibid. viii. p. 498, and see the character of des Marais in St Simon, i. p. 295.

practices' of its diocesan, the Bishop of Chartres,[1] and Fénelon, well knowing that his own name had been made the standard of revolt, had seen himself forced to apologize to the foundress for his teaching. It was not high spirituality, he said, but, rather its absence, that had made Maisonfort untrue to her Grace, which was amiability and good breeding.[2]

But M$^{me.}$ de Maintenon's suspicions of the prophetess only increased, and during the summer she collected a number of opinions on her writings from Bourdalone and other eminent divines. Their answer was so uniformly unfavourable as to quench the cooling embers of her interest in that lady's fortunes; henceforward Cæsar's wife cut herself loose from all association with so dubious a character, and began to take counsel with Bossuet how they might oblige Fénelon to do the same.

M$^{me.}$ Guyon herself supplied the weapon. In June she petitioned for an enquiry, by a mixed commission of ecclesiastics and laymen, into both her doctrine and her morals. The prayer as it stood could not be granted; since any enquiry into her morals seemed both unnecessary and dangerous—unnecessary, because her virtue had not, as yet, been seriously impugned, the evidence against her was admittedly slight, the witnesses unworthy of credit[3]—dangerous, because a verdict of acquittal would have blinded Fénelon all the more.

But an examination into her doctrine promised very differently. There the evidence was all the other way, and the judges, without indecently condemning her unheard, could be made to 'express themselves forcibly' against her before the trial began.[4]

Nevertheless, M$^{me.}$ Guyon and her books were to play but a secondary part in the Enquiry; she was canonically answerable only to the Archbishop of Paris, and no one wished to draw so notorious an evil-liver as Monseigneur de

---

[1] Phélippeaux, p. 50.
[2] Fén. Wks., ix. p. 15.
[3] So thought Bossuet, Wks., xviii. p. 458.
[4] Fén. Wks., ix. p. 24.

Harlai into discussions on the Love of God. But her writings might well form the pretext for a general investigation into the new spirituality; the Commissioners, sitting as doctors rather than judges, might define its boundaries and condemn its excesses, embodying their conclusions in a code of rules for the use of mystical souls and their Directors. In this way they would at once perform a useful public service and secure effectually the object that Mme. de Maintenon and Bossuet really had at heart, the rescue of Fénelon from his own extravagances.[1] For he could be associated with the Commissioners, not as judge, but as advocate in his own cause and Mme. Guyon's, could be encouraged to set out his own views in all their length and breadth, till the Commissioners understood exactly what he meant. Then they would draw up their Formulary with eyes really fixed on him and bind his conscience for the future by compelling him to sign it. His honour would not be wounded, his future prospects not be marred, for Mme. de Maintenon undertook to hide from the King all he need not know,[2] and Bossuet was so to draft the judgment as to safeguard his old pupil's faith, while sparing him the shadow of a retractation or a censure.

For Bossuet presided, though Mme. Guyon herself had named the judges, and with him sat, as assessors, Louis de Noailles, Bishop of Châlons (soon afterwards made Cardinal and Archbishop of Paris), and M. Tronson, Fénelon's old tutor at St Sulpice. Owing to the great age and infirmities of the latter, the sittings were held at Issy, a village within a walk of Paris, where the Seminary had its country house, and thence the resulting Articles have taken their name.

Fénelon, well knowing that his own future and his doctrine's were at stake, made haste to assure the Commissioners of his perfect docility. Before the proceedings began, he gave into M. Tronson's keeping a written document in which he took God to witness that he would accept

[1] See Memoirs of Le Dieu, ii. pp. 216 ff, where Bossuet expressly admits this.
[2] Geffroy, i. p. 317.

without equivocation or reserve whatever the Commissioners might decide.¹ He promised Bossuet to be like a little child in the hands of one who ' in these days, was the chief pillar of the Church's tradition, and spoke to him, not with the authority of a man, or even of a very great Doctor, but as the oracle of God.'²

Once the sittings had begun, Fénelon wrote ' prodigiously,' still defending Mme. Guyon's doctrine, but chiefly busied with his own : she was as nothing in his eyes, he told M. Trouson, now that the Interior Life was on its trial.³

The examination dragged wearily on during the latter half of 1694. At Christmas Mme. de Maintenon persuaded the King to give Fénelon the rich abbey of St Valéry, as a reward for his docility, and as compensation should another project miscarry. For the Archbishopric of Cambrai was vacant, and she had already decided on her candidate. In the end, little as he loved her *protégé*, the King raised no objection; no whisper of Quietism reached his ears; on the 4th of February, 1695, Fénelon was named Archbishop. He at once resigned St Valéry, but remained Preceptor to the Princes.

Just a month later, the Commission finished its work ; on the 6th of March the Articles were ready for signature. What really happened during the next four days will never be known ; the truth has been smothered under a cloud of most bitter controversy, coloured on one side by Fénelon's desire to exaggerate his own part in the final arrangement of the Articles, on the other by Bossuet's equal anxiety to show that he had never differed from his colleagues or himself in rejecting all that made in Fénelon's favour.

According to Fénelon, thirty Articles were first offered him, and these he refused to sign except out of deference to their superior authority : the Commissioners then added four more Articles, which met his objections, and he signed the whole ' with his blood.' ⁴ But Bossuet and de Noailles

---

[1] Wks., ix. p. 22.
[2] *Ibid.*, pp. 29, 48, 50, etc.
[3] *Ibid.*, p. 37.
[4] *Ibid.*, iii. pp. 25, 72.

deny that he had any part whatsoever in the composition of the Articles; there had never been less than thirty-four, and these Fénelon only signed with great difficulty and against his own conviction.[1]

On the whole, the latter story is the more credible. The Thirty Articles, objected to by Fénelon, and disowned by de Noailles and the Bishop of Meaux, seem to have been no finished product, but a rough draft by Bossuet, to which he added, at his own or his colleague's instance, and far more unwillingly than he would have it appear,[2] four more Articles, all favourable to Fénelon, before the latter was invited to sign.[3] One or two small points were conceded to him at the last moment, but the bulk of his proposed alterations was overruled—they would, as de Noailles said, have nullified the Articles,—and on the 10th of March he signed with the rest.

So Bossuet won the first battle, though his victory was very far from complete. For the Articles, drawn up ' with so many prayers and sacrifices,' were a compromise between a great power and a growing one, a treaty of peace of that aimless sort, which is commonly the best incentive to future war.[4] Their chief characteristic was their want of character; they condemned certain Quietist errors, but they were not a censure, they laid down certain regulations, but they were not a code of doctrine or of practice. The more crucial the question, the more oracular was their reply; they struck out Disinterestedness with one hand (9th Article), but wrote it in again with the other (33rd Article); they gave no definition of Passive Prayer, yet explained that it was as rash to deny its existence (21st Article), as it was dangerous to engage in its practice (29th Article). They went too far for Bossuet, not far enough for Fénelon; each found himself irresistibly tempted to write a commentary upon

---

[1] Bossuet, Wks., xv. 237, 339; and see de Noailles' version in Fén. Wks., ii. p. 520. [2] Boss. Wks., xviii. p. 454.
[3] As to the draft see Bausset, i. p. 396. See also Fén. Wks., ii. p. 224, for the text of it. [4] See the analysis in Bonnel, p. 38.

them, that should wrest their amiable incoherence into conformity with his ideas.

For the moment, indeed, there was peace and apparent restoration of harmony. In July Fénelon was consecrated by Bossuet and de Noailles in the chapel of St Cyr, 'that spot so precious and so hard of access,' in the presence of his royal pupils and M$^{me.}$ de Maintenon's inner circle of friends. In September he set out for Cambrai to take formal possession of his diocese.

Yet the note of danger had already been sounded. Bossuet was hard at work on a treatise, intended to utterly confound the Quietists and explain the true doctrine of the Interior Life, and this treatise Fénelon, in common with des Marais and de Noailles, had promised to officially approve. He could not well refuse the compliment, although he knew that Bossuet had been screwed up in the Articles to a point far above his usual dogmatic level, at which he certainly would not long remain.[1] But he had unbounded faith in his own powers of persuasion, if only he were allowed to collaborate in the book, and therefore made haste to offer his services, not, as he said, to enhance its value, but simply as a pledge of his perfect docility. He is still full of respect for Bossuet, still proud to call him master, still glad to defer to his opinion, after he has explained to him his own. Yet through his letters breathes a new-found independence: he can adjure the old Dictator to listen sometimes to the poor in spirit and obey the Heavenly Voice that speaks within. For the whilom disciple is become a brother Bishop, the 'little child' is grown a man.[2]

Bossuet, however, declined his assistance, and immediately Fénelon's suspicions deepened into alarm, and his alarm thereafter into panic. The humiliation of the signature still rankled deeply in his mind and prompted the fear of another worse disgrace in the future—what if Bossuet, M$^{me.}$ de Maintenon and the rest were no more

[1] Fén. Wks., iii. p. 27. Wks. ix. p. 103.   [2] Wks., ix. pp. 76, 77.

than a band of pious conspirators, pledged to tie his hands yet more tightly, to make him solemnly approve a book that pared the spirituality of Issy to the quick?[1] Yet he had given his promise, he had signed the Articles and could not raise dogmatic objections to their author's exposition, though to approve it was to cut away the ground beneath his feet, and stultify his own forthcoming Treatise. At all hazards an independent pretext for refusal must be found, and at once his thoughts fell on M$^{me.}$ Guyon and the injustice that Bossuet probably would do her. Six months before the prelate's manuscript was in hands, he told M. Tronson that he should not approve it, if it attacked either her writings or her character.[2]

The position was shrewdly taken. Bossuet's first kindness to M$^{me.}$ Guyon had melted away during the six months (January to July, 1695) that she spent, half willing penitent, half prisoner, under his charge at Meaux; it changed to violent indignation when she escaped from her convent without his leave, full of wild impossible accusations against him, and flourishing in his face his garbled attestation of her perfect orthodoxy.[3] Bossuet could spare the fallen, but not even the weakest and most contemptible of rebels; he had treated her, he said, according to rule, had accepted her entire submission, and, if she had lied to him, she must be handed over to the police.[4] A little later he wrote again: "The efforts made on the part of this woman are astonishing. Clear as are her attempts at evasion, her followers do not notice them. If I were to give way, all would be lost, but that, while life is in me, I shall never do."[5]

For Bossuet did not scruple to turn all the artillery of Heaven against a fly. The Saints, he said, had not thought it beneath them to attack the feeblest errors, if only they were widely spread, while those who were for despising everything let every madness reign.[6] And even

---

[1] Wks., ii. p. 249. *Ibid.* ix. p. 79.
[2] *Ibid.* ix. p. 79.
[3] Phélippeaux, pp. 149 and *ff.*
[4] Wks., xviii. p. 478.
[5] *Ibid.* p. 483.
[6] *Ibid.* xiv. p. 31.

for his anger we can find excuse; a charitable understanding of the mentally unsound is a virtue younger than the seventeenth century, and, without it, what was to be made of a woman who was at one and the same time an *Illuminata*, guided only by the Inner Light, and a humble Catholic Christian, subject to the canonical authority of her Bishops? Bossuet might draw up condemnations as he pleased; subscriptions to a censure, even solemn avowals of error, were nothing to her, whose doctrine was not her own, but God's, who, as His unerring messenger, His chosen Spouse, owed only formal outward obedience to His Church's Law.

Nevertheless, Fénelon was mistaken in his reckoning. Bossuet could descend to virulent personalities in a pamphlet; he had no place for them in the solemn dogmatic treatises addressed to the City and the World. And to this class belonged the forthcoming Instruction on the States of Prayer; though it dealt largely with M$^{me.}$ Guyon's writings, it had no word against her candour or her morals; it did not even mention her by name. For Bossuet was at war, not with the woman, but with the books, and with the books only in so far as they formed part of a system of extravagant and innovating spirituality, common in principle to a great number of writers, though expressed with very different degrees of clearness, with varying proportions of malice or ignorant presumption, of aversion or inclination to sexual excesses.[1] Some might not see whither they were drifting, but Bossuet was not concerned with their intentions; he had not to decide on the guilt or innocence of individuals, but to prove that all alike were hurrying to a goal outside Christianity, beyond the Trinity and the Incarnation.[2]

In July, 1696, Fénelon received the manuscript of the Instruction, but returned it after a very cursory inspection, explaining that he could not approve a book which attributed to M$^{me.}$ Guyon monstrous and diabolical errors, of which the rudest countrywoman would not have been guilty; nor would he have anything to do with a dis-

---

[1] Wks., xiv. pp. 32, 209.   [2] *Ibid.* p. 5.

guised retractation of his own opinions, but would bide his time and set matters before the public at a favourable opportunity.[1] Deaf to all entreaties and suggestions of compromise, his gathering feverishness saw more and more clearly into Bossuet's fiendish treachery and vanity, that yearned after the *spolia opima* of the Quietist War, and, not content with present triumphs, was determined to feast the eyes of his creatures with the richer spectacle of an Archbishop crushed and beaten, driven into a thinly veiled abjuration of his errors, and publicly owning himself a partaker in this wretched woman's iniquities.[2]

Doubtless, in these protestations there was an element of real sympathy for $M^{me.}$ Guyon, a feeling that Bossuet had treated her harshly, and mistaken her vaporous inconsequences for artful and deliberate errors. Still Fénelon's apologies for her are not the work of a whole-hearted confidence; only too often does their halting incompleteness betray a knowledge of the badness of his cause. Against the justice of the censure he can only plead the purity of her intentions, an issue never raised by Bossuet, nor considered by the general jurisprudence of the Church. Or else he takes somewhat firmer ground, admits the reasonableness of Bossuet's attack, is ready to sign a Formulary imposed by lawful authority, yet excuses himself from taking an active part against her, lest he should seem to be wantonly flouting a former friend.

And Bossuet, it seems, would have admitted the justice of this argument, and been satisfied to forego his demand for an official approbation, if Fénelon had promised to express general agreement with his censures, whenever conversation turned on $M^{me.}$ Guyon and her books.[3] But Fénelon was too filled with terror for the safety of his doctrine to consent; to utter even informally one word of censure on her seemed, in his present state of panic, like the suicide of his independence, his abject confession of defeat.

[1] Wks., ix. pp. 87, 100, 104. [2] *Ibid.* ii. p. 48, iii. p. 31. [3] ix. p. 81.

And therefore he did not pronounce it, though his silence caused unspeakable dismay to M. Tronson, lost him Mme. de Maintenon's friendship, meant an open breach with Bossuet. At this great price he had bought his freedom, the coast was clear, he could publish what he pleased.

Nor did he long delay. In October he sent to de Noailles (now Archbishop of Paris) the manuscript of a book dealing with the whole question of the Interior Life, a domain, he said, little understood by those who did not love it, and never before sufficiently explained by those who did. He had therefore set himself to reduce to rule the experiences of many Saints, welding them into a reasonable coherent system, that bore no traces of illusion or extravagance. Nor need the timorous de Noailles fear his vital disagreement from his brother of Meaux; he had only accomplished with thoroughness and good-will what Bossuet would do grudgingly and under constraint, less keen to affirm than to deny, readier with his refutations than his proofs.[1]

Luckless de Noailles could never follow an argument or see a difficulty, but he knew it, and sent the book back with a few vague compliments and an earnest recommendation not to publish till Bossuet's Instruction had appeared.[2] This advice Fénelon promised to follow; he spent some time collecting opinions from other theologians, but, at last, grew impatient, and went back to Cambrai, leaving Chevreuse to settle the date of publication.

This last manœuvre had its advantages. Under cover of an agent, Fénelon could slip, if need be, out of his promise to de Noailles, and be the first to publish; for Chevreuse was told nothing of a definite undertaking, and only knew that de Noailles, like Tronson and others, was urgent for delay.[3] Nay, Fénelon himself gave the same advice to his follower, well knowing that the Duke's precipitate zeal would be sure in the end to assert itself, if there were anything to be gained by being beforehand with Bossuet.

And matters fell out exactly as he had intended. Chev-

[1] p. 105.   [2] Wks., iii. p. 38.   [3] *Ibid.* ix. pp. 120-122.

reuse, in time, got tired of waiting; "without my knowledge and in my absence" the book was sent to the printers; furtively and in haste—for there was fear lest Bossuet should set the police in motion—it was smuggled through the press, Chevreuse himself, to the great scandal of St Simon, sitting in the printer's office to correct the proofs; and on the 1st of February, 1697, afterwards the saddest of anniversaries, Beauvilliers presented to the King the first copy of the Maxims of the Saints.

CHAPTER VIII

AT WAR WITH BOSSUET

> Dans ces combats où nos prélats de France
> Semblent chercher la vérité,
> L'un dit qu'on détruit l'espérance
> L'autre que c'est la charité ;
> C'est la foi qu'on détruit, et personne n'y pense.
> —*Contemporary Epigram.*

FROM the first moment of its appearance the Maxims was doomed. The world had looked for something worthy of Fénelon's name : it found the Interior Life reduced to a code of forty-five dreary theorems, 'all phrases and subtleties and abstractions.' And it was drawn up in a style that invited hostility ; Fénelon, as his enemies said, arrogated to his book all the authority of a Pontifical Definition and dealt out approbations and censures with no sparing hand, giving to each proposition its false as well as its true meaning—this last, 'the voice of a tradition uninterrupted between the Apostles and St Francis of Sales,' the other its heretical counterpart, its caricature by the Quietists.[1]

The book shocked everyone, said St Simon, the ignorant because they understood not a word of it, the more intelligent because they could not accustom themselves to its strange and barbarous terminology, the bishops because they believed that even under the Maxims so-called 'True' grave errors lay concealed.[2] Some thought the book very bold, others very heterodox, others that the design was bad but the execution subtle, others that Fénelon would have done

---

[1] Bossuet however, said with some truth that the False Maxims were mere dummies, meant to satisfy the popular hatred of Molinos without seriously condemning his doctrines. Works, xv. p. 280.

[2] St Simon, i. p. 409.

BOSSUET

FROM AN ENGRAVING AFTER THE PORTRAIT BY RIGAUD IN THE LOUVRE

better, now that so much false mysticism was abroad, to limit himself to attacks on that and leave the rest to God.¹

Nearly all Fénelon's friends forsook him, feeling sure, said one of the most pious, that he was embarking on a voyage which would bring him no profit and was not called for by God's glory;² there remained only a few faithful intimates such as Beauvilliers, who cared nothing for his place at Court, but believed that Fénelon was in the right, and would do nothing that might embitter his hour of death.³ Some enemies of his enemies also gathered round Fénelon, chief of them Cardinal Bouillon, nephew of Turenne, Sub-dean of the Sacred College and lately appointed French Ambassador at Rome. Bouillon, a prelate of the old worldly school, cared little for theology, but he sided naturally with a man of rank, whose family had for centuries been friendly with his own, against the middle-class Bossuet or that 'snob in purple,' the Bishop of Chartres. And his help was well worth having; however great his 'ridiculous vanity,'⁴ it went hand in hand with a zealous friendship for Fénelon and a kind of paradoxical Quixotism, an adventurous championship of losing causes, that was marked rather by energy and dash and worldly wisdom than by the scruples of a too sensitive conscience.⁵ Moreover, at Rome, said the Abbé Bossuet, an Ambassador was almost of more consequence than the Pope himself.⁶

The Jesuits lent more dubious support. They had always been friendly to mysticism, none the less because the Jansenists, their enemies, were its inveterate foes; and though they could not now row outwardly against the stream, it was easy to let Bourdalone and a few independent

---

¹ Bossuet Wks., xviii. pp. 528, etc.
² The Abbé Brisacier, joint-head of the Missionary Order of Lazarists. Fén. Wks., ix. p. 132.
³ St Simon ii. p. 47.
⁴ *Ibid.* i. p. 409. M$^{me.}$ de Maintenon is still more severe, and calls the Cardinal un pantalon suisse. Geffroy, ii. p. 253.
⁵ See Le Roy, France et Rome, p. 422 *note*. Bossuet Wks., xviii. p. 733.
⁶ *Ib.* p. 616.

spirits thunder against Quietism, while the bulk of the Society secretly supported Fénelon both in France and Rome. Père La Chaise combined both policies in his own jovial person; he told the King that the book contained forty-three grievous errors, yet wrote, as if by Louis' authority, to the outgoing French Ambassador at Rome, to order its defence.[1] There was no help for it—the King's Confessor was a Jesuit like the rest.

Of the adversaries Bossuet was the life and soul. Until he declared himself, they had been full of doubt and hesitation: even Fénelon's most implacable enemy, the King, was inclined to go no farther than an icy silence of disapproval.[2] But Bossuet had foretold a terrible scandal, if ever the Maxims was published, and now he was grimly determined that history should take him at his word. To convert the King to violent measures was no difficult task, for in Louis' eyes a man accused of heresy was already condemned; and Bossuet need only fling this dead accusation on the gale to change his doubts into furious anger, not only with Fénelon, but also with those who had conspired together to get him made Archbishop.[3] M$^{me.}$ de Maintenon, even saw herself compromised, and followed trembling in her husband's wake; for some time past she had shown coldness to Fénelon and his circle, and now, under the stress of open scandal, the rift soon widened into a breach. It was not without pain that she broke away from her friends—the memory of M$^{me.}$ de Chevreuse haunted her for years [4]—but she feared, at first, for her own reputation, and presently came pique at the behaviour of those who, as she thought, had not been frank with her, but had used her as a stepping-stone to establish

---

[1] Bossuet Wks., xviii. pp. 536, 543; and see Le Roy, p. 77.

[2] Bossuet, during the controversy prided himself on his moderation, and said that he was 'the last to speak' to Louis (Wks., xv. p. 265). After it was over, he told Le Dieu that it was only his own firmness which had overcome the King's irresolution. See Le Dieu, ii. p. 228. The reader should remember that a book may well be dangerous and 'erroneous' without deserving all the pains and penalties of 'heresy.'

[3] Geffroy i. p. 304. [4] *Ibid*. ii. p. 37.

their own doctrine at the Court.[1] As to the place-hunters and hangers-on of Versailles, it was incredible, wrote Bossuet complacently, how odious Fénelon had become to them, now that he was fallen into disgrace.[2]

Once installed at the head of his forces, Bossuet's plan of action was soon made up : with de Noailles and Godet des Marais of Chartres—henceforward the Triumvirate of Quietism—he would draw up a list of erroneous propositions, to to be handed to Fénelon by the King together with a demand for explanation. Fénelon had promised to submit, if the Bishops could prove him in the wrong, and they intended to put him to the test, acting in all moderation, but with no undue regard for his feelings; nor would anything short of a retractation serve their purpose, for Quietism would be held in honour until this book was crushed.[3]

But Fénelon would neither confer with Bossuet nor be judged by him; in April he got the King's permission to carry his cause to Rome. For the time, indeed, negotiations were still kept up with the two other Bishops; Fénelon had some hope of winning over two friends of his youth whose feeble inertia was already calling forth Bossuet's complaint.[4] But with him also they were one thing in the morning and another in the evening—all that was certain about them was that they would commit themselves to nothing—des Marais murmured ' correct, explain, suppress '; de Noailles and his admirers spun elaborate notes and emendations — cobwebs, as Fénelon said himself, that Bossuet would sweep away with a single blow of his brush.[5]

On the 15th of July Bossuet sent his ultimatum through de Noailles. The book was utterly bad, odious, and inexcusable, the explanations no better,[6] but Fénelon was invited to a friendly conference, where the truth might break out of itself, and his eyes be opened to errors, which, grave

---

[1] Geffroy, i. p. 289.
[3] B. Wks., xviii. pp, 563, etc.
[5] Wks., ix. p. 173.

[2] Wks., xviii. p. 561.
[4] *Ibid*. p. 562.
[6] B. Wks., xiv. p. 481.

as they were, would soon be atoned for by a humble submission.¹

But Fénelon saw no use in further parleying—not a line of his book would he alter, or even admit that its meaning was ever dubious; all he asked for was leave to go to Rome, there to defend his case himself. Louis answered him with a curt command to go to his diocese and stay there; with his own hand he wrote to the Pope, begging a speedy judgment on this scandalous book.

So Fénelon was banished from the Court (August 1st), yet his cause was still far from desperate. The matter was going to Rome; he had gained time to prepare his defences, had turned his judges into prosecutors, was to appear before a friendly tribunal. If the Roman authorities were not very mystical themselves, they had lately canonized a number of mystical Saints; moreover, they could not but feel kindly to an Archbishop of France who had appealed to them of his own free-will, and was known to be utterly unlike 'those Gallican *frondeurs*,' in that he ascribed the fullest authority to the Holy See. The Pope might well take Fénelon's advice and seize on this opportunity of reading a lesson to the Gallican Church, always so jealous of its privileges, so hostile to the power of Rome; might show that he also was guided only by the truth, yet could be merciful to all his children when they called upon him.²

So strongly was this danger felt at Court that the King would not have sanctioned the appeal, had not Bossuet guaranteed a condemnation. Even Rome, said the Bishop of Meaux, was better than a National Council; alone among Frenchmen, he could not believe that the Pope would make himself a partaker in Fénelon's iniquities; it was not yet time for those in Judæa to flee to the mountains.³

---

¹ B. Wks., pp. 473, 483.
² Wks. ix. p. 198-199. These are Fénelon's suggestions of arguments to be employed by his agents in Rome.
³ B. Wks. xviii., pp. 633, 658. See Phélippeaux, pp. 287-288.

AT WAR WITH BOSSUET 149

The appeal once lodged, Fénelon's courage began to revive. At first he had bent before the storm of troubles that fell so thickly upon him, first, the icy reception of his book, next the burning of part of his palace at Cambrai (Feb. 1697) a few months afterwards, the expulsion by the King in person of Mme. de la Maisonfort from St Cyr—the prelude, as all the world suspected, to the dismissal of Beauvilliers and Burgundy's other tutors from their place.[1] At Easter-time, he had moved even Bossuet's compassion, shut up, sick and dispirited, in a little cottage near Versailles and venturing neither to Cambrai nor to Court. But he was slowly gathering together his forces; soon Bossuet reports him full of pride and with no notion of surrender;[2] his conduct becomes a map of trickery, artifice and mystification; he plays the part of the martyr with the most surpassing arrogance.[3] His voice had lost those tones of strained, hysteric vehemence, of plaintive, regretful insincerity, which marred all his defences of Mme. Guyon; now there was no more cause to think of her—the fight was all his own, and with the need of combat came the power. Bossuet, St Simon, all were startled by that Letter to a Friend, in which he bade the Court farewell.

"Pray, my friend; there is nothing left but silence, obedience and prayer. Pray for me in my hour of need, for the Church afflicted by these troubles, for those who are warring against me, that they may correct me if I am astray and do me justice, if I walk aright; pray for prayer itself, that stands in peril and must needs be justified. Perfection has fallen under a ban; Disinterestedness has become a source of error and impiety; Christians are taught to seek God for their own sakes, for the pleasure that they find in Him; even the best among them may not serve Him for Himself. What if hypocrites have misused Pure Love, have overthrown

---
[1] Mme. de Maintenon herself thought so, and later did her best to force the King to dismiss Beauvilliers. See Geffroy, i. p. 304. To the unhappy Maisdefort she behaved abominably, see p. 285.
[2] B. Wks., xviii. pp. 540, 542.
[3] M. de Cambrai est inexorable et d'un orgueil qui fait peur, p. 579.

the Gospel under its specious name?—It remains none the less the perfection of Christian Truth, nor is any error worse than to destroy the holiest, lest it turn to evil uses : it is God, not man, who best watches over His Own. Let us be silent, let us be humble, let us pray, rather than wrangle over prayer ; it is thus that we shall best defend it ; in silence we shall find our strength." [1]

In reply, the three Bishops published 'an atrocious document,' the Declaration of Fénelon's errors, and the war of pamphlets began. For eighteen months it raged unendingly, and always in the same narrow groove.—In Fénelon's system was there room for Hope? Did his various explanations tally with the Maxims or with one another? What part was played by Nature, what by Grace, in determining man to the Love of God? Des Marais and de Noailles took part, as well as Bossuet, in the struggle ; indeed St Simon awards to the former the chief honours of the war : he was the rock against which Fénelon always dashed in vain.[2] And even gentle, embarrassed de Noailles has lately found an admirer in M. Crouslé—perhaps because Fénelon thought his pastoral more full of poison than even the utterances of Bossuet.[3]

There were many reasons for Bossuet's wrath. Like his friends at Versailles, he thought mysticism rare and not very necessary ; it should not be paraded in the streets, but be kept carefully hidden from the eyes of a world that would neither value nor understand it. He had little of the mystical temper himself ; his magnificent imagination fastened only on hard realities, seeing far deeper into these than other men, but never travelling beyond them. He was no master in that vague cloud-land of Fénelon's, where one chance word could stir whole tumults of emotion, set loose

---

[1] Wks., ii. pp. 283 and *ff*. The Friend was Beauvilliers. [2] i. p. 416.

[3] The Pastoral, out of a helpless desire to spare Fénelon's feelings, avoids mentioning him specially, and attacks Disinterestedness under the general head of Quietism, thus classing Fénelon with Molinos. Bossuet on the other hand, attacks the Maxims openly, but distinguishes between Quietism proper and the " Semi-Quietism " of the Maxims. See Fén. Wks., ii. pp. 463 and *ff*.

whole trains of echoing fancy ; his words were keen to hold the hearer tightly gripped, spell-bound before the majesty of fact. We must go to Parma and the Sistine Chapel for our parallel ; if Fénelon was a Correggio in religion, Bossuet was its Michelangelo.

Yet the painter of the Last Judgment stood higher than its orator—

> Wer nicht sein Brod mit Thränen ass,
> Wer nicht die kummervollen Nächte
> Auf seinem Bette weinend sass,
> Der kennt Euch nicht, ihr himmlischen Mächte,[1]

and Michelangelo had gained a diviner instinct, a more universal enlightenment, among those sorrow-laden nights of weeping, which mystics call the dark waters close to God. But Bossuet was a mirror of calm unhesitating certainty, of serenity unruffled, of confidence unassailed, perhaps the supreme representative of a common sense that lives only in and for the Present, the fathomable, the near at hand, that gathers up into itself, and becomes the incarnation of all the wisdom of an age, yet leaves upon posterity a feeling of mingled reverence and regretfulness, of sorrow that so stately a temple can be the dwelling-place for but one generation of minds. Bossuet had never wavered, never doubted, never stumbled in his course, knew nothing but by hearsay of the agonies of a moment through which the mystical spirit must pass, when the soul ' becomes a stranger to the usual sense of things,'[2] when its landmarks are uprooted, its rules of conduct overthrown, when men appear to it ' as trees walking,' and the understanding swims, and the judgment totters, and the senses are in uproar, when the soul snatches vainly at stones or brambles

---

[1]   He who with tears ne'er ate his bread
        Who never through the long night-hours
        Weeping has lain upon his bed
          He knows you not, ye heavenly Powers.
—Wilhelm Meister. Book ii. ch. xiii. Translated by Mr Alison Phillips.

[2] St John of the Cross, ii. p. 90.

as it falls headlong over the cliffs, down into that awful Silence, "whose anguish is no more comparable to grosser pains, than an incorporeal spirit to a body all of earth."[1]

Non sinimus scribere de sancto nisi sanctum. To such a man as Bossuet even the greatest of the mystics necessarily seemed full of 'amorous extravagance and pious excess.' Fénelon may not have been as great a master of the Interior Life as his epitaph declares, but he had good reason to charge his adversary with ignorance of the mystical writings, with unreadiness to make one allowance for their language, with hasty indiscriminate censure of all he did not understand.[2] For the genius of mysticism is a thing apart, not to be grasped by casual reading of St Teresa, or even by controversial study of St Francis on the love of God.

Again, the first of mystical virtues was Charity, a Charity that had for its outward sign the singular knowledge and sympathy for human character, that has turned many a dreamy monk into a forcible realist. But Bossuet's virtue was Faith, not Charity; he was a preacher rather than a counsellor, an abstract thinker, strong on the type, but for whom the individual had scarce an existence, a man of reason, order, and traditions, loving to go forward *bonnement, rondement, simplement,* in the accustomed ways.[3] He was a dogmatist, not indeed in the word's most vulgar sense, but as one who saw in creeds an institution rather than an idea, a measuring-rod rather than a lever, an abstract of all human duties, not their bare beginning. Creeds enshrined for Bossuet that idea of Unity, of which his mind was so full, and his life so true an exemplification; he could not bear to see the white radiance of Eternity stained by the many-coloured dreams and fantasies of men; from the strange records of the mystics he turned back to the Apostles and the Prophets; for him their 'experiences,' together with the Fathers, were enough.[4] It was not for

[1] St Teresa Autobiog., ch. xx.
[2] See esp. Fén. Wks., ix. p. 141.
[3] See Lanson's Bossuet, p. 486.
[4] Wks., xiv. p. 16.

AT WAR WITH BOSSUET

Bossuet to see that there was a Unity still higher than the noblest uniformity of Faith, a Unity whereon these mystics strove to build the Freedom of the Children of God, that Unity in Charity, where all things are allowed.

In short, had Fénelon been the very greatest of the mystics, he would have made no convert of Bossuet; as it was, the awkward crudeness of his system seemed to its critic to endanger the whole oneness of the Christian life. There was no longer any law true for the whole of mankind; the one broad rule was garbled away into a chaos of exceptions and distinctions; the Righteous were split up into classes, each with their several aims and motives, their several rules of guidance—here the Perfect, living by Pure Love alone, there the Hireling Just, still tainted by the leaven of Hope and Fear. Between them rose a spectre of metaphysical Disinterestedness, an idea so abstract that it could be intellectually grasped by few, and practically followed out by none; yet this invention was the bar, that shut out countless numbers from the higher spiritual state.

And to Bossuet, above all men, this exclusiveness was detestable, for he had ever been the friend of the many, had ever walked in the safe middle of the path, pitching his demands neither too low nor too high, but ready even to sacrifice something of the ideal, if he might be the better understood of the people. He had asked for no Disinterestedness, but, like another great Bishop, had "treated the favourite passion of self-love with the utmost tenderness and concern for its interests," [1] had thrown over in the many's favour the common doctrine of the Schools, and taught that the desire for pleasure was an unalterable law of nature, true even for spiritual men, who could not love His God unless He made him happy. The earliest statements of his doctrine are distinguished by an almost brutal frankness— there was no love without hope, no hope without self-interest, therefore no love without desire of heaven—and from this

[1] See Bishop Butler's 11th Sermon.

first position he never swerved, though, as the quarrel went on, an eloquence which never touched without adorning, threw veil after veil of increasing grandeur over its original nakedness.[1] Might not the holiest ever reflect, he asked, that God had meant them to be happy? Might they not yield a free consent to this wise provision of their nature? Where was the harm, where was the peril, provided that they found their only happiness in God? To wish to be happy was implicitly to wish for Him, to wish for Him was to wish intelligently to be happy.[2] Theorists might draw their careful distinctions between the love of Hope and the love of Charity, between love of Him as good in Himself and love of Him as good to man, but practice gladly seized on every motive and held him best who loved the most, whatever the reason of his love.[3]

Fénelon might call this merchandize, might hunt innocent self-love through all its fastnesses, might call himself the champion of true Prayer,—but whither, asked his critic, did his system lead? What was his Disinterestedness but a vain and frivolous imagining, a love that knew no Gospel, no Saviour, no Christ, that would subsist unchanged if all God's care, His mercy, His Goodness were forgotten,—nay was the more perfect, the more it strove to forget them and kept its purity untarnished by any remembrance of His Grace. Worse than the heathen Socrates, who had at least a Providence, Disinterestedness clung to nothing, hoped for nothing, said no prayers, but 'wished its God a stone,' a barren Entity unknowable, careless of its creatures' welfare and all unheeding of their love. It was not Christian, it was not even a religion, it was simple Deism in a theological dress.[4]

And what was Fénelon's Passivity but a shameful inaction, an indolent waiting on Grace, that made no resistance to sin or temptation, that never stooped to co-

---

[1] See Bonnel, pp. 217 and *ff*.   [2] Wks., xiv. p. 250, *cf*. pp. 626, 699.
[3] *Ibid.* p. 407, *cf*. p. 242.
[4] *Ibid.* pp. 692 and *ff*., and see Wks., xv. pp. 118, etc.

operate with God, but stood aside in craven trembling from the battle of life, under pretence of leaving all to Him.[1] Fénelon's mouth might be full of Charity, of the need of exercising all the virtues in its name and in its strength, but Charity, though the Queen, was not the sum of the virtues ; each had its special place and value—the tree was not dispensed from growing because its leaves and branches were virtually contained already in the root. Nay, cried the great defender of the active life, it was this ordered progression, this harmonious development from one seminal principle that gave, not only its beauty and perfection, but its very being to the tree.[2]

And so Bossuet girded himself up for the struggle and proclaimed *qu'il y allait de toute la religion*[3]—that the whole of religion was at stake. The world might call the controversy an affair of words and personal interests and technicalities, 'just a Bishop's quarrel, all intrigues and ambitions, with nothing of religion in it but the name'[4]— the world had said the same thing of the rise of every heresy, and Bossuet was determined to prove it in the wrong.[5] Earlier in life, he might have been, perhaps, less precipitate, have asked himself whether the Maxims was really more than an academic thesis—itself no cause, but one of the symptoms of a *maladie du siècle* not to be cured or even reached by papal censures, from which, moreover, since the fall of M$^{me.}$ Guyon and Molinos, the world was already beginning to recover. Or he might have reflected that violent and prolonged attacks would give the book a notoriety unobtainable on its own demerits, would bring into chief prominence its most mischievous features and awaken new sympathy for its author—he might have trusted more generously to his countrymen's good sense and let the weight of its own extravagances bury Fenelon's ill-starred volume in oblivion.

[1] Wks., xviii. p. 538. [2] Wks., xiv. p. 75. [3] *Ibid.* p. 489.
[4] So the cynical Duchess of Orleans, Letters (Ed. Jaeglé), i. p. 199.
[5] *cf.* Wks., xv. p. 440.

But he was growing old, and with advance of years came increasing disinclination to let things find their natural level, greater intolerance, greater anxiety to protect the public against themselves, greater hatred also of that easy accommodating secular spirit which called itself judiciousness or worldly wisdom or sense of proportion. Its votaries might judge things by their practical workings instead of by first principles, might spare bad books out of regard for their author's name, or because they were dull and unintelligible and seldom read—but Bishops, he cried, enter into no such cynical connivances: with them truth is truth and error error; they speak to one another *apertè apertè*, with all the holy rigour of the theological tongue.[1]

And Bossuet was troubled by the new conditions of the warfare. Heretofore he had fought against open enemies and in purely theological battles; now he was at war with the master of a great cabal, who had a hundred voices tuned to sing his praise, a hundred busy hidden hands to scatter his answers throughout the Court, the Town, the Provinces.[2] Now every courtier at Versailles was a party to the struggle and many were banded together against the truth, for on the first great outburst of instructive orthodoxy had followed a period of darkness and reaction, when parties were formed, Dialectic laid traps for the unwary, and Eloquence led the simple astray, when men knew no longer where they stood or what were the principles involved, but took sides simply as their humour bade.[3]

And present intrigues seemed but the earnest of a greater future danger. What if Fénelon's real aim went beyond mere devotional innovations, what if the Maxims and its cryptic language were the password of a great political conspiracy, if behind this prodigious versatility and cleverness, behind the genius that struck terror into the heart,[4] lay all the worldly

---

[1] Wks., xiv. pp. 486, 710, and see M. Rebelliau's little work on Bossuet, chs. viii., ix.   [2] *Ibid.* p. 489.   [3] *Ibid.* xv. p. 266.
[4] Qui lui conteste l'esprit? Il en a jusqu'à faire peur, et son malheur est de s'être chargé d'une cause où il en faut tant. Wks., xv. p. 448.

AT WAR WITH BOSSUET

ambitions of a scheming and meddlesome priest? The tutor of Burgundy had seized with the son an opportunity that Bossuet had let slip with the father; this rash reformer, this high-priest of every novelty, was heir to all and more than all his senior's influence at the Court, and Bossuet might well look forward with a real concern, sharpened, it may be, by more human envy and annoyance, to the day when Fénelon would return to Court in triumph 'after I and two or three others are dead,' and there, brushing aside the God-appointed order, in which the priest stood second to the law-giver, would rule from his confessional everything, even the State.[1]

And if Fénelon's new principles overspread the Church, Bossuet foresaw the ruin of almost every project near his heart. Though never a Gallican in the stricter sense, he had gloried in the honourable independence of the Church of France; but the helm of power was now falling to an Ultramontane, a friend of the Jesuists, for whom the Gallican liberties were 'a very servitude.'[2]

There would be no reconciliation with the Jansenists. Port Royal's stern belief in man's corruption would never be converted to Pure Love, nor listen to a doctrine of Perfectibility in a world where even the holiest could scarce be saved. And Fénelon's mystic outbursts shocked its grave sobriety; they were a triumph of the Imagination, that bold Pretender ever on the watch to steal from Reason the Empire of the soul.

Bossuet, again, had striven for a reunion with the Protestants on terms of a moderate and reasonable orthodoxy. But now the solid basis of Catholic unity was cracking; and Lutherans and Calvinists grimly smiled as they saw the Romish Babel rent again asunder by a new strife of tongues. Nay, Quietism had brought about one more division within the Protestant camp itself; while the great Huguenot, Jurieu cursed it for a monstrous heresy, Bishop Burnet and the German Pietists were welcoming even Molinos and

[1] See Wks., xix. p. 147. [2] Fén. Wks., vii. p. 315.

Mme. Guyon as deliverers of the people from the bonds of Rome.¹

All these things gave to Bossuet's voice a certain savage harshness, a brutal irony unknown to his earlier controversies with the Protestants and Jansenists. There, as he said, there was plenty of moderation;² there he had borne himself with all the dignity of a great Ambassador treating with a hostile power, or of a mediator bringing peace and contentment to the disaffected party in a State; here he was at best a Brutus, doing justice on the body of a single traitor, and that traitor a son, who once had been near to his heart.

It is hard for us Englishmen, for whom ecclesiastical discipline has ceased to be even an impertinence, rightly to appraise the conduct of one who had not only grown up under its shadow, but had become its very embodiment, its almost infallible mouthpiece, who was called by his own contemporaries, and that in no spirit of imbecile flattery, the last of the Fathers of the Church. No man was ever more convinced than Bossuet that his was God's and the Church's cause; he thought himself the apostle of Christian manliness and courage against a gospel of nervous debility that found its highest perfection in despair,³ of reverence against the ignorant presumption that 'laid God down a method and mapped out His Graces in degrees,'⁴ the champion of universal objective Catholicism against that rebellious spirit of individuality which had been the mother of all the heresies. And it may be granted that Bossuet did right to be angry, that to the great master of solid argument Fénelon's ironical deference, his quibbles and irrelevancies, his saintly airs of martyrdom, were a provocation intolerable, that by the disposition of nature Bossuet could never be reasonable without being passionate or passionate without being reasonable—it may even be well that beneath the writer we should find the man, behind the majestic impersonal dogmatist the

---

¹ See the introductory chapter of Scharling's Molinos.
² Wks., xix. p. 250.   ³ See Wks., xiv. p. 552.   ⁴ Wks., xviii. p. 136.

AT WAR WITH BOSSUET

ardent pamphleteer, 'flinging his fury into theses,' thirsting,[1] despite all protests, for a personal victory, alive with human passions like our own.[2]

Yet there is danger in too much excusing. It must not be forgotten that Bossuet carried himself with something of the *bourgeois* insolence of a prelate in the right towards the gentleman in the wrong, that he hectored, threatened, plotted, violated confidences, made accusations as base as reckless, hated impersonally, by hideous distortion of the *errores odi, errantes diligo*, as only a priest could hate. No artifice of the historic imagination, however abounding in explanations, however easy of pardon to all unlovely sincerities, can altogether avail to clear him, to prove that he did not sacrifice the honour of his methods to the greatness of his cause.

And if Bossuet, the frank and open, is a difficult problem, what must be said of Fénelon, who was a standing enigma to his own conscience, whose organism was so delicate, so strained, that to him the common rules of morality scarcely apply—he must be judged by a code peculiar to himself. 'He lost his way on the highroad,' said his enemy, 'and was drowned in a drop of water; had he only been able to be simple for a single moment he would have been saved.'[3] On his side there was scheming, shuffling, downright lying, mystification for its own sake, pamphlets barbed with an irony benignly outrageous, at times, even, outrage without the benignity, as when he charges his adversary with employing to write down falsehoods the same hand which at the Altar offered the Incarnate God of Truth,[4] or begs him remember how great is his age, how soon he will be answering before a Judge Whom reputation does not dazzle nor eloquence appease.[5]

Or he teems with the *superbia quæsita meritis*; the tale of

[1] Luther met en thèses ses fureurs, said Bossuet in the Variations.
[2] I summarize some admirable pages of Bonnel, pp. 255-259.
[3] Boss. Wks., xix. p. 16.
[4] Quoi, Monseigneur, vous dites la messe et vous parlez ainsi. De la même main, etc. Fén. Wks., iii. p. 344. [5] *Ibid.* p. 54.

his hardships never loses in the telling, often bids a bold defiance to the facts ; as his enemy complains, he could obscure the clearest reasonings, embroil the simplest issues, never spoke without glancing over his shoulder to find some loophole of retreat.[1] He was a master, too, in all the arts of anonymity, in shifting on to other shoulders the burden of his actions, in letting his own fingers weave the rope that was to drag him, a seemingly bound and helpless victim, into some underhand trick.

And yet M$^{me.}$ de Maintenon was right—with him also there was perfect sincerity ; no impostor could have been so obstinate, have piled up such masses of relentless tortuosity in defence of his opinion. Through all this coil of tangled falsehood runs a thread of higher feeling, a real desire to spare his enemies, to give back peace to the Church, a real consideration for Beauvilliers and Chevreuse, a fear lest too great vigour on his part should be visited on their heads by the King.[2] In this strange character, where all contradictories were reconciled, virtues could lie down peacefully beside their opposing evils, merits became failings and shadows lustres ; there was no disengaging the good from the bad, no frontier post to watch where generous forbearance ended and where the pose of 'dove-like' uncomplaining martyrdom began.[3]

It was a poor quarrel and a sign of degeneracy, says Dean Church, and few will wish to set his verdict aside. Only the Genius of Misdirected Energy can take pleasure in the spectacle—on one side Fénelon's brilliant persuasiveness and sleight-of-hand wasted on the explaining of problems either insoluble or beneath solution, on the other Bossuet's majestic eloquence and logic breaking these airy phantoms on his wheel. There is something more than mournful in the hundreds of pages that discuss whether the desire of happiness is necessarily an imperfection in the sight of God, or

[1] See Le Dieu's conversation with Bossuet, ii. p. 242.
[2] See *e.g.* Wks., ix. pp. 436, 498, *et passim*.
[3] 'The meek and dove-like Fénelon,' says Mr Vaughan. Hours with the Mystics, ii. p. 264.

AT WAR WITH BOSSUET 161

determine the precise degree of beatitude sacrificed by St Paul when he wished to be accursed for his brethren's sake —St Paul of whom one antagonist allows that 'he never exactly measured the value of his acts,'[1] whose words, said the other, were a mere transport of ecstatic love, meaningless because beyond possibility and impossibility alike.[2] Well might Fénelon declare that both of them would have been happier, if, instead of becoming the laughing-stock of infidels by this war of words, they had spent their time teaching the Catechism to the poor children of their villages![3]

And the tactics were more than worthy of the cause. Even while doctrine was alone in question, the moral level was low enough; there was a misuse of authorities hardly even to be justified by the unscholarly erudition of that age,[4] accusations, both founded and unfounded, of garbled quotations and faithless rendering into Latin, dark hints from Bossuet that he was attacking only on the surface, that beneath lay heresies too black for charitable lips to tell.

Round one point alone grew up a whole jungle of denials and counter-assertions.[5] Fénelon declared that a passage in the Maxims which ascribed '*involuntary* trouble'[5] to Jesus on the Cross was no more than a note on the margin of his manuscript, incorporated by a mistake of Chevreuse with

---

[1] Fén. Wks., ii. p. 410.   [2] Boss. Wks., xiv. p. 227.
[3] Fén. Wks., iii. p. 354.

[4] "Bossuet," says Bonnel (p. 218), "made the Fathers speak his language," with results that do not approve themselves to more dispassionate scholars. See Deharbe, Volkom. Liebe, pp. 50 and *ff*. Fénelon seems deliberately to have used a spurious edition of St Francis of Sales, whenever it suited his purpose, and Baudry charges both Prelates with having read St Francis superficially indeed, though they quote him on almost every page. See Wks. of St Francis, ed. Migne, ix. pp. 510, 661.

[5] Maxims, p. 122. The whole proposition, as condemned by the Pope, runs: Inferior pars animœ Christi in cruce non communicavit superiori suas involuntarias perturbationes. The whole difficulty was about the adjective. Reading the whole matter in the light of the solemn declaration in Fénelon's Will (Wks., x. p. 135) it seems probable that he began by hesitating to use the word, but plucked up courage, on re-reading his draft, to put it down tentatively in the margin, and neglected, either by accident or design, to strike it out when the manuscript was finally sent to Chevreuse.

the text, though he was willing to take a modified responsibility for it and argue that it was understandable in a lawful and Catholic sense. But Bossuet would have none of his explanations or his denials of authorship, and answered that this, in whatever sense taken, was the most abominable heresy in the book, and in far too close agreement with its context and with the whole system of the Maxims, to be shuffled off lightly on to a proof-reader's shoulders.

But it was far worse when the Abbé Bossuet, his uncle's Roman agent, had his way, and to disputed points of dogma succeeded wrangles over facts. Now began the reign of innuendo, of vague suggestions flung with careless artifice upon the air, to be lovingly dwelt on or ignored or denied just as the environment might demand, in themselves mere bodiless nothings, whispers with only half a meaning, that lodged without effort in the reader's brain, their service more than rendered when they had called forth a shrug of the shoulders or an indolent 'Who knows?'[1]

And for this work Fénelon was pre-eminently fitted by a quality of character which was not all, or even chiefly, artifice but, rather, a constitutional infirmity of his nature, a powerlessness to see things in their true proportion, whenever his sympathies or his interests were deeply engaged. The emptiest compliment became a solemn attestation, the most accidental slight a mortal injury; Louis XIV.'s grudging allowance of his appeal to Rome grew into a kindly warning, almost an order, to carry his cause away out of Bossuet's intolerant reach, to the calm unbiassed judgment of the Pope.[2]

And as the quarrel went on, Fénelon drifted into a bottomless sea of unrealities, where doubts appeared more certain than a demonstration, suspicions surer than a proof, where from an assemblage of true particulars some strange half-conscious alchemy distilled a whole of wild impossible falsehood. Some of his accusations almost pass the limit

[1] See a really forcible letter from Chanterac to Fénelon. Wks., ix. p. 468.
[2] Boss. Wks., xix. p. 131, and see Fén. Wks., iii. pp. 41, 44.

of sanity—what are we to say when, not content with branding Bossuet's wrongful publication of some private letters as a gross breach of confidence, he invests one of them, long after it was written, with the mysterious glamour of a 'general confession,' and weakly and indecisively charges his opponent with the most grievous crime a priest can commit—the violation of the secret of the Confessional?[1]

Without his excuse of temperament, that opponent was not far behind him. Seventy-two witnesses were needed by the Roman Courts to establish a charge of sexual vice against an Archbishop, and 'God forbid' said Bossuet, once he was pressed, 'that I should say a word against M. de Cambrai's morals.'[2] Yet it was ingenious to drag M$^{me.}$ Guyon from her prison to confrontations with Lacombe, to wring from this wretched man, now ripening fast for a lunatic asylum, confessions of guilty commerce with his friend, to remind the world that by her own avowal she had *another* spiritual son who stood even nearer to her than Lacombe.[3] It was wise also to make much of the trial of the filthy Curé of Seurre, condemned at this very time to the stake for Quietism and spiritual incest,[4] to hunt up the records of mystical scandals in Italy and Spain,[5] to keep the Roman gossips agog for new letters, new discoveries, new abominations, but especially for that imaginary correspondence between M$^{me.}$ Guyon and Fénelon which was so terrible that it could only be printed at the last extremity.[6] And there was policy even in calling Fénelon the Montanus

---

[1] The formal accusation is made in Fén. Wks., iii. p. 18, but it had been whispered about long before. See Wks., ix. p. 205. Chanterac's language (*Ib.* p. 581) made it clear that Fénelon really meant a sacramental confession, though, as Bossuet complained (Wks., xv. p. 381), the accusation was never exactly formulated and Fénelon afterwards denied (Wks., iii. p. 66) that he had meant a sacramental confession.
[2] See Wks., xv. p. 378, and see Wks., xix. pp. 494, 502.
[3] *Ibid.* xix. p. 260.
[4] Fén. Wks., ix. p. 517. The Curé, according to Chanterac, was well known to M$^{me.}$ Guyon.   [5] Boss. Wks., xix. p. 248.   [6] Fén. Wks., ix. p. 464.

of this new Priscilla;[1] not all the courtiers who chuckled over the *Relation du Quiétisme* had read their Eusebius, or knew that the Phrygian heretic's virtue was sounder than his doctrine.[2]

It was at Rome that this crop of weeds grew thickest. There each prelate had his confidential agents, at the head of a whole battery of subterranean wires, of spies and secret allies, of the hundred voices tuned to sing his praise at Rome, at Paris, at Louvain, Florence, Salamanca, even, in Fénelon's case, in all the newspapers of Holland.[3] Each took particular count of the other's correspondence; Bossuet had his sandalled detectives to pry into every letter that came or went from Cambrai;[4] Fénelon was indebted for many kind offices to the master of the Brussels post;[5] over the secrets of his Embassy mail-bag Bouillon reigned supreme.[6] There was much intriguing, also, for a sight of the enemy's defences; for the short and piquant narratives, 'better than anything in Terence,' that Bossuet intended for the Pope's ear alone, for the innumerable answers and apologies which Fénelon would not publish in France, but sent direct to Rome.[7] Or arrangements were made with some discreet and friendly Jesuit for denouncing Bossuet's doctrine of Charity to the Holy Office;[8] pamphlets from Cambrai, whose Ciceronian style would fatally betray their origin, were to be broken up into the kitchen-Latin of the Propaganda, printed and returned to France as evidence of the trend of Roman opinion.[9]

But above all there must be abundance of such facts as every Monsignore could understand. Bossuet's whole

---

[1] Wks., xv. p. 285. Père de la Rue, an anti-Quietist Jesuit and a friend of Bossuet, compared Fénelon and Mme. Guyon in the pulpit to Abelard and Héloïse. See Fén. Wks., ix. p. 516.

[2] Of Montanus' innocence Fénelon's friends were not so confident. See Wks., ix. p. 580.

[3] Fén. Wks., ix. p. 321, *cf.* p. 227 and the note. Boss. Wks., xviii. pp. 633, 651.   [4] Wks., xix. p. 90.   [5] *Ibid.* ix. p. 637.

[6] Boss. Wks., xviii. p. 614.   [7] p. 637, *vide* post.

[8] Fén. Wks., ix. p. 648, *cf.* p. 676.   [9] p. 648.

AT WAR WITH BOSSUET

conduct must be explained by jealousy, and Fénelon's by love of Mme. Guyon; the quarrel must become an organized plot to ruin Fénelon, who alone had stood out for the honour of the Crown, when Bossuet and de Noailles were urgent for the proclamation of Mme. de Maintenon's marriage with the King.[1]

And every prelate's taste was carefully consulted. To Scholastic logicians Fénelon was pictured as a follower of Descartes,[2] to strict disciplinarians as a lax administrator, to the secular clergy as a friend of none but monks and friars;[3] the Roman ladies were assured that de Noailles did not love the Madonna;[4] the many friends of Jansenism learnt that Bossuet was no better than a Jesuit, admirers of the Society that he was the worst abettor of Port Royal.[5]

Even the history of Mme. Guyon was transformed in this marvellous crucible; it was Bossuet, not Fénelon, who had been her friend, had treated her during her six months' stay at Meaux with a warm indulgence strangely contrasting with Fénelon's invariable coolness and reserve.[6] The more light-minded among the Cardinals even had their jests about Bossuet and this pretty woman, to the no small scandal of Fénelon's agent, the Abbé de Chanterac, who could not bear, good honourable respecter of dignities as he was, that even the arch-persecutor should be suspected of impropriety.[7]

Yet Chanterac was far from being the prolix simple-minded fool the Abbé Bossuet thought him. Certainly he was no match for the Abbé in unscrupulous diplomacy nor for Bossuet's second agent, the shrewd and caustic Phélippeaux, in his knowledge of theology; yet that mattered little when Fénelon himself controlled the arguments, and Bouillon was at hand to manage the intrigues. Chanterac's

---

[1] Boss. Wks., xviii. p. 625.   [2] p. 650.   [3] Fén. Wks., ix. pp. 331, 353.
[4] Boss. Wks., xix. p. 362.   [5] *Ibid.* xviii. p. 781.
[6] *Ibid.* xix. p. 14.   *cf.* Chanterac's letter in Fén. Wks., ix. p. 471.
[7] Fén. Wks., ix. p. 312.

business was to excite compassion, to enlist the sympathy of the Cardinals on behalf of dignity and virtue in distress, nor could Fénelon himself have better played the part than this loyal, modest and single-minded gentleman, as he wandered sadly round from prelate to prelate, bewildered at their florid Italian politeness which said so much and meant so little, and told in stumbling Latin his little touching stories of his master's goodness and misfortune.[1]

And all was told in simple unsuspecting faith; Bossuet was a hard, jealous, arrogant man, not even quite as truthful as might be wished; Fénelon was a saint over whom Providence was watching; his day of trial would soon be ended, for even in that land of riotous ambitions God's glory and His truth would triumph in the end.[2]

The Abbé Bossuet shared neither in Chanterac's scruples nor in his pleasant illusions; right was on his side also, but he thought less about truth and more about the power of France, about those thunderbolts from Louis which alone could rouse the Pope from his slumbers, and prevent him from shielding Fénelon at every turn of the game.[3] With this enormous power behind him, with a Nuncio at Paris entirely after his uncle's heart, it was easy to bribe and intimidate and threaten, 'not exactly to embitter the Italians, but to make them feel the power of France,'[4] to persuade them that Louis would rather hear of the condemnation of the Maxims than see his grandson on the throne of Spain.[5] And the vulgar, blustering Abbé was just the man for the work; in him not a little practical energy and astuteness were hidden away behind the exterior of a foppish clerical cad. The Romans made merry over his gorgeous lackeys and pages, over his nightly adventures 'with the little dark lantern,' over the social attractions, so dangerous to young ladies, that got him "the entry to the very best houses, because, to speak frankly, I know how to

---

[1] Fén. Wks., ix. pp. 206 etc.   [2] *Ibid.* p. 375.   [3] Bossuet Wks., xix. p. 408.
[4] The euphemism is de Noailles'. Bossuet Wks., xix. p. 94.
[5] Fén. Wks., ix. p. 504.

AT WAR WITH BOSSUET   167

talk and have seen something of the world."[1] But, if they laughed, they also trembled. His bluster disquieted the Cardinals, a set of old men 'timid as hares, never free from panic, who would only believe what was immediately before their eyes'; he broke in rudely on their courtly leisure with violent unaccustomed language—the devil was the chief defender of the Maxims, Fénelon was a very great liar, a wild beast who must be hunted down and speared for the honour of the episcopate, the worst enemy the Church of France had ever had.[2]

Nor could they ignore him as an empty boaster when letters and peremptory messages kept pouring in from Versailles. Rome, as a friendly prelate said to Chanterac, could not answer France with cannon-balls[3] or throw away her friendship for a book, for a scholastic quillet that hardly even touched on doctrine, when any moment Charles of Spain might die, and plunge the world into war for his inheritance.[4] Louis XIV. might not be to Rome the best loved of Most Christian Princes; Bossuet was still remembered by many as the author of a certain noxious Declaration of Gallican Right, but not a few of their Eminences were *papabili* and dared not mortally offend a Sovereign who carried the Triple Crown in his pocket.[5]

Other Courts also had an interest in the struggle. Although the Imperial Ambassador worked hard for Fénelon, the Spanish deserted to Bossuet,[6] and zealously on this side was a smaller potentate, Cosimo III., Grand Duke of Tuscany, a famous dabbler in theology, whose word had no small weight in Roman counsels, for many of the Cardinals had been his subjects.[7]

But Bossuet's firmest allies were the enemies of the Jesuits, and above all the Cardinal Casanate, "to whom,

---

[1] Boss. Wks., xviii. p. 740. See Fén. Wks., ix. p. 308 etc.
[2] Boss. Wks., xix. p. 236 etc. Fén. Wks., ix. p. 423, etc.
[3] Fén. Wks., ix. p. 671.   [4] See Fén. Wks., ix. pp. 454 and *ff.*
[5] See Bouillon's candid remarks on his brethren, p. 699.
[6] Boss., xviii. p. 805.   [7] Fén. Wks., ix. p. 348.

under God, we owe everything,"[1] a dictatorial old man of high character and strangely catholic sympathies, for he had once been a friend of Molinos and was now the chief patron of Jansenism.[2]

The Jesuits, on their side, had taken up the matter as a personal challenge. It was not without fear that the Abbé Bossuet saw their 'black moles' working everywhere against the interests of France, for the Society, though hated and cried down by Bishops and laity and rival Orders, generally arrived by subterranean channels at its end. And behind the Jesuits there was Bouillon, more violent and more crafty than the Abbé Bossuet himself, who 'almost told the Cardinals they were asses,' and turned on the senile Pope himself with the fury of a wounded boar.[3] And he could play more adroitly on the timid Roman's fears; it was no small matter, he told them, to condemn an Archbishop of France; Fénelon would prove a terrible fellow when roused; he would set the whole kingdom in a blaze of schism.[4]

And these, as all our Frenchmen contemptuously agreed, were the right kind of arguments for Rome. Interest in theology the Monsignori had none; they were born diplomatists who had never studied anything but law, for the road to the purple lay through nunciatures and administrative offices, while Divinity was left to the Friars who had no other means of advancement.[5] The Pope himself, Innocent XII., understood but little of the controversy, though that, said the Abbé Bossuet, did not matter, for he had great confidence in the Holy Ghost.[6] He was an old man, often ailing, and with none too clear a head, very anxious to be civil to the King of France, to whom he owed his election, though on the whole his sympathies were for Fénelon, who had erred, as he said, from loving God

---

[1] Boss. Wks., xix. p. 184, and *cf*. Chanterac's confirmation of this fact, Fén. Wks., ix. p. 738.   [2] See Fén. Wks., x. p. 17.
[3] The comparison is the Pope's, Boss. Wks., xix. p. 184.
[4] *Ibid*. pp. 360, 367 and *ff*.
[5] Phélippeaux, Relation, pp. 299 and *ff*.   Chanterac says the same thing, Fén. Wks., ix. p. 662.   [6] Boss. Wks., xix. p. 361.

too much, just as Bossuet had erred from loving his brother too little. But the Pope was a reed on which neither party could lean with safety; his yielding temper and failing memory left him helpless in the hands of others; he was always on the side of the speaker who had just sat down.¹

Nevertheless, Innocent and his Cardinals were somewhat nettled by Bossuet's pretensions to dictate to them— *Episcopus Meldensis*, they said, *est Papa Gallus*, and were resolved to show the great master of Tradition that they could be as accurate as he.² The Maxims was thrice examined, first by a committee of monastic experts, who, after hearing the parties 'as in a murder-trial,' drew up a list of propositions to censure, though care was taken that the balance of opinion should be neatly trimmed; since nothing, said Chanterac, was more intolerable to Rome than having to make a definite pronouncement.³ One judge was removed to please the Bossuets, but when the Court seemed to be inclining too strongly to their side, Bouillon suggested that no one in France thought much of the theology of monks, and two Bishops, both favourable to Fénelon, were promptly added.⁴ This manœuvre had the desired effect of equally dividing the judges; in May 1698 five reported for the Maxims, five against, and the matter went up to the Cardinals of the Holy Office, with whom 'prudential' rather than dogmatic considerations were expected to weigh.⁵ Last of all the question came before the Pope, who, with the assistance of his Cardinal Consultors, pronounced the formal judgment.

Except to Fénelon and his immediate following, the real issue of the struggle was never for a moment doubtful. At times even the invincible hopefulness of Chanterac was

¹ Wks., xviii. pp. 634 and *ff*.
² See Fén. Wks., ix. p. 413.   ³ *Ibid*. p. 385.
⁴ Even the Abbé Bossuet was obliged to admire this master-stroke of diplomacy, Boss. Wks., xviii. p. 696.
⁵ These prudential considerations were Chanterac's terror. See Fén. Wks., ix. pp. 489, 643.

overcast, especially when events in France made too plain that tide of outside opinion, with which it was at once the policy and the glory of the Roman Court always to coincide.[1] Such were the marriage of de Noailles' nephew to Mme. de Maintenon's niece,[2] (April 1698) the dismissal of Burgundy's inferior tutors from their place, and with them Fénelon's brother, an Exon of the Guard, for the sole crime of his relationship. (June 1698) Still worse was it when this lightning was followed by thunder, by the expulsion of Fénelon himself from his nominal preceptorship (January 1699), but worst of all was the appearance of Bossuet's *Relation sur le Quiétisme*, which covered Fénelon and Mme. Guyon with ridicule, and something more than ridicule, till even Bouillon half-doubted of his innocence and the Beauvilliers circle hid their heads for shame.[3]

But Chanterac found some crumb of comfort everywhere. Italy was a country of great and sudden changes where Pontiffs died, and black in a moment turned to white:[4] a censure of the Maxims was not to be thought of—had not the General of an Order told him that this would lead to schism in the Church, to the uprising of Doctors of every nation, to the death of all belief in the infallibility of the Pope?[5]

And Fénelon himself was not many degrees less optimistic. He an Archbishop, a Mystic, an Ultramontane, head of a diocese teeming with heretics, close to infidel Holland, could never be condemned—Rome would never give this handle to the Protestants for saying she had varied, one moment canonizing the mystics and the next anathematizing their doctrine—she would never set the stamp of truth on Bossuet's lying assertion that the true root of Quietism was Disinterested Love.[6]

---

[1] Fén. Wks., ix. p. 305.
[2] This blow was all the more crushing, since, according to Le Dieu (ii. p. 229), Fénelon had himself, in happier days, had a large part in negotiating the marriage.
[3] Fén. Wks., ix. p. 421.
[4] *Ibid.* p. 661.   [5] *Ibid.* p. 340.   [6] *Ibid.* pp. 199, 542, etc.

Yet, although he had persuaded himself that the conscience of Rome was in his favour, Fénelon went in no small terror of her cowardice. He knew that, if she could, she would escape without deciding, would take refuge in some 'prudential *mezzo termine*' or patch up with his enemies a compromise wherein Bossuet would figure, not only as a conqueror, but as one who could make a merciful use of victory, and Fénelon himself would be judged to have fallen —fallen, not by open graceful submission to the voice of God's infallible Vicar, but in an ignoble scuffle behind the scenes, by the unworthy hand of Bossuet.[1]

His first aim, therefore, was to guard against this danger, his second to inveigle Rome into openly becoming his Protectress, to melt her by the tragic pathos of his bearing, and yet by the fiery energy of his defences encourage her to pluck up heart of grace. Was she afraid of public opinion in France?—Fénelon scoured the Universities for proselytes, filled his letters with assurances that Paris was veering round to him, and did his best to hasten on the change by wearing his most fascinating air of martyrdom.

For in the two countries Fénelon played two different parts. To his Italian judges he was innocence meekly but bravely fighting for its rights; to his own countrymen at home he was helpless, uncomplaining, innocence oppressed. In France, as Chanterac noticed with horror, appeared none of his valiant Roman pleadings for the Truth; there silent at first for the sake of Beauvilliers and Chevreuse, he became still more silent as a matter of policy; there he let the three Bishops run their course unchecked, counting securely on the reaction that must follow when men grew tired of Bossuet and of this warfare so eternally one-sided, and began to think compassionately of its victim. There he was determined that the world should see him as in his letters he pictured himself, sitting stricken but silent in his Palace at Cambrai, peacefully indifferent to the sounds of far-off battle, forgetful of the ill his enemies wished to do

[1] Fén. Wks., pp. 264, 367, 501, etc.

him in the remembrance of the good they had done him against their will.[1]

Still there remained two men in France, Louis XIV. and Bossuet, who were wholly impenetrable by his gentler arts, and Louis XIV. and Bossuet were the two men whom Innocent feared the most. Yet even these Goliaths had a joint in their armour—'There are two sides,' he told the Romans, ' to the character of the King of France; with him the self-willed autocrat is doubled by a timorous devotee; the first will bribe and threaten unscrupulously, so long as the final decision goes unpronounced; the second will bow before the lightest whisper from St Peter's Throne. And once the King has failed them, my adversaries' sole support is gone; whatever the verdict, neither the clergy nor the Sorbonne will open their mouths; de Noailles is a man of peace and Godet des Marais an Ultramontane, while Bossuet himself is a cowardly bully, ready enough to bluster while he has an army at his back, but when he finds himself alone, he will become meek and supple as a glove.' [2]

There was but one drawback to this brilliant strategy—it was built up on an entire illusion. Rome, though full of sympathy for Fénelon's woes, was not led captive by his logic, nor—to borrow one of Bouillon's choice expressions—could she send such prelates as Bossuet and de Noailles flying from the Vatican *à coups de pied par le derrière*.[3] Long before the end, Infallibility had made up its mind; Fénelon's enemies were to win, but not to triumph,[4] and the one object of his allies was to make that victory as cheap as possible, to narrow down the Papal utterance from a solemn Bull to a more informal Brief, from a detailed condemnation to a vague censure " in the globe " or to a simple prohibition of the Maxims " until it was corrected." Hence Bouillon's

---

[1] See Wks., vii. p. 526. This aspect of the case has been dealt with brilliantly but unfairly by M. Lanson (Bossuet, pp. 404, and *ff.*) who adopts in all seriousness Bossuet's stock accusation against Fénelon of having every gift except the power of admitting himself to be in the wrong. See Wks., xviii. pp. 643, etc.

[2] *Ibid.* ix. pp. 252, 429 and esp. p. 543.   [3] *Ibid.* p. 482.

[4] Vinceranno, ma non trionferanno, said a Cardinal to Chanterac, *Ibid.* p. 673.

AT WAR WITH BOSSUET 173

long duel with the Abbé Bossuet, each striving to hurry on a judgment when the stream of opinion seemed making in his favour, each anxious to 'eternalize' the matter, whenever the verdict was going against him.

But Fénelon himself was obliged to allow that, the longer the battle, the more envenomed did his enemies become. The Romans, too, were weary of the whole affair;—even the Pope was wakened by intense anxiety to be rid of it to a degree of energy which—Bouillon told the King—was wholly supernatural in one so placid and so shy of thorny questions.[1] By the middle of February, 1699, Chanterac had given up all hope; a few days later Bouillon's last resistances were overcome, and on the 12th of March the Abbé Bossuet could raise his song of victory: " God is stronger than man ; the Truth has triumphed ; the gates of Hell have not prevailed against the Church."

Albano, the most judicious of the Cardinals, aided, however, by Fénelon's great enemy, Casanate, drew up the Brief of judgment. The Maxims was prohibited, twenty-three extracts from it specially condemned, though the Pope refused to brand them as heretical, or to order the book to be burned by the executioner. Dogmatically speaking, too, the Brief walked in the safe path of Roman precedent and decided as little as possible ; Disinterestedness, in the larger sense was neither asserted nor denied nor even defined, and all that was done was to prune Fénelon's system of its wilder extravagances. Habitual Passivity (Prop. 16), Indifference to Self (Prop. 4), to Hope and Fear (Prop. 1), neglect of virtues other than Charity (Prop. 18) went the same way as deliberate sacrifice of all wish for Heaven (Prop. 6) though perhaps the last article struck the heaviest blow, when it laid down that Disinterestedness by itself is not the sum and essence of the Gospel (Prop. 23).

Yet the Brief was not without some of the 'solid consolations' that Bouillon had promised Chanterac beforehand:[2]

[1] Fén. Wks. ix. p. 689. [2] p. 676.

Fénelon's enemies had charged him with a great crime; the Pope had only found him guilty of a small one. And in pronouncing against the Maxims Rome had not declared for Bossuet; Fénelon could lawfully tell his friends that Disinterestedness was not condemned, but only its exaggerated statement: self-interest had not been made the essential condition of our love of God—it was still possible to love Him for Himself, provided that Hope and desire of Heaven were not habitually of set purpose excluded.[1]

The news of his condemnation reached Cambrai on the morning of the 25th March, Lady Day, just as Fénelon was preparing to mount the pulpit of his cathedral. An hour sufficed for him to change the plan of his discourse and give an earnest of his future submission by preaching on the obedience that Christians owe to their superiors.[2] And, on the whole, he worthily redeemed this pledge, by submitting 'simply, humbly and without restriction,' yet also with a certain protest and unwillingness, that—so far from attenuating the value of his action—is, in such a man as Fénelon, perhaps the strongest proof of its sincerity. For the saintly idol of Cardinal Bausset, renouncing in one moment forever the cause he had fought for during two years with all the passion of his soul, and the conscienceless hypocrite of M. Crouslé, revolted in heart yet submissive in tongue, put equal strain on our credulity; the real man stands revealed in the letters to Chanterac, here, as ever, a mass of contradictions, in which the nobler elements fitfully preponderate, recognizing the errors of the Maxims but insisting that he never meant them, acknowledging the Papal judgment yet resolute to go no step beyond it, anxious to show no bitterness or wounded pride to Rome though also determined not to flatter it or fall in grovelling abjection at its

---

[1] The exact bearing of the judgment, which Bossuet and his modern apologists have enormously exaggerated, is made clear by Deharbe, pp. 179 and *ff.* See also the account of Fénelon's conversations with the Chevalier de Ramsai, Bausset, ii. p. 410, and iii. p. 346. See also Fénelon's later Epistola Secunda de Amore Puro (written in 1712). Wks., iii. pp. 563 and *ff.*

[2] See Chanterac's letter to him. Wks., x. p. 8.

AT WAR WITH BOSSUET 175

feet. 'I adhere to the decision, he wrote, to his agent, but there is no good reason why I should be pleased with it or why I should act as if I were. Show no unnecessary civility and leave as soon as possible, though it would be well if you could get from Rome some assurance of the underlying purity of my doctrine and intentions. But do not wait one quarter of an hour for a papal message simply praising my piety and submissiveness; if Rome is resolved not to bear witness to me, I fancy I can do without it; my patience, my moral standard, my labours in my diocese, will prove my innocence far more effectually than a few vague compliments in a Brief.'[1]

Bossuet, on hearing the judgment, was overjoyed. The Brief, he said, would have a universal welcome; it was long since Rome had given so good or so precise a judgment.[2] Nay, in this first outburst of triumphant relief, he could be merciful even to his adversary, and rejected his amiable nephew's proposals to work for a second, stronger, condemnation, on the double ground that he was sure Fénelon meant to submit, and that to ask Rome for more than Rome had given would seem like a confession of failure.[3] Besides, he held it right, for the sake of peace, not to look too closely into retractations, if once the essential point were there.

But this mildness vanished so soon as Fénelon—to use the famous phrase of Fontenelle—began to import coquetry into his submission. Bossuet's wrath was easily kindled by his rival's cool placidity and airs of resignation, but especially by the official Pastoral of submission, wherein, as he said, Fénelon had simply tried to set himself right in the eyes of Rome, and dwelt on nothing but his own docility, the one thing that redounded to his credit. 'It was not thus,' he cried, 'that men recanted in the Early Church'—forgetting that, as Fénelon had not been declared a heretic, there was no need for recantation.[4]

[1] See Wks., ix. pp. 717, 730, and Wks., x. p. 6.
[2] *Ibid.*, xix. p. 426. [3] p. 438.
[4] p. 456. Recantation involved an avowal of past error, as distinct from submission, which meant mere acceptance of the judgment.

But Bossuet was haunted by a fear, which the Chanterac letters show to have been not wholly groundless, that Fénelon would manage, even now, to slip the cable of his condemnation, by obtaining the Pope's approval of his explanations and defences. Indeed the struggle at Rome was not yet over; both parties still laid eager siege to Innocent's ear; Chanterac besought him to 'establish forever the doctrine of the Saints' by declaring that Fénelon had erred only through inadvertency of language, while the Bossuets begged that the bad and wicked arguments, by which the Maxims had been defended, might be delivered over to a similar condemnation.

And when Rome preserved a prudent silence, Bossuet, determined to leave no loop-hole to his enemy, appealed to Louis and the Bishops of France, whose ratification was necessary on the Gallican principle, before the Papal Brief could have the force of law. Out of sixteen Provincial Assemblies, eight, acting on a hint from Versailles, asked for the suppression of the defences, and Bossuet did not scruple to stir up one of Fénelon's suffragans, Valbelle, Bishop of St Omer, to demand it in the Metropolitan Assembly of Cambrai itself.[1] And he was delighted when Valbelle exceeded his instructions, and dashed into the fray, says Chancellor d'Aguesseau, with all the hot-headedness of a Southerner, and all the chicanery of a Norman, and, not content with seeing his Archbishop drink the cup of humiliation, made him drain it to the very dregs, in that he threw unworthy suspicion on his good intentions, and robbed him of the paltry consolation of saying that, if his words were bad, his thoughts were good.[2] Saint Simon also joins with d'Aguesseau in blaming the conduct of this courtier in purple [3]—but neither Saint Simon nor the Chancellor knew that St Omer's inspiration came from Meaux.

Thus ends a long and painful story, and only those who

[1] Fén. Wks., x. p. 29. See Bossuet Wks., xix. p. 501.
[2] Wks., xiii. p. 182.   [3] ii. p. 189.

are free from the *banalité écœurante* of believing that there are generally two sides to a quarrel¹ will be ready with their judgment. To many the whole matter will seem a mere futility, a dispute over things that pass man's understanding, conducted on one side by a pragmatical bully, and, on the other, by a hysterical hypocrite. And not a few must have risen from its study to find new zest in a saying of the great contemporary sceptic, Bayle, that God is too essentially good and reasonable to be the author of a thing so charged with odious sophistries as a positive religion.

Yet, if the Quietist battle brings its warriors no new glory, at least it must not be suffered to obscure the glories won on other fields. All human idols have their feet of clay, yet he is not a noble-minded critic whose spying-glass is always turned towards the mud. For all his false steps in this dismal quarrel, Bossuet may still remain to us by far the greatest Churchman modern Europe has produced, of Bossuet's rival the famous paradox² may still be true: Fénelon might almost have become a Saint, had it not been for Disinterested Love.

¹ Thus the Abbé Delmont ends his spiteful little book on Fénelon and Bossuet by declaring that la grande mémoire de Bossuet a souffert de cette banalité écœurante : Il y eut du tort de part et d'autre.
² See M. Caro's Nouvelles Etudes Morales, p. 186.

CHAPTER IX

TÉLÉMAQUE

> Les peuples verront aux montaignes
> La paix croistre et meurir,
> Et par costaux et par campaignes
> La justice fleurir.
>
> De peu de grains force blé ; somme,
> Les espys chascun an
> Sur les montz bruyront en l'air, comme
> Les arbres de Lyban.
>
> Sans fin bruyra le nom et gloire
> De ce roi nompareil
> De son renom sera memoire
> Tant qu'y aura soleil.
> —CLÉMENT MAROT, *72nd Psalm.*

TÉLÉMAQUE, wrote Fénelon to Father le Tellier, Confessor of Louis XIV., ten years after his book's appearance, is a fabulous narrative in the form of a heroic poem, like those of Homer or Virgil, in which I have set down the truths most necessary to be known by one who is about to reign ; there also are described the faults that cling most closely to the sovereign power. But I have borrowed from no real persons, I have sketched no characters of our own time ; my book was written at chance moments hurriedly and piece by piece ; it was sent to the press by an unfaithful copyist, and was never intended for the world.[1]

Enmities, contemporary and modern, have raised more than one objection to this account. Fénelon, it is said, lays on the copyist or the proof-reader the burden of all his literary indiscretions ; it is the same story here as with the Maxims ; both were hurried untimely into the world without

[1] Wks., vii. p. 665.

his knowledge; neither owed its most dangerous passages to its author's hand. But there is no good reason here to disbelieve him, or even to set down the publication to the pious treachery of his friends, acting in the hope that this new marvellous work of genius would blot out all memory of the Maxims of the Saints.[1] The venal transcriber was not unknown to an age guiltless of all respect for copyright; others besides Fénelon had suffered from his machinations, though on none had the blow fallen at a more disastrous moment. For the existence of Télémaque first became known in the autumn of 1698, just when the Quietest controversy was at its fiercest; it was published by the piratical booksellers of Holland early in the following year, at the time that Fénelon was making his submission to the Pope.[2]

Even without Télémaque, Fénelon could never have returned to Court; as it was, the book filled the King's cup of wrath to overflowing. For in those days it was difficult to treat of courts and governments without writing a satire; Fénelon had wished to "say everything," and, in the cautious, measured undertone, befitting a royal antechamber, everything had been said: Louis, his Court, his Ministers, his mistresses—all were there.[3]

Yet Fénelon had neither the bitterness nor the entire absorption in the ills immediately around him, that go to make the satirist: he had no wish simply to hold up a mirror to the vices of his age, still less to indulge in the timid realism of the contemporary novelists, and exhibit, for the mere pleasure of the showing, the chief figures of his own day in a Greek or Persian dress. Real men and women

---

[1] Le Dieu, ii. p. 12, reporting some remarks of Bossuet.

[2] The printing was begun in France, but the sheets were seized by the police. Bausset, iii. p. 12.

[3] Louis is Idomeneus, the Dauphin Boccharis, Louvois, the great War Minister, is Protesilas, Mme. de Montespan Astarbe, William of Orange is Adrastus, Tyre is Holland, the League of Augsburg against Louis is the coalition against Idomeneus. As to the various contemporary keys to Télémaque, described by Fénelon's friend and editor de Ramsay as 'low and malignant inventions,' see Hist. Litt., p. 155.

are present in Télémaque, but only as a lesson or a warning : the true sting of the book lay, not in any spiteful portraiture or epigram, but in the idealism that portrayed a commonwealth where virtue had her own again, where, as the coming age of sentimentalists could boast, all was attuned to the harmony of Nature, kings and peoples turned to agriculture and the necessary arts, where, above all, a sense of the Divine was once more restored.[1]

Nevertheless, Télémaque was more than a scholar's dream, more than an imaginary City of the Sun. The book that for us is the very symbol of elegant monotony, had for contemporaries all the interest of a political manifesto, all the terrors of a threatened Puritan reformation. If Salentum, as a whole, had scarcely even the vitality of the might-have-been, many of its principles were in danger of actual transplantation to France, were foreshadowings of a very possible future, when Louis and two or three others were dead, and Fénelon stood on the steps of the Duke of Burgundy's throne. Many a courtier groaned in spirit, as he foresaw the changing of the grandfather's tiresome outward decorum into the intense moral inwardness of the grandson, the rise of a new spirit of unwearying insistance on duty, on forced simplicity of life, of an Inquisition into conduct almost Genevan in its severity.[2] Bondholders in darkness heard the doom of their privileges and places and tax-farms pronounced in this apostolate of abstract superhuman Justice, which bowed before no old traditions, stayed for no lawyer's parchment explanations, but turned on every sullen fog-bank its search-light of unfaltering Truth and Reason. With Fénelon Letters ceased to be the hand-maid of the Court, and became the mouth-piece of a¹ new era of criticism and change ; Télémaque is a prelude to the Eighteenth Century, the first low

---

[1] See the incidental panegyrics on Télémaque in Bernerdin de St Pierre's Etudes de la Nature. Wks., iii. pp. 86 and *ff.*
[2] See the Domestic Inquisition recommended by Mentor. Bk. x. (Wks., vi. p. 483).

muttering of a storm that was to end with Rousseau and the Revolution.

For Fénelon's book is one of those outbursts of saddening hopefulness, that indict the whole Present at the bar of a fancied glorious Past, that cares nothing for the laws of organic growth or development, but strike out with a simple *Appello Naturam* all the complexities of our modern civilization. Like the writers of the dawning Age of Reason, Fénelon strained his eyes back to the first beginnings of the world, back to a Golden Age whence man by his own fault had issued, trailing behind him in his progress through the centuries a lengthening chain of laws and customs and traditions that shackled more and more his first divine sympathy—this cherished darling of Catholicism was one of the earliest to teach mankind to cry:

> Es erben sich Gesetz' und Rechte
> Wie eine ewige Krankheit fort
> Sie schleppen von Geschlecht sich zu Geschlechte
> Und rücken sacht von Ort zu Ort.
> Vernnuft wird Unsinn, Wohlthal Plage ;
> Weh Dir, dass Du ein Enkel bist.[1]

And as in these ideal politics no thought is taken of the lapse of Time, so also Fénelon looks away from Space: Télémaque is a sermon on the fraternity of nations, on the whole human race regarded as one vast family, bound together by ties of natural law and affection that rise superior to the petty ordinances of any single State. 'Limitless as is our debt to our own country,' he cries, 'we owe far more to the great fatherland, Mankind ; all men are brothers, all wars are civil wars, whose necessity is the reproach of man, whose

---

[1] Laws are a fatal heritage
Like a disease, an heirloom dread,
Their curse they trail from age to age
And furtively abroad they spread.
Reason doth nonsense, good doth evil grow,
That thou'rt a grandson in thy woe.

—Gœthe, Faust, i. 1973-8 (trans. Miss Swanwick). See Télémaque, bk. vii. p. 451 ; and the 13th Dialogue of the Dead, p. 250.

continuance is a stain upon our race. Even the savage, though he seems to civilized warriors little better than a beast, scorns to wanton in the murder of a fellow-creature: it would be well if we could blot out history and save all future generations the shame of knowing that man has shed the blood of man." [1]

Yet, if history itself must remain as a warning, to erase its results from the brains of its makers was no difficult task; Fénelon uproots all the inherited instincts and characteristics of the man as easily as he sweeps away the traditions and customs of the nation. He has the true eighteenth century belief in the *tabula rasa*, in a state of human intelligence born clear and vacuous into the world, and marked for the first time for good or evil when institutions and surroundings have begun to write thereon. Man, made in the image of God, was in himself a feeble helpless creature, with no instinctive bias or disposition of his own, but at the mercy of habit and caprice and the promptings of others, clay to be moulded at the law-giver's will. And therefore, Fénelon says, 'we, the masters, should seize on our subjects in their early youth; for the King, father of all his people, is in a special sense the father of the children; to the commonwealth, rather than to their parents, belong those future citizens who are already the flower of the State. Thus we shall change the tastes and habits of the whole people: we shall build up again like some Solon or Lycurgus, from the very foundations, and teach the people to live a frugal, innocent, busy, life after the pattern of our laws.' [2]

All must be done from above, for the people could not be leaders in the work of their own regeneration: though all were by nature reasonable animals, they could take no step forward by themselves; the thoughts of the many were the heritage of fools. They could never rise above certain virtues of custom and tradition, mutilated fragments of more general truths; they would be just where they had been

[1] Bk. ix. p. 462, and see the 17th Dialogue of the Dead, p. 256.
[2] Bk. xi. p. 495. Bk. xvii. p. 548.

taught to be just, generous to a fellow-citizen and inhuman to a stranger, jealous of their country's honour and unrighteous despoilers of a neighbouring people. They would never shake off prejudice or hope of reward, never do good out of simple conviction, never follow the True and Beautiful to its source, heedless of the worldly advantage it might bring.[1]

This path could be trodden only by their master, the disinterested law-giver, Plato's philosophic King. Through good report and evil he would go forward alone, looking for no return of gratitude, expecting from his servants nothing beyond what he had taught them, rewarded only by the increase of their virtue, or, if that was wanting, then, at least, of his own, and by the favours of the gods, who would console him in every adversity.[2]

For Fénelon has broken irrevocably with the ideas of the closing age and its belief in absolutism tempered by fear of God. Bossuet had made the King a splendid viceroy of the Almighty, responsible to no man, but only to the great Liege Lord above, had glorified before Louis XIV. his royal right and privilege of ministering to the necessities of his people. But Fénelon alters 'right' to 'duty': though the prince is still the mainspring, the tireless pivot of the State, it is only that he may the better bear its burdens, may be the steward of the national upbringing as the mother was the servant of the education of her girls.[3] The old theological sanction of royal virtue was no longer enough, now that the Rights of Man are making themselves heard beside the claims of Heaven; Télémaque's rule of conduct must rest on surer foundations than the good-will of angry fickle deities, gods of like passions with his own; he must become a paladin of duty, a drudge of philanthropy, his task-master no captious Jove, but an Eternal Law of Right and Wrong.[4]

And of this Law Fénelon's Olympus becomes the inter-

---

[1] Bk. xvii. p. 547, and see the 7th Dialogue of the Dead.
[2] Bk. xviii. p. 561.   [3] Bk. xvi. p. 542.   [4] See Bk. xviii. p. 558.

preter. Louis XIV. had thought himself an exception to all rules of morality : his grandson is reminded that the gods are no respecters of persons ; there is little difference in their eyes between the theft of a vineyard and the theft of a province ; their Imperative speaks to all alike in the same tones of calm and passionless authority.[1]

Louis had always acted as if the famous phrase were true, and he, and he alone were the State. Mentor answers that a King cannot be King by himself : he is great only through his subjects, through their numbers and contentment ; neither breadth of lands nor gorgeous palaces can save him, when once the tale of his people is dwindling, and commerce and husbandry wither away.[2]

Louis, again, had been the King of Pleasures, but Fénelon teaches that happiness is only for those who live *procul negotiis* ; the Prince's life is a state so burdensome that it will only be entered upon at the call of necessity ; no man need barter his independence for the slavery of a foreign crown.[3]

Louis had thought himself infallible : his critic holds that even the best sovereigns are unprofitable servants ; they pass their time alternately repairing one fault, and falling into another ; if Kings are to be pitied for having to govern men, so men are also to be pitied for having to be ruled by Kings.[4]

Precept and example are heaped up, one on the other, to awaken Burgundy to the perils of his state. Pygmalion shows him the fate of the tyrant, Idomeneus the danger of luxury and arrogance, Sesostris of bland mediocrity on the throne. He is shown how Princes are corrupted by the false and wicked maxims of Mazarin and Mazarin's master, Machiavel, and taught that probity is a pretty fable, and cynicism the only truth, till they think they have reached the summit of political wisdom, when they say in their haste : ' All men are liars.' Or they are told that Plenty is

[1] Bk. xvii. p. 553. [2] Bk. x. p. 473.
[3] Bk. v. p. 443.   [4] Bk. x. p. 476.

the mother of Revolution, that, for the sake of safety, the people must be weakened and brought low. As though rebellions were not born of the despair of an ill-treated people, of the harshness and arrogance of their rulers, of the nerveless brains at the head of the State, that can neither watch for trouble nor prevent it! " These," cries Rousseau's great forerunner, " are the true causes of Revolution, and not the bread the labourer is suffered to eat, after he has earned it with the sweat of his brow."[1]

But Fénelon does not paint always in such gloomy colours; he could bless, as well as threaten, could hold out to his pupil a vista of triumphs, paler, indeed, but far more lasting, than any won by Louis the Great. Idomeneus' grasping pride and love of conquest had united all other peoples in league against him, but Burgundy would assert for France in another fashion a glorious primacy of peace. The sword, indeed, could not be wholly allowed to rust— for was not the best school of peace the assiduous cultivation of arms?—Burgundy would be himself a captain, his people must be trained to valour, his arsenals be always full. But he would wage no war without necessity, would keep his treaties, and live at peace, remembering that the best of frontier-fortresses is good faith, the only link between nations is a mutual confidence. Thus he would come to be the universal peace-maker, the counsellor of other nations and their judge, ruling over his neighbours by persuasion, even as he governed his own people by authority.[2]

For the author of Télémaque was not always in the clouds; linked with the philanthropist was a patriot, unable to forget, even in his dreams, the maritime arch-enemies of France. Not by warfare, but by rivalry, would Burgundy break the pride of London and Amsterdam; what Tyre had been, the city of Idomeneus must become; ships would pass in and out of its harbours like the flux and reflux of the sea, for in its port dwelt justice, stern and even-handed;

---

[1] Bk. xi. pp. 487 and *ff*.   [2] Bk. ix. p. 464.

under the shadow of its stately towers each alien found himself at home.

On behalf of the trader Fénelon would even abate some of his besetting love of regulation. " Commerce," said Narbal, " must be free, for it is like those rivers which dry up, when men try to alter their course." Strange merchants must be burdened by no vexatious dues or inquisitions, native industries be encouraged, not hampered by authority; it was enough if frauds and bankruptcies be punished, and all excessive hazards be forbidden—no man might risk his neighbour's fortunes, or more than half his own.[1]

Thus was Fénelon the Memnon, through whom first breathed the new economical gospel of *Laissez faire*. Yet it was not to Free Trade alone that he looked for social salvation; in matters of commerce he was no more than a humane keen-witted observer, but it was from his heart that he was speaking when he bade France make fast her ascendancy over other nations by ensuring the moral and physical welfare of her sons. And the true cure for all her evils he found in agriculture, a pursuit ever dear to reformers, that had been called by an old author, much loved of Burgundy, *res sine dubitatione proxima et quasi consanguinea philosophiæ*, that could offer to the husbandman " the most natural and best natured of all delights, the satisfaction of looking around him and seeing nothing but the effects and improvements of his own art and diligence, and seeing, like God, that all his works were good." [2]

It is easy to make merry over forgotten ideals, and the vogue of agriculture is among them. Pastorals and Theocritean idylls have long lost their savour; we do not now believe that the Earth becomes more bounteous to the farmer, the more mouths he has to feed, nor do all the miseries of our modern Wessex finish before the fall of night. Yet, although, in Fénelon's eyes, the country was

---

[1] Bk. x. pp. 478, etc., *cf.* Bk. iii.
[2] Abraham Cowley, Essay on Agriculture, to whom I am indebted for the quotation from Columella.

still the home of streaming udders and unwithering fruits, of songs and rustic flute-playings and tranquil sleep, it was not merely a townsman's banal Paradise, but a land where food was plentiful and life was free, where the healthy freshness of the body was but an outward index to the healthier freshness of the mind, where the humblest might marry when and whom he would, unchecked by hope of dowries or fear of master's dues, for avarice was banished, the old degrading servitude was gone; the calling of the labourer was no longer a disgrace.[1]

Blurs and extravagances in the picture there were bound to be, for Fénelon's ends were always wiser than his means. Political Economy brings many reproaches against him—the clashing of the patriots' wish for commerce with the Churchman's scruples against money lent at interest, or again, an ill-kept balance between the claims of rustic simplicity and trade. If luxury is forbidden, what is the need of commerce? Who will be its servants, if almost all the workmen are drafted on to the fields? And what shall we say when Fénelon passes beyond these general precepts to construct his famous Dream City of Salentum, a State where life is brought back to the level of Homeric simplicity, and discipline enforced with the rigidity of Plato's Laws, where the legislator runs riot in edicts against vice, and edicts against extravagance, clothing the citizens all alike, each in the uniform appointed to his rank, banishing all gold and silver ornaments, all perfumes and embroideries, all highly seasoned dishes, reserving the Arts for the service of the gods or the commemoration of the heroes of the State? The moral philosopher will be ready with still weightier accusations; Fénelon, he will say, has piled up law upon law and rule upon rule till the citizens' private liberty is lost, till the harmonies of the Perfect State are lost behind its whirring mechanism, its leading melody is drowned beneath a brass accompaniment. He makes no provision for change or development, forgetting, as all theorists of

[1] Bk. x. p. 481.

optimism, before, or after him, forgot, that the good Present is the worst enemy of the better Future, that there is no custom so sacred but it will, in time, corrupt the world. And, for all his patriotism, he stands further away than other political dreamers from the realities around him; the Republic could have been written only by a Greek, or Utopia by an Englishman, but Télémaque owes nothing to the seventeenth century or France—it is a triumph of timeless cosmopolitanism, a book neither ancient nor modern; in the streets of Salentum every nationality feels itself *dépaysé*, every generation homeless and astray.

But the blemishes in Télémaque must not blind us to its greater merits, to the pulse of generous large humanity that beats through every page, self-denying, yet not ascetic, tender, yet not sentimental, passionate, yet not unreasoning, to the voice that made reach, even to Kings' houses, the cry of that helpless hopeless downtrodden class, which was fast losing, not only the rights and dignity, but almost the outward semblance of man. Even its errors are not the follies of an irresponsible visionary; from out of every one of them France might have gleaned a seed of useful truth. A 'rigid police of morals' was not health, but it was sounder than the licence of the Regency; to depopulate the towns was a scheme impossible, yet Paris has not always belied the saying that a great town, full of ministers to the wants of the rich, is like a huge misshapen head, set on a feeble and ill-nourished trunk.[1] Nor has every modern Acanthus, when accused on slender evidence of spying, found a Télémaque to argue that denunciation is not proof, nor mere suspicion worthy of death, that there is no maxim so barbarous, no policy so inhuman, as that which offers up a possible innocence to the Moloch of the Public Weal.[2]

Nor is it just to blame its author because the ideas of Télémaque are not excepted from the operation of the laws of nature. Books that have profoundly influenced their age

---

[1] Bk. xvii. p. 547.   [2] Bk. xv. p. 532.

must, in like measure, seem stale and lifeless to posterity, when once all that was best in them has passed into the world's common stock of knowledge, their boldest paradox become a truism, their startling prophecies a common-place reality. And yet it is by its ideas that Télémaque still lives, ideas whose dim grandeur casts upon the reader of to-day a spell whose secret easily eludes his power of definition, ideas that still claim our reverence for their service in the Past, dying ashes from a camp-fire where our fathers warmed their hands, as they journeyed on to deeper Truth and higher Justice.

Beside the political significance of Télémaque, its dramatic interest is but small. Fénelon, whose letters are a gallery of speaking portraits equal to the pages of St Simon, could not endow the personages of his story with life; Télémaque, Mentor, Philoctetes, Idomeneus, flit by us cloudy and impalpable, the baseless fabric of a vision.

Not once in all those eighteen books does their hero rise to the dignity of a real existence. Setting out, like Bunyan and Goethe, to embody a moral doctrine in the history of a single character, Fénelon has missed the peculiar excellence of each : Télémaque is too vague to be a royal Wilhelm Meister, a figure typical, yet also flesh and blood ; he is too heavily coloured by the idiosyncracies of Burgundy to rank among such purely abstract figures, such allegorical presentments of a whole epoch of human experience, as the Christian of the Pilgrim's Progress.

At bottom, he is the boy whom Fénelon had once taught at Versailles, brilliant enough and ready of speech, even, at times, perversely ingenious and quick to argue with his master, but passionate and impracticable, thorny, self-centred and neglectful of others, arrogant in the last degree. But, grafted on Burgundy as he was, is sometimes Burgundy as he should not be, and sometimes Burgundy as he might become ; and there results from the mixture a shadowy, inorganic, whole, as lifeless as those creations of the unskilful novelist, which are drawn from a half-made fusion of several living persons.

And confusion is made greater by the presence of Mentor. This strange amalgam of a philosopher and a goddess plays in Télémaque all, and more than all, the part taken by his creator in the real Burgundy's life—if, indeed, he does not recall some spiteful sayings about the Fénelon of the confessional, anxious to impose himself on his penitents as 'the very oracle of God.' He is the lodestar of his charge's existence; it was Mentor whom Télémaque was always going to follow, Mentor to whom he turned as a deliverer, whose eyes he always sought, whose thoughts he always tried to guess. Once separated from his master his character is robbed of all polarity: one moment he will be an angry boy, stung to fury by the insults of a bully, and dashing through the camp of the Allies 'like a mad-man or a raging lion.' Two days later, having repented and confessed his fault, he is taking his place at the head of the forces, 'so cool and thoughtful and considerate, that Philoctetes, Nestor and the other chiefs give way to him; the captains forget their wisdom and experience, and rally round their beardless leader, as though, during all their lives, they had been under his command.'[1]

But the rudeness of the contrast had no terrors for Fénelon—rather does he use it to point an unexpected moral: this nursling of a heathen goddess was become inspired by powers akin to Christian Grace. "You have done great things," said Mentor, when his pupil returned to him in triumph, "but the force was given you from Above; Minerva stilled the violence of your passions, as Neptune stilled the swelling surge, when he bids the waters sink to rest."[2]

And this emergence of Christian ideas was no accident in Télémaque. Seldom was Voltaire wider from the mark than when he named the book a Greek poem written in French prose. It is throughout a pedagogic epic, too

[1] See Bk. xiii. [2] Bk. xvii. p. 546.

motivé, too full of ingenious contrivance to be really Greek ; as Homer's chief merit is his 'amiable simplicity,' so Fénelon's is the art which gives to each adventure its hidden meaning, to every landscape its sly reflexion on Versailles. Echoes of the Ancients there are in plenty, and Fénelon's love of *il costume*[1] has gathered a surfeit of gods and nymphs and pagan temples round him, but, at bottom, his theme is purely Christian; Mentor is an allegory of the Catholic Church ; his deities are attributes of the One True God, and if, in his moral teaching, there is much of Socrates, there is more of the distinctive lessons of the Gospel, Sin, Repentance and Forgiveness. The wisdom of the Ancients, when it enters, is subordinated to this higher Law ; Socrates and Homer are called upon to help in the upraising of Salentum, only because Fénelon saw the great foreshadowing of a greater Future, almost a first Divine Revelation of Reason, pending the second, greater, Dispensation of Life, in the 'contempt for riches, the frugal manners, the happy peaceful simplicity, which the Ancients bring before our eyes.'[2]

And there are moments when Fénelon would unite the two religions still more closely, and christen the heroes of antiquity themselves. Philoctetis, in his hands, becomes a type of the soul, already purified by sorrow, awaking to the active life of Grace ; Hercules dies no longer as the innocent victim of a woman's treachery, but offers himself, a willing sacrifice, in atonement for his broken conjugal faith.[3] And yet in this transfusion there is no absurdity or violence ; far as we may be from the gloomy netherworld of Homer, even from the *lucis tam dira cupido* of Virgil's Shades, there is room for Plato beside the Christian Mystics in Fénelon's Elysian Fields. "There a celestial radiance ineffable, a light beside which the sun's rays are but dark-

---

[1] See Wks., vi. p. 640, for Fénelon's extraordinarily modern view of the importance of 'local colour.'   [2] *Ibid.* p. 646.
[3] Bk. xii. pp. 497 and *ff*.   See Boulvé, Hellénisme de Fénelon, pp. 196 and *ff*.

ness, clothes, as with a garment, the bodies of the Just. In it they move and have their being; they breathe, they feel it, they are plunged in this ocean of delight. Into this happy land pain and death may not enter; remorse and hope and fear are banished, sorrow is cast out; desire is dead, for, having nothing, they yet have everything; the hunger of their soul is stayed, for all their happiness wells up from within." [1]

For the Fénelon of Télémaque was still the young Sulpician who once had dreamed of a missionary journey to the Levant. Still, at no great distance after 'the Sacred,' followed 'the Profane'; still he turned to his Classics as no study, but a loved diversion and refreshment. And Télémaque is the measure of his love. Itself perhaps Greek in no one single feature, there yet hangs round it an atmosphere, a moral fragrance, only to be called out by one who had fulfilled the wish of his youth, and learned to breathe, as purely as 'on the double summit of Parnassus,' the very essence of the antique.

And it was this that earned him the disfavour of those rigid spirits who had forsaken Cicero for the Bible. Easy to imagine, if harder to share, is Bossuet's scorn for the 'florid effeminacy,' the 'amorous gallantries' of 'M. de Cambrai's romance'; [2] and certainly, here and there are passages which, even to a milder censure, seem scarcely worthy of a Christian priest: the loves of Jupiter might have been less frequently paraded, nor need Calypso have lusted quite so openly to forget the father in the embraces of the son. But these are passing faults of taste, of a kind not uncommon in Télémaque; hereditary kingship might have been left uncriticized in a book intended for the son of kings, and there are more dignified ways of saving a youth from temptation than casting him violently into the sea.

And the chief cause of Bossuet's anger will seem to modern readers an absurdity; to-day the most prudish

[1] Bk. xvi. p. 524. [2] See Le Dieu, ii. pp. 12 and *ff.*

cheek need scarcely blush at Fénelon's mention of the
blind and shameful tyrant Love. For his aversion to this
monstrous vice was little less strong than Bossuet's own.
Not out of inclination did he write the history of its ravages
on Télémaque, since he held it unworthy of its place in
literature; the great dramatists of antiquity had never
borrowed from it, nor would he now have sullied his pages
with the poison, had it not been for his royal pupil at
Versailles.[1]

But how would Burgundy withstand the temptations of
the Court, if he knew nothing of this fearful appetite? In
a book destined for his private eye alone, Télémaque must
pass by impurity in all its forms, must hear of an adulterous
demigod writhing in the Centaur's poisoned shirt, would
himself become the object of an abandoned older woman's
passion, and breathe for a while the sensual, wine-sodden
air of Cyprus, sacred to Venus and her train.

But the least of his dangers was naked, shameless, brutal
vice. Burgundy's real enemy was Love itself, the Desire
that shelters under a more mystic name, quick to don the
semblance of an innocent modesty and present itself clothed
in virtue's garb, yet is, none the less, the arch-deceiver, the
first-born child of madness, the crown and citadel of earthly
appetites. In Love was embodied the triumph of the
Animal, Nature's victory over Spirit and Pleasure's over
Duty; in Love was drowned the pure, sweet, tranquil joy
of Reason under the whirling, drunken paroxysms of Feeling.[2] And so it is that Télémaque turns away from the
lovely face to the lovely mind, from the playful, smiling,
butterfly Eucharis to the chaste, severe, Antiope, away from
a rudderless passion that mocked restraint to a sober attachment, that gloried in its reverence for authority. Mentor's
violence alone had torn him from Eucharis; her image
never left his heart, he could scarcely bear to utter her
name. "But for Antiope I have no such feeling, only
respect and esteem, and the belief that my life will be

[1] See Wks., vi. p. 633.   [2] See Bks., iv. and vi. *passim.*, and Bk. xvii.

happy, if it is passed in company with her. I shall never cease to love her, though I could resign her if I must, nor will she delay, even for one moment, my journey home to Ithaca."[1]

So spoke the model lover of the seventeenth century, applauded by all those critics, who, with Fénelon himself, preferred 'the amiable to the surprising or the marvellous,' or, like Boileau, saw more beauty in a brook rustling softly through the meadows than in the furious downrush of a muddy mountain-torrent. Yet few things change more surely than men's estimate of passions, and the chaste Antiope leaves upon the reader of to-day a sensation of intolerable weariness and chill. Cut from the purest, veinless marble, 'more like a goddess than a woman,' 'adorned less chiefly by her beauty than by the good order of her father's house,' she is a statue hardly even Grecian, but fitted only for an alcove in some frosty convent garden. And Télémaque himself is no small tax upon our modern patience and credulity—where, outside a seminary's walls, did a lover ever reproach the gods with their gift of youth, or pray that he might become old and bowed and fit for the tomb?[2]

Yet there are also moments where the writer gets the better of the moralist and Fénelon loses some little of his priestly scruple and reserve. There is real vividness about the portrait of the baffled Calypso, as she stands watching the escape of her prey: 'her face suffused with rage, she casts hurried furious glances from side to side; a livid circle forms about her trembling lips; her colour, sometimes pale as death, changes with each moment; her voice is tremulous and harsh and broken; her tears no longer flow abundantly, for wrath and despair have dried them at their source.'[3] And there is an ugly reality, too, about the gaudy flowers of Cyprian vice, as they flit across the stage 'with dissolute air and flaunting dress and wanton gait, their eyes wandering over the men in search of an answering look, their hearts

[1] Bk. xvii., p. 550.   [2] Bk. iv., p. 422.   [3] Bk. vi., p. 440.

agog to rival each other in the kindling of some lawless passion.' [1]

And with the most hazardous figure of all Fénelon's discretion has played him false. Eucharis, indeed, is carefully hidden from the reader's eye; he catches only distant glimpses of a girl with hair flying idly in the breeze, wrapped in a long light robe drawn carelessly around her; he knows her graces only by the havoc that they make with Télémaque. And yet so faithfully are all his transports drawn, with such unconscious subtlety are all her charms suggested, that Eucharis is, of all Fénelon's characters, the most lifelike and the most attractive, worthy of a place, if not among the heroines of literature, at least among the attendant maidens of their train.

And some little of the vividness of Eucharis has overflowed on to Fénelon's pagan deities. True they are not the gods of Homer, 'so gross and sensual as to seem invented by the Enemy of Mankind in order to turn into derision the very idea of a Divinity,' nor had Fénelon the idealizing warmth and vigour that could recall the *Götter Griechenlands* to one fresh hour of life. Yet there is a dim reality about them, uncommon enough in the poetry of that age; their creator knew his Classics far too well to treat them as simple *dieux éclos du cerveau des poètes*, decorative synonyms invented by Homer for the virtues or the forces of the earth and air. No product of Boileau's frigid receipts would have drawn the following strange confession from Joseph Blanco White: [2]

" I read Télémaque so often when only six or seven years old that I knew it almost by heart. Its effect on my imagination was very powerful: my first doubt of the truth of Christianity originated in that book before I was eight years old. My delight in the description of the sacrifices offered to the gods was intense; I felt, besides, a strong sympathy for the principal personages of the story; the

---

[1] Bk. iv., p. 421. [2] Quoted in Dr Mozley's Essays, ii. p. 73.

difference between their religion and my own struck me very forcibly, and my admiration of their wisdom and virtue suggested the question—Why should we feel so perfectly assured that those who worshipped in that manner were wrong? The next time I went to confession, I perceived the necessity of accusing myself of doubts against the Faith. The priest's astonishment was unbounded, but, on learning that I read no books but Télémaque, he told me not to trouble my foolish head with such subjects, gave me absolution and did not even interdict the book."

Our Northern coldness is less fortunate, and to the English reader of to-day the moral earnestness of Télémaque must be, in a sense, the measure of its comparative literary insipidity. All great religions have their epic, but natural virtue has inspired never a one; too cold, too abstract, too lacking in picturesqueness and variety, its powers are soon exhausted, it can bear no imagination through any lengthy stretch of flight.

Nor can a poem be 'complete in all but metre,' when its author must apologise to Roman Cardinals for its existence, and explain that it was written to charm the ears of young Princes with song, while it instilled into them the purest and most weighty principles of Kingly rule.[1] True literature cannot be content to have only a moral end; not of necessity indifferent to ethics—for our humaner generation will comply no longer with Goethe's invitation to the sight-seer and leave its conscience behind in the vestibule whenever it visits a gallery—it has, nevertheless, its own independent aims and methods, its own beauties and perfections, and to these the writer's moral enthusiasm must bow down: his virtue, welcome as the tranquil ally, must not become the mistress of his art. Fénelon's purely theocratic principle is too hard for human backs to bear; there are few would echo his wish that Homer could have had Socrates or Marcus Aurelius as his heroes, instead of

---

[1] Wks., vii. p. 555, in a letter to Cardinal Gabrielli.

Achilles or Odysseus,[1] and we should look in vain for a defender of his thesis that the Arts were invented to express, and, in expressing, to inspire the passions, to warm man's heart to noble feelings, and to set before him in noble and touching pictures, the beauty of virtue and the ugliness of vice.[2]

And Télémaque suffers somewhat in modern eyes from its faithfulness to seventeenth century tradition. "Modern poets," says Novalis, "pray to chance," but Télémaque moves on in stately slow procession from shipwreck to battle-scene, from love-scene to battle-field, and thence to the triumphs of Salentum. It is the realization of its author's ideal of a work where the reader can advance continually without distraction, can see how each fresh incident grows out from the last, and be always on the watch for an ending that escapes him the more skilfully the more he strives to grasp it. And, at the last, he may turn and look about him, like a traveller, who, being arrived at the summit of a mountain, takes pleasure in surveying the road he followed and the places passed along his route.[3]

Only at rare moments does the style of Télémaque rise to warmth or brilliancy of colouring. For the most part Fénelon is faithful to his literary canons, prefers the amiable to the surprising or the marvellous, graceful tranquillity to hard endeavour; harmony is his watch-word and serenity his peculiar note—not the serenity that comes from victory over strong emotions, but the peaceful efflorescence that has never known a struggle. His own style carries to perfection a quality he much admired in others, 'that noble and ethereal diction which sets no foot on earth, but, like the divinities of fable, wings its course lightly through the air.'[4]

And he pays for this aloofness by monotony. There is little to arrest the reader's mind; the weightiest incidents rise to the surface and sink again without a splash, and, as the tale draws

---

[1] Wks., vi. p. 646.   [2] p. 572.   [3] p. 639.
[4] *Ibid.* p. 606, speaking of his predecessor in the Academy, Cardinal Pellisson.

on, the force of its most vigorous passages is smothered more and more under the cadence of the words, as they fall in one unending stream of soft and even melody.

Yet there is a curious richness in this prose so full of rhythm and harmony that breaks at every instant into verse, as it drags itself along its slow and weary way, fainting under an overload of epithets.[1] Its periods have the ease and fulness of one who, while drifting down the stream of his fancy, was ever mindful of Augustine's rule—*Elocutionis pulchritudinem si occurrerit, vi rerum rapit, non curâ decoris assumit* [2]—all naturally and unconsciously he stretches out his hand and takes it.

For Fénelon, at once a man of genius and a man of rank, claimed his double privilege of peerage, left scrupulous accuracy to the professional writers or to 'such purblind critics as had no taste for the Sublime, and indulged himself in a nonchalant freedom sometimes to-day resented in the Land of Equality, as savouring both of literary heresy and of aristocratic impertinence. But it was this independence of established order that made him a discoverer of the possibilities of language ; he is one of the first of his countrymen to make music in his prose, the first to treat it as of itself a thing of beauty, fit to rival Poussin in the painting of a Tyrian market-place or to draw a landscape with the breadth and light and dignity of Claude Lorraine.

" From Télémaque," says Ernest Renan, " I first learned to paint Nature by moral traits. Before I saw it, my only notion of the island of Chios was drawn from Fénelon's three words : *l'île de Chio, fortunée patrie d'Homère*. These three words, rhythmical and harmonious, seemed to me a perfect picture, and, although Homer was not born at Chios, though, perhaps, he was never born at all, they brought that fair and now so ill-starred island before my eyes better than a thousand little material details would have done." [3]

---

[1] I paraphrase Ste Beuve's famous definition. See Causeries du Lundi, ii. p. 20, and see Crouslé, i. p. 267.
[2] Quoted Wks., vi. p. 619.   [3] Souvenirs d'Enfance, p. 254.

And this power of painting landscapes in a single word, this almost mystical control of language, must be our compensation for the absence of a higher mysticism,— that reverence for Nature as its Maker's chosen dwelling-place, 'the mirror of His unseen Beauty, the screen of an unknown Reality, whom all creation touches by the hand,' that meets us in so many schools of Christian literature, from the Psalms of David to the Hymns of St Patrick and St Francis, from the poetry of Spenser to the poetry of Wordsworth, and seems as though half-promised by the Treatise on the Existence of God.[1] But of this feeling there is not a trace in Télémaque; there Fénelon looks at Nature only through the Ancient's eyes and paints his landscapes with a Homer open before him, just as he valued his own Cambrai garden chiefly for its living comments on the Georgics.[2]

And never did he imitate the Greeks with less success; his landscapes differ from his masters' by all the gulf that separates the modern from the ancient world. "Greek literature," says Schiller, "was naïf, but ours is sentimental; *die Alten empfanden natürlich, wir, aber, empfinden das Natürliche.*" The Greeks had seen no special charm in natural scenery, because to them all things alike were natural, the seas and forests of created nature no more so than the sculptured glories of creative Art. But Fénelon headed a long school of writers with whom the Natural and the Artificial stood in sharpest contrast; he was the prophet of an Exodus back to rustic simplicity, away out of the Egypt of the seventeenth century, where Nature had become the foil of man, the humble background of his dignity and pride, abandoned to the gardener and the architect. Round Calypso's grotto Télémaque saw no marble columns, no strangely lopped trees, no artificial rockeries or cascades, only a cavern hollowed out of the rock, adorned with many shells and pebbles and tapestried with a vine. And in the blessed

[1] Wks., i. p. 44. See the excellent chapter on Fénelon in Laprade's Sentiment de la Nature, ii. p. 125.   [2] Wks., vii. p. 476.

land of Bætica, Fénelon's vision within a vision, a commonwealth so ethereal as to be inimitable even at Salentum, the very art of architecture was unknown, for the inhabitants never built a house. It was enough for them to be sheltered from the wind and rain; they would not bind themselves too closely to the earth by building dwellings that would last beyond their lives.[1]

Thus there enters a note of polemical bitterness into Fénelon's pictures of the Golden Age. His love of Nature was not wholly single-hearted; with his invectives against "sumptuous gardens and rich parterres" mingles the childish petulance of Perdita among her gillivors, needing to be reminded that

> We marry
> A gentler scion to the wildest stock
> And make conceive a bark of baser kind
> By bud of nobler race: this is an art
> Which does change nature, mend it, rather, but
> The art itself is nature.

And already in Télémaque are traces of the morbid spirit of the coming century, powerless to enjoy a forest solitude without thanking God it was not in a city, or to admire the foliage of a tree without plucking a switch to belabour the back of mankind. Only too often does Fénelon's Nature approach the veiled and shadowy goddess of the preaching Rousseau, no living reality lovely in herself, but a lifeless, dead imagining, the sum of all the qualities that man has not, a pattern of silence to his vain discourses, of frugal manners to his spendthrift richness, of generous bounty to his grasping selfishness.

And Fénelon, looking on Nature as a moralist, was led to make her incomplete, to forget her cruel, savage grandeur, her iron exactitude of rule, her wanton squanderings of life and force, before the image of a Power beneficent, the Teacher and the Friend of man. His favoured countries

---

[1] Bk. vii., p. 451.

know no thorns or briars, no jagged mountains, no pestilent south-wind; they are the home of everlasting flowers and sunshine, where 'Spring and Autumn celebrate a peaceful Hymen and walk together hand in hand.'

A view of Nature so amiably imperfect bears the marks of poetical weakness on its face. Fénelon's landscapes have their beauty, but it is beauty only of a superficial kind; they are a sentimental gloss on his teachings, a decorative adjunct to his story, *horizons formés à souhait pour le plaisir des yeux*. Except, perhaps, for Philoctetes' farewell to Lemnos and 'the sweet waters that his misery found so bitter,'[1] there is no sign in Télémaque of that inward modern feeling for Nature, which converts a landscape into a mood, bids Rousseau appeal to trees and flowers, not as witnesses only, but as sharers, as accomplices in his emotions, or creates out of one country scene a Paradise for the hopes of Werther, but, for his despondency, a Hell.[2] Still less does Fénelon rise to the heights of that purer, nobler, school of poets who see in Nature 'a presence far more deeply interfused,' whose task it is to 'wed this goodly universe to man in love and holy passion,' whose recompense lies in this, that they

> in times of dereliction and distress
> Despaired not of our nature, but retain
> A more than Roman confidence, a faith
> That fails not, in all sorrow my support
> The blessing of my life. The gift is yours,
> Ye winds and sounding cataracts! 'Tis yours,
> Ye mountains, thine, O Nature! Thou hast fed
> My lofty speculations, and, in thee
> For this uneasy heart of ours, I find
> A never failing principle of joy
> And purest passion.

And yet the final victory of Nature owes not a little to Télémaque. Here, as in much else, its author was a prophet,

---

[1] See Bk. xii., p. 503; and Laprade's comments, p. 131.
[2] See Sorrows of Werther, letter of 18th August; and *cf.* Laprade, pp. 196, 323.

fated to lead others to a Promised Land, which his own feet might never tread. It was Fénelon who, in a Golden Age of artificiality, first preached the graciousness of simple Nature, Fénelon whom Rousseau made his idol, and—is not the writer of the *Nouvelle Héloise* a lineal ancestor of Wordsworth?

CHAPTER X

CAMBRAI

On my word, I must quit this place as soon as possible, for if I stay here another week, I shall be a Christian in spite of myself.—LORD PETERBOROUGH, *writing from Cambrai to John Locke.*

THE disgrace brought on by the Maxims and Télémaque was the great turning-point in their author's life. Taken by himself as the most disastrous of calamities, under a wide view it bears good witness to a saying often in his mouth, that only through their trials and misfortunes do men rise to moral dignity and worth.

For the stroke brought Fénelon just what his character needed. Banishment from the Court freed one who was by nature an intriguer, from the temptations of the place, where, as Bossuet said, all the affairs of the Universe have their starting-point and centre; shame and wounded honour and sense of failure broke through the crust of dilettantist affectation and unreality, which had numbered even religion among its provinces, and laid out the very Love of God according to the four-square measure of its rules. Under stress of his troubles Fénelon gained new breadth and depth of piety, new self-reliance, self-control; a moral unity never before observable, began to draw together the scattered fibres of his mind. Heretofore he had lain himself under the condemnation his lips had more than once pronounced on others; he could not make his own heart his home, but was driven thence, a houseless vagabond, compelled to wander between two spheres, between an upper realm of cloudy hopes and fancies, too unsubstantial for the solid earth, and a nether-world of mean realities, of daily action, pitched too low. But in these later years the gulf of separation was bridged over; Fénelon's ideals became more practical, his practice grew more ideal; the dreamy Utopian, the supple smiling courtier, met in the high-minded, generous-hearted counsellor of ministries; mystic enthusiasm joined with worldly graces to make the great, devoted, idolized Archbishop.

Two of his letters mark the contrast. A few days after his nomination to Cambrai he wrote that: 'my life has been full of liberty and pleasantness, of congenial study and delightful friends; I am leaving them for a life of ceaseless slavery in a foreign land.' Hardly had the blow of condemnation fallen, when he wrote again: 'Nothing now remains to me but a perpetual silence, wherein the one consolation will be the labours of my diocese.'

Cambrai, a town of no great size or beauty on the Scheldt, was the ecclesiastical centre of the Flemish provinces conquered during the earlier half of Louis XIV.'s reign, and confirmed to France by the Treaty of Nymwegen in 1678. Formerly a dependency of the chaotic Empire, there still clung round it some of the perfume of departed glories, of days when its Bishop's jurisdiction extended over Brussels and Antwerp, and he governed the territory immediately around him as an almost Sovereign Prince, with his own fortresses and garrisons and mint.[1] Fénelon himself ranked both as a Prince of the Holy Roman Empire and as a Duke of France, and, though all feudal privileges had long been lost, was still the principal landowner of his province, with a floating revenue of 100,000 francs, perhaps about £20,000 in modern English money.

But the position though one of the most splendid in Louis' gift, was not without its geographical thorns. Quite half the arch-diocese lay altogether beyond the frontiers of France, and Fénelon's administration had much to suffer from its local government, the jealous Hainault Estates, and

[1] See Fén. Wks., vii. p. 179, and Wks., viii. p. 293 for a history of the vicissitudes of the diocese.

from the indolence of the dispossessed Bavarian Elector, then Spanish Viceroy at Brussels. And matters became far worse with the outbreak of the War of the Spanish Succession. The capture of Tournai in 1709, and the subsequent flight of its Bishop, led Fénelon into interminable negotiations with his not very heroic suffragan, who could not be persuaded to return, and fight out with the Dutch States-General 'a cause stronger than that of St Thomas of Canterbury.' And for several years his own arch-diocese was a principal theatre of the war, the great battles of Malplaquet and Denain being fought within its borders.

Nor were the inhabitants of Cambrai, Flemings not Frenchmen in their language, their habits, their modes of thought, very eager to welcome an Archbishop born in southerly Périgord, and coming to them straight from Versailles. Fénelon's predecessor M. de Brias, had been one of themselves and a prelate altogether after their heart, good and firm and wise and boundlessly charitable, an excellent Flemish gentleman, says St Simon, as highly thought of by the French Government after the taking of Cambrai as he had been by the Spanish before it.[1] But Fénelon, on his first appearance, overawed them by his elaborate courtesies and delicate fine gentleman airs; perhaps, too, he did not hide his low opinion of their capacities or his amusement at their blunt straightforwardness of speech. There were no refinements of piety at Cambrai, he told M$^{me.}$ de Maintenon, nor indeed, was their refinement of any kind; the virtues of the natives were as coarse-fibred as their manners. The ecclesiastical arrangements, in particular, struck him by their primitive simplicity; the nuns received whom they would in their parlours, without a thought of gratings or enclosure, and many of the country priests engaged a fiddler on winter evenings, and gave dances to their servants and parishioners and friends. But, on the whole, Fénelon thought the moral level fairly high;

[1] i. p. 271.

the heavy Flemings were neither as virtuous nor as vicious as the French, but there seemed to be more innocence and honesty among the mass, and especially among their nuns.[1]

And friendlier relations were soon established; two years after his arrival Fénelon could flatter himself that he was already fairly popular. Even the affair of the Maxims, which had, at first, threatened to wreck his authority, became in the end a new source of strength; for his edifying submission, and—St Simon would add—extraordinary adroitness in making a merit out of his tribulations, won him the heart of every party and of every rank.

Moreover, as the great caviller himself allows, Fénelon's episcopal duties were perfectly performed. To his clergy he professed himself, and was, a Father and a Brother in God; the laity adored him for his charities, for the gentle firmness of his government, for the natural grace of manner that enhanced an hundredfold the value of everything he said or did. Always ready to help, yet always modest in offering assistance, he seemed, when about some kindly action, to be receiving, rather than doing a favour; in visits to the sick at home, to the hospitals and wounded soldiers, he was indefatigable, nor was he a stranger to the Cambrai prisons. Tours of inspection, repeated several times a year, brought him into touch with every corner of his diocese; it was administered with great strictness, and yet on broad and liberal lines; there was no harrying of Protestants or Jansenists, no bureaucratic fussiness, no seeking after popularity, but every man, whether great or small, was treated exactly as became his station in the world.[2]

To certain more rigid spirits, indeed, Fénelon's administration seemed almost wrongfully tolerant, *une pure politique*, said Bossuet, full of concession to the prejudices of the Flemish law-courts, or to those detestably irregular practitioners in souls, the Jesuits and the other Religious Orders. But, as Fénelon urged in self-defence, the Friars and the

[1] Wks., ix. p. 71. [2] St Simon, xi. p. 62, and see viii. pp. 469, etc.

Douai Parliament had proved too strong for every prelate who stood up against them, nor was it wise to claim the full privileges of a Gallican Bishop in a jealous and newly conquered country where the Gallican Canon Law did not run.¹ At Cambrai, he said, there was no room for *tranchots*, slashing young reformers red hot from the Sorbonne;² every matter of importance went before the Vicariate, a Board chiefly composed of native Church-dignitaries, by whose decisions he felt himself often disagreeably bound. All local customs, down to the humblest, were handled with a delicate touch, as the priest of Jument found to his cost, when he quarrelled with his flock for joining in a certain Church-procession with drums and flags and arrows in their hands. 'Speak to the parishioners very severely in my name,' Fénelon wrote to the Rural Dean, 'but also try to make the rector see that he will never gain any authority over them, or win their confidence, unless he learns to meet them half-way over these little pardonable eccentricities of usage.'³ And in the still more delicate matter of patronage Fénelon was careful that no outsider, still less a relative of his own, should swoop down on his richest livings, and secure by interest what the natives looked on as their own by right.⁴

But Fénelon could also speak hard words in his *Mandements*, or official pronouncements to his diocese. If it cost the philanthropist a sigh to impose the law of fasting on those whose life was a perpetual fast, he could turn fiercely on the workman who preferred the alehouse to the happiness of his family in this world, and the joys of Paradise in the world to come, or slouched idly through six days of labour, that he might turn the Lord's Day into a feast of devils.⁵ But far more readily did he bestir himself to be the *malleus vitiorum* of the rich, and remind them of the lessons of his Epiphany Sermon of long ago, how it was vain to look for almsgiving from men whose social code made ruinous

---

¹ Le Dieu, ii. pp. 167 and *ff.* ² Wks., viii. p. 395.
³ p. 342.   ⁴ p. 385.   ⁵ Wks., vi. pp. 186, 187.

extravagance the first necessity, and the last duty of the gentleman the payment of his debts.[1]

And it is characteristic of their difference of temperament that, while Bossuet willingly put the Bible into the hands of the unlearned, Fénelon, with less faith in human nature, as willingly took it away. This was no time, he thought, to sow the Holy Scriptures broadcast, when the Socinian, the Protestant, the Jansenist, were quick to turn and twist them to the profit of their own imaginings, when the shallow worldly wisdom of the sceptic measured all things in heaven and earth by a string of narrow fantastic prejudices, and deemed itself insulted, if it were asked to believe such old wives' fables as the story of Eve and the Serpent, or other 'extraordinary and mysteriously inspired passages of Holy Writ.'[2]

Nor, in fulfilment of the duties of his office, did Fénelon shrink from their very *exuviæ*. Thus in March 1700, he wrote to the Intendant of Hainault, proposing to restore the ancient discipline of the Church with regard to the eating of eggs in Lent, because after several years' indulgence, a prescription was arising in its favour, just as had already happened in the case of butter, milk and cheese. 'I am sorry,' he said, 'to trouble you with these tiresome details, and fear I may cause inconvenience to many excellent people, but that we Bishops are often bound to do in spite of ourselves—besides, if we once proved unfaithful to the law, who would be left to keep it?'[3]

Yet his heart was not in this religion of the buttery-hatch, but was resolved that Cambrai, at least, should not share the common impression that a Bishop was a rich gentleman who lived in a Palace, and governed severely, and did nothing useful, except give dispensations and blessings and indulgences.[4] And it was not merely for his spiritual services that he deserved the praises of St Simon; being, as Le Dieu will tell us, on the best of terms with the

[1] Wks., v. p. 623.   [2] *Ibid.* ii. p. 197.
[3] *Ibid.* viii. p. 344.   [4] *Ibid.* ii. p. 201.

Governor of Cambrai and the Intendant, with the nobles and Government officials, not only of his diocese, but of all Flanders, even as far as Brussels, Fénelon used his influence with them to beg many temporal favours for his people, got his village schoolmasters exempted from service in the army, saved the farmers and their horses from forced labours in the winter, even warned the Ministry at Paris that that devastated country could be the theatre of no more campaigns.[1]

Fénelon governed his household on the same principles as his diocese. There he lived, says St Simon, with all the piety and dignity of a true Pastor, yet with the splendour of a great nobleman, who had renounced nothing, and was still on excellent terms with the world. But his magnificence made no one angry, for it was kept up chiefly for the sake of others, and was exactly proportionate to his place; with all its luxuries and courtly ease, his house remained a true Bishop's Palace, breathing the strictest discipline and restraint. And of all this chastened dignity, the Archbishop was himself the ever-present, ever-inimitable, model, in all that he did the perfect Churchman, in all things the high-bred man of rank, in all things, also, the author of Télémaque.[2]

But St Simon only judged from hearsay. An observer of a very different order, Bossuet's gossiping and inquisitive secretary, the Abbé Le Dieu, managed to penetrate to the Cambrai Palace, and has sketched its master from the life. Finding himself at that city in September, 1704, a few months after Bossuet's death, he called on Fénelon to pay his respects and, timing his visit opportunely, was invited by the Archbishop to remain to dinner. "On arriving at the dining-hall," proceeds this incomparable narrator, "we found the other guests awaiting us, washed our hands without ceremony, and the Archbishop, taking the head of the table, said Grace. M. de Chanterac sat on his left

[1] Wks., viii. pp. 356, etc.   [2] xi. p. 59.

hand, the rest of the party placed themselves indiscriminately, I taking a humble seat among them, and soup had already been handed round, when the Archbishop signed to me to take the vacant chair on his right. I objected that I was already served, but he politely insisted, so I obeyed him and changed my place, my soup being carried after me by a servant."

"The dinner was very abundant and magnificently served, several soups, good beef and mutton, game of all sorts, splendid grapes and peaches, and excellent red wine; the bread was good, the table-linen clean and there was a great quantity of costly silver plate. There was a great array, also, of footmen in livery, who waited noiselessly and well; the butler was a man of very imposing appearance and seemed to be a great authority in the household."

"We were fourteen at table and sixteen in the evening, although, except myself, not a single stranger was present; they were all nephews of the Archbishop or intimate friends who never leave him, or else his chaplains and secretaries and equerry. The talk during dinner was quite easy and unconstrained, the Archbishop taking his part with the rest; even the chaplains joined in freely, much to my surprise, for few prelates of the rank of M. de Cambrai allow their household officers to dine regularly at their table."

"The Archbishop ate very little, and only of dishes very plainly dressed, in the evening nothing more than a few spoonfuls of eggs cooked in milk, with a glass or two of weak white wine—it is no wonder that he is so thin and pale. But, for all his sparseness, his complexion is clear and his health pretty good; though he had only that morning returned from a three-weeks' visitation, he did not show the slightest sign of fatigue. I think that it is really chagrin which gnaws him, for, kindly and courteous as he was, he had an air of extreme mortification and the drawn face of a St Charles.[1] When we were alone together, he talked on

[1] St Charles Borromeo, the famous ascetic and reforming Archbishop of Milan in the sixteenth century.

none but spiritual subjects, as though he wished to keep up his reputation of a man altogether mystical and holy, wrapped up entirely in another world."

"After dinner, we adjourned to his great state-bedchamber, where he never sleeps, and the Archbishop, taking a chair before the fire, began to sign some documents which had to be sent off at once. Coffee was then brought in; there was some for all, and the Archbishop gave orders that mine should be served with a napkin. The conversation turned chiefly on the Archbishop's recent pastoral visitation, and from what was said I gathered that he was the only prelate in Flanders looked upon as capable of doing much for religion. Presently the Archbishop left us, to visit M. de Montbéron, the Governor of the place, with whom he is on very friendly terms, and left me free to wander about and inspect the buildings of the palace."[1]

With these the Abbé was much impressed, especially with 'the superb edifice of brick, faced with stone-work elaborately carved,' which Fénelon had put up on the site of the old council-hall and library, destroyed by the great fire of February 1697; though perhaps a modern taste might have found its Renaissance decorations sadly out of keeping with their huge Gothic neighbour, the Cathedral. But in those days neither Le Dieu nor his betters thought much of mediæval architecture; did not Fénelon himself consider it the very type of all that was pretentious and unmeaning, a twin-sister of bombastic, meretricious eloquence?[2]

Le Dieu has much to say, also, of the interior arrangements of the palace, of its stables, 'full of post-chaises, in which so many poor country curates had travelled at their ease,' of its halls of reception with 'their beautifully polished floors, their marble chimney-pieces, their upholstery of crimson velvet fringed and garlanded with gold.'[3] But he agrees with the Abbé Galet, Fénelon's contemporary

---

[1] Le Dieu, iii. pp. 156-160.
[2] See the Second Dialogue on Eloquence. Wks., vi. p. 590, and *vide* ch. xiii.
[3] Le Dieu, iii. pp. 161-164.

panegyrist, that, however grand and commodious the outside, the Archbishop's personal appointments were modest indeed ; in the meagre simplicity of his private living-rooms, 'fitted up plainly in serge,' of his dress, 'a long violet cassock, trimmed with scarlet but without gold tassels or lace,' even of his ecclesiastical vestments, Fénelon 'did homage to that idea of Holy Poverty whose actual practice was forbidden by his station in the world.'[1]

But for others Fénelon loved to do things *un peu largement*, to obey the generous impulse of a moment and take the burdens of his clergy on himself, offer to pay more taxes than he need, or even squander money on the beggars whose appearance moved him. Yet he could also practise a sounder economy, held a careful audit of his household accounts, set aside large portions of his income for the starving soldiers, or the necessities of his diocese and seminary, or the education of his nephews and their maintenance in the army.[2]

These last, with one or two of his old subordinates of the Preceptorship, Langeron, the witty and cheerful 'Little Abbé' of his correspondence, and Dupuy or 'Puteus,' 'the easy-chair in which one could be sure of finding rest at any moment,' formed almost the whole of Fénelon's society during the early days of his disgrace. At their head was the 'Big Abbé,' or 'Panta,' Pantaléon de Beaumont, a nephew scarcely younger than his uncle, a jovial energetic personage, not without learning, though 'rather simple-minded, perhaps, for at Cambrai we all wear our hearts upon our sleeve.'[3] To Beaumont, as controller of the household and one of the Vicars-General of the diocese, many of Fénelon's letters are addressed ; uncle and nephew took counsel together about appointments to the Seminary or on the vagaries of the Dean and Chapter, or, again, on the far more delicate matter of the servants, how they might introduce into the Palace kitchen an assistant to the sick

---

[1] Galet. Principales Vertus de Fénelon, publ. 1725, reprinted in Works, x. p. 144.   [2] Wks., vii. p. 435.   [3] *Ibid.* viii. p. 48.

head-cook, without running the risk of hurting his feelings by appearing to give him a successor.¹

And, as time went on, a whole string of nephews and grand-nephews gathered under Beaumont's charge. First the favourite of all, the *très-cher Fanfan*, Gabriel, Marquis of Fénelon, afterwards his grand-uncle's first biographer and faithful guardian of his memory; and, next to him, there came his brothers, 'Alexis and Lobos,' 'poor little younger sons, who must early learn that they would have no other fortune than what was brought them by their merits and hard work.'² Or there was his cousin, young Laval, 'horribly dull among a crowd of priests,' or the Abbé de Salagnac, a youthful student destined for the Church, whose frivolous brain, however, did not take kindly to the Schoolmen, and needed the reminder that if they sometimes talked transcendental nonsense, they were, in this respect, no worse to blame than the new-fangled philosophical romances of Descartes.³ And Fénelon's study was seldom empty of some younger *non-vénérable marmot*, arriving at Cambrai in a state of boundless ignorance, and set down promptly to make his first acquaintance with the Greeks and Romans and learn to love the paths of virtue from those who strove to make them pleasant.⁴

And presently the little circle was widened by all who had not blushed for Fénelon at the time of his disgrace. Beauvilliers, though, as a Minister, he wrote no more, still thought it a crime not to be Fénelon's admirer;⁵ Chevreuse's pen was never idle, and, before long, Beaumont was drawing up with Mme. de Beauvilliers a list of those who might safely come, as well as write, to Cambrai.⁶ At first there was good reason for precaution; but, as time went on, and Louis showed no fresh aggressiveness, fear of his postal detectives dwindled to a pleasant sense of mystery, honoured only by a little cryptic language and copious use of *noms de plume*.

[1] Wks., vii. p. 420.   [2] p. 481.   [3] p. 438.
[4] p. 481.   [5] St Simon, ix. p. 4.   [6] Fén. Wks., vii. p. 421.

After six years of waiting, Chevreuse ventured over to Cambrai from his not very distant country-house of Chaulnes, and later, received Fénelon there on an annual visit, paying, however, for this last privilege, on his return to Court, by some weeks' quarantine from Burgundy's society.[1] Otherwise, Fénelon's sentence of banishment was strictly enforced, its only formal relaxation in eighteen years being a permit to go to the Baths of Bourbon (1706), and even so late as 1713, he had to apologize to the Minister for having *seemed* to wish to visit a sick niece in Paris.[2]

For with the knitting up again of friendships came no slackening in the enmities. Louis XIV. was adamant, and Mme. de Maintenon made no sign for good or evil, nor is it any great reproach to Fénelon that he had no thought of reconciliation with the Triumvirs of Quietism. They, it is true, had made advances; hardly was the Maxims condemned, when Bossuet sent word through Beauvilliers that he was ready to do whatever the tenderest charity might inspire,[3] and de Noailles' feckless amiability planned various little childish and vexatious stratagems, in the hope of entrapping Fénelon into a correspondence.[4] But Fénelon had no patience with the fool, and the great man's warm assurances were in signal conflict with his acts; each of them had his answer in the words of Abraham: "Is not the whole earth before thee? If thou wilt take the right hand, then I will go to the left."

With the Bishop of Chartres, alone of the three, Fénelon entered into an exchange of letters, 'not without their thorns'; but the anti-Jansenist polemic, which brought them together, widened more than ever the breach with Bossuet and de Noailles—there is a world of meaning in

---

[1] Fén. Wks., vii. p. 295.

[2] *Ibid.* viii. p. 181. Strictly speaking, he seems to have been banished to his Province, rather than his Diocese. On the Spanish side he was entirely free.

[3] Boss. Wks., xix. p. 441.

[4] *e.g.*, refusing to give a formal *Exeat* to one of Fénelon's clergy who had studied in Paris, in order to compel Fénelon to write and ask for it.—Wks., vii. p. 554.

one of Fénelon's questions to Le Dieu—"Who helped M. de Meaux to die?"[1] And the two surviving enemies, Louis XIV. in the later political writings, and Cardinal de Noailles in the Jansenist campaign, fared at his hands even worse than Bossuet.

Not that Fénelon was ever 'a good hater,' in the word's vulgar and perhaps most pardonable sense : his heart was shielded alike from violent enmities and from violent friendships by an all-absorbing interest in himself, which left it little room for other company. This was not the brutal egoism of a Louis Quatorze—it was hardly an ethical quality at all, but, rather, a weary indifference to outside things, part intellectual self-sufficiency, part stoical pride, and part ascetic religion, a feeling that "I hold a little to everything, and yet again to nothing, but turn easily aside from all that flatters me, except from a rooted attachment to myself."[2] And, with it, went the exceeding self-confidence whose seamy side is disbelief in others, that perfect contempt for the brains of mankind, which, as the great Napoleon once complained, made it so difficult to treat them seriously. 'I make no demands on my fellows,' Fénelon wrote, near the end of his life, 'I try to do my best for them, and to ask for little in return. I should like to oblige the whole human race, but there is no man to whom I would be under an obligation. Is this pride and vanity? Nothing could be more ridiculous; but, in growing old, I have learnt to know mankind, and to understand that the best thing is to do without them.'[3]

And it is no paradox to say that this detachment from men and things, hallowed in Fénelon's mouth as 'the love of our neighbour for the love of God,' was one of the secrets of his far-famed amiability—since who could show a serener front to the world than the man who continually practised what he preached to Burgundy, and 'seemed to give himself

---

[1] Le Dieu, iii. p. 169. Le Dieu himself saw that the question implied that Bossuet had a great deal to repent of.
[2] 219th Spir. Letter. Wks., viii. p. 589.   [3] Wks., viii. p. 207.

to all, while, in reality, he gave himself to none?' For Fénelon's indifference was far from being isolation; though the deeps of his nature were seldom stirred, he was easily responsive to the impressions of his environment, took a pleasure almost physical in seeing, in creating, a gay well-ordered world around him, was, as he said, of a temper flattering and complaisant, even to the point of over-indulging his company, when nothing interfered to weary him or try his patience.

Again, little as he could acknowledge an equal or ask for reciprocity in friendship, Fénelon had an eager hunger for disciples, adapted himself with unvarying insight to their different temperaments, re-fashioned and controlled their characters with a master's skill, and loved them with all a master's fondness for his handiwork. For Fénelon the friend is never to be separated from Fénelon the educator and Fénelon the priest, the universal Mentor, Ste Beuve's perfect unsurpassable Director of Consciences, 'the coachman,' as he said of himself, 'charged to drive other souls to God.' And, as spiritual counsellor, the world's one grievance against him is that he did his work too well. For he was still, among a circle of maturer dependents, the *esprit dominateur* he had been with Burgundy. With all the force and authority of the greatest moral teachers, he stands below them in that he had not their supreme impersonality, that "humble effacement of the actor in his work, which makes their inward longing for a living place in the thought and future of mankind little else than self-identification with the recognized purposes of God." [1] 'Direction,' he cried indeed, 'should be an intercourse of pure faith, all fidelity and death to self, unto which nothing human may enter;' [2] but the voice which spoke to Beauvilliers and Chevreuse was too often the voice of a very human Fénelon, the hand of guidance he reached out to them too seldom strengthened while it led, the

---

[1] See Martineau's Types of Ethical Theory, ii. pp. 208, 209.
[2] Fén. Wks., viii. p. 65.

obedience he exacted from them was a blind surrender, *divinisé en eux pour M. de Cambrai par religion*.[1]

Yet if Fénelon, by his masterfulness, often abused a system of Direction, that was always trembling on the verge of abuse, it is impossible, also, not to find in his Letters a spirit of large and generous practical piety. Once absolute submission had been made, Fénelon spared no effort to requite it, listened with tireless patience to the irrepressible Chevreuse, spreading himself out over reams of futile ingenuity, where theories on gout jostled theories on Jansenism, and 'my good Archbishop's' advice was asked on every kind of question between the Interior Life and sales of land and mortgages, between the probable fortune of a Cambrai heiress and the moral guidance of the Duke of Burgundy. And Fénelon's authority must be exerted in as many spheres, to persuade the Duke, who had often been cheated, not to draw up his children's marriage-settlements himself, but to leave them to a 'conveyancer afraid of his own shadow,' to prevent the incorrigible theorist from applying to his daughters-in-law either the 'repressive' or the 'laissez-faire' system of education, by insisting on a happy union of both, to beg him bring some steady method and application into his affairs, and leave hair-splitting and rhetorical artifice alone. 'You waste too much time on everything,' he wrote; 'you are not slow, but you fly rapidly from one thing to another, and yet let each one carry you too far. Sobriety is what you chiefly need, sobriety of thought and language, and that is only to be gained by prayer; you should proclaim a solemn fast from argument and cut things short from morn to night.'[2]

As the father sinned through logical irrelevancy, so indecisiveness was the capital error of the son; the Vidame d'Amiens could neither enjoy the world nor quit it, but halted uneasily, a Mr Facing-both-ways, between the life of

---

[1] St Simon, x. p. 285. St Simon is here blaming, and with reason, Fénelon's behaviour during the anti-Jansenist campaign.
[2] Wks., vii. pp. 219, 221, 246, etc.

pleasure and devotion. Him Fénelon pursued with a genial unrelenting patience, ran after him the faster the more he fled, and twitted him with the mingled conscientiousness and terror that used to bring him to the Cambrai Palace-door and send him away again rejoicing, whenever the Archbishop was from home. For the Vidame was not without a likeness to that elder brother who once had written to Fénelon to beg to be excluded from his prayers, as he was afraid that they were curing him of a too delicious vice.

But when the young man married and reformed, Fénelon began to tighten his grasp, none the less because the son showed signs of following in his father's traces, and losing himself among letters and documents and stewards' reports. 'You will be failing in your duty to God and man,' wrote Mentor, 'if you bury under a pile of papers the talents that were given you for your country's service. You cannot choose your own path in life—it is appointed for you by your rank, and for sins against one's worldly station there is no excuse and no forgiveness. Get a good secretary and leave the details to him; read and pray and go out into the world; see others and be seen of them—that is your vocation, as it is mine to be your tormentor.'[1]

And the same counsels are repeated in a warmer tone to the young Marquis Gabriel de Fénelon, the Archbishop's nephew and adopted son, the only living soul, perhaps, for whom he had that quite unmeasured affection, which 'neither thanks nor lets itself be thanked.' For the Marquis, though a brave, almost foolhardy, soldier was poor and ill-educated, and by nature stiff and gloomy and silent, fond only of such company as let him feel at ease, and afraid to adventure himself in that greater world, in which it was so very possible not to succeed. But Fénelon had no mercy on the youth who was at once his best-loved penitent and the solitary hope of their house's restoration: the Marquis must put his pride and indolence in his pocket and make up his mind to

[1] Wks., vii. pp. 383 and *ff*.

cultivate the great. 'At your age,' wrote the uncle, 'it is easy to break the ice of Society, but, as the years go by, you will find it harder and harder, till at last you find yourself without friends and without reputation, without means of advancing your family. Try to gain some little victory over yourself every day; go into the world as a penance for your faults, as a duty to your house and name, and rid yourself of that hidden selfishness, which pretends to be taste for a quiet serious life.' [1]

For Fénelon had no patience with the bastard devotees who despised the world because the world despised them. Detachment was the fruit of religion, not of shyness or indifference; there was no merit in the ill-grown weeds that worldliness flung over the church-yard wall. Far more than the licence of the unregenerate, more than the Pharisaism of the Jansenist, Fénelon hated the *sérieuse mollesse* which would like to enter Holy Orders because it found itself useless in the world, or turned a self-righteous back on Vanity Fair because it had neither wit nor elegance nor fashion. "Such a man," he cried, "is so lukewarm that neither God nor the world will have him; he becomes a mere thing, and as though he were not, the world only speaks of him to say that 'This is not a man.'" [2]

It is in very different language that he speaks to a charming and illustrious correspondent, who did not love the world too little, but too much. Mme. de Grammont, wife of the hero of the Grammont Memoirs, was neither soft nor serious, but a lady famous for her wit and beauty, and vain of her great position at the Court. To her, as not exactly a penitent, but one of the friends he used to meet in Mme. de Beauvilliers' *entresol*, or 'around the little marble chimney-piece,' Fénelon uses a tone of gay decorous pleasantry, that 'little air of playful flattering banter,' he was so anxious that his nephew should adopt towards the great. Often *angloise et insupportable* in the eyes of her friend, *quelquefois déni-*

---

[1] pp. 432, 446. [2] 34th Spir. Let. Wks., viii. p. 471.

grante, hautaine et rampante,[1] he rallied her on the petulant unreasonableness in herself, which made her neighbours' failings seem intolerable, called her a good watch that soon runs down, and must often be wound up by the key of piety, or lapsed occasionally into the tumid style of M$^{me.}$ Guyon, and spoke of her as a naughty child, that must be swaddled and given its soup and put to bed.[2]

Not, indeed, that he would have her become the sport of evil tongues, all too prone to make a mock of virtue; she might 'repair the breaches which the world had made' by stray quarters of an hour of meditation, entered upon at times when her friends thought her more becomingly engaged, at her dressing-table, out driving or even at dinner, 'during that first course which hunger generally devours in silence.' Or this Director, who was himself a fellow-sufferer from *la démangeaison de la critique*, finds her means of mortification in the little tedious duties of Society, bids her remember that 'God often hides His Presence under bores,' and imposes on these caustic lips, that never spoke without their point, a self-denying ordinance of silence. 'I do not think,' he wrote, 'that you can possibly talk too little, provided you are silent out of deference to others; I should be charmed to hear that you never opened your lips except to praise or edify your neighbours, though I am sure that, if you lay this constraint on yourself, you will never talk at all, and will find listening very dull.'[3]

And Fénelon's letters range over a wider field than his later spiritual correspondence. M$^{me.}$ de Grammont's soul is not alone in question; there is time to moralize a little over passing events, over the falling away of M. de Tréville, or the conversion to piety of M$^{me.}$ de le Sabliere. Or else some worldly disappointment becomes the text of a little sermon on the spiritual meaning of the Universe, and the

---

[1] So, at least, thought M$^{me.}$ de Caylus, p. 124. See St Beuve. Lundis, x. p. 23. The letters to M$^{me.}$ de Grammont, possibly to an earlier period than the other letters here referred to, and end with Fénelon's disgrace, in 1697.

[2] 235th Spir. Lèt. Wks., viii. p. 598.   [3] *Ibid.* p. 599.

Countess is bidden remember that all the world's contradictions, its fickleness, its injustice, nay, our own imperfections and passions, are nothing other than effects of the Wisdom and Justice and Goodness of God, hiding Himself under blind and sinful man, to purify us and make us worthy of Him. "Only under this view," cried Fénelon, "can we advance beyond the tinsel decoration to the hidden purpose, can we make the world become to us a great reality, worthy of praise eternal as the scheme of God."[1]

And there is many a gleam of this breadth and humour in Fénelon's letters to another lady, M$^{me.}$ de Montbéron, wife of his friend the Governor of Cambrai, the most doleful and exacting of all his penitents. For this poor woman had many troubles, her husband's debts, her own ill-health, and, worst of all, a jealous, unrestful feverishness of temper, which turned in religion to a wearing scrupulosity, and in daily life became a martyrdom to social usage and 'to a certain super-excellent politeness.'

Of the more fanciful terrors Fénelon made short work. 'For you,' he wrote, 'doubts and scruples are a forbidden fruit; let them buzz in your imagination like bees in a hive; if you excite them, they will get angry and sting you, but if you leave them alone, you will be quit for the buzzing and the fear. If they come upon you in prayer-time, try to follow the example of St Bernard, who, on being assailed in the middle of a sermon by admiration of his own eloquence, said to himself: Vanity did not bring me here, and vanity shall not drive me hence.'[2] And when her husband and her doctor wished to prevent excessive church-going, Fénelon loyally came to their assistance, and bade her sacrifice a sermon to her husband's wish, and 'fast from masses,' just as Chevreuse had been told to fast from reasoning. "In future," he said, "I shall judge of your spiritual by your bodily state, and not believe that God is pleased with you, until I know the doctor is. But I shall think you a very Saint in Paradise,

[1] 260th S. L. Wks., viii. p. 610.
[2] 340th Sp. Let. and see 359th. Wks., viii. pp. 652, 661.

when you can sleep well at night, and be free of scruples in the day-time."[1]

Nevertheless Fénelon did not speak always in these breezy tones. Like his other penitents, M[me.] de Montbéron must mortify the flesh, and lay the axe to the root of her favourite vices. Over-refinement of manner must give way to simplicity, and striking extremes to a mean, not golden, but dowdy; nay, this all-governing Director will descend to the details of her wardrobe, and bid her wear dresses neither magnificent nor yet of a conventual simplicity, but such as would suggest an absence of all taste, and give her the appearance of a tradesman's wife.[2]

And from her, as one of the chief, and most 'interior' of the penitents, mortification asked for more than trifles; it was no longer what it had been with M[me.] de Grammont, or the Vidame d'Amiens, a simple discipline, a healthful correction of their faults, but widened into that whole system of sacrifice and death to self which circled round the Maxims of the Saints. And the change of spirit was wholly for the worse; the more Fénelon left the solid earth, the more did his kindly reasonableness desert him, the more he held up to this wretched scrupulist a cruel ideal of Detachment for Detachment's sake, of egoism painfully subdued by resignation, not egoism vanquished and transformed by Love.[3]

Nay, the ideal itself, as preached to M[me.] de Montbéron, has no small tinge of supernatural selfishness; for Fénelon, the semi-Quietist Director of Consciences, was far indeed from the philanthropic Fénelon of Télémaque. Ridden by one idea, he had taught his royal pupil to strain every nerve in the service of humanity; ridden by another, he bade M[me.] de Montbéron cure herself of such 'romantic ineptitudes,' since there was no worse pasture of self-love than the wish always to neglect oneself for others.[4] This peremptoriness, doubtless, had in view no more than the

---

[1] 338th and 450th Sp. Lett., pp. 651, 695.   [2] 269th Sp. Lett., p. 618.
[3] Naville, Christianisme de Fénelon, p. 15.   [4] 417th Sp. Let., p. 680.

hysterical excesses of altruism ; but his counsels, as he might have foreseen, were turned by his penitent into a law, and carried out to the uttermost scruple. After eight years of his almost daily Direction, she was afraid to nurse her own daughter through a confinement, because uncertain whether the call to do so came from God, or from a merely natural, and therefore selfish, impulse. 'I assure you,' the author of the Education of Girls was obliged to write, ' that you cannot be wrong in performing one of the essential duties of a mother towards a most excellent and deserving daughter. Remain with her till she is out of danger ; meanwhile, I promise to send over constantly for news of you, and, at the first call, to come myself—indeed I would come without a call, were not my presence at such a moment likely to be a burden on the household.'[1]

For Fénelon's Direction had done more than purge M$^{me.}$ de Montbéron of unselfishness ; it had spellbound her judgment and eaten away her will till she could exist no longer for an hour without him. ' Cursed be he that maketh flesh his arm,' was a text often, but vainly, in Fénelon's mouth ; the history of M$^{me.}$ de Montbéron's conscience, with its nightmare terrors, its frantic yearnings after the Director and no less frantic repugnances, is the history of the penalty paid by all those who yield up to another the key of their heart, and listen to the precepts of a man as always and necessarily the oracles of God.[2] . . . Let us hurry away from these pitiful scenes to company with whom Fénelon could again be human.[3]

For Fénelon is not to be found whole and entire among his penitents and priests at Cambrai ; he was too good a Frenchman, says M. de Broglie, ever to forego the national

[1] 447th S. L., p. 694.
[2] *Cf.* 435th S. L., p. 689. "J'ai la clef de votre cœur. . . . Vous ne sauriez nier que Dieu vous a unie à moi, et que vous me trouverez *en lui sans* distinction, dès que vous revenez à votre oraison. (Italics as in the text).
[3] Avec vous je m'humanise, wrote Fénelon to the Chevalier Destouches. Wks., p. 48.

taste for gaiety and wit and conversation. Throughout his exile he still kept touch with Paris, corresponded with many men of mark and bade them welcome at his Palace, amongst others two dispossessed Potentates, Joseph of Bavaria, the frivolous young Elector-Archbishop of Cologne, whom he persuaded to submit to Ordination,[1] and the Chevalier de St Georges, the Old Pretender to the English Crown. Of the latter he was at pains to send a portrait to the Duke of Burgundy, which would be flattering even to Stuart powers of fascination, were not the ease and grace of manner, the vigour and decisiveness he singles out for special praise, the very qualities most desirable for his own royal pupil to acquire.[2] To Cambrai also came the famous and eccentric Peterborough, and, later, a long train of diplomatists on their way to Utrecht, among them, perhaps, an old acquaintance, 'M. Prior, an Englishman known throughout Europe for his wit and parts.'[3] And from our own country came a stranger figure, a young Scottish Jacobite, known in France as the Chevalier de Ramsai, who, after scouring Protestant Christendom in search of a religion, found it at Cambrai on the lips of Fénelon, and settled there—a kind of Boswell without the genius—to stenograph his master's table-talk.

But the chief among those outside friends was a certain Chevalier Destouches, a brother-officer of his nephew Gabriel, although already entering on middle life. The bond between them was entirely mundane, for Destouches though singularly pleasing in manner, and not without pretensions to scholarship, was a great glutton, and worse things besides —indeed, as Fénelon said, there was nothing respectable in his manner of life, except its absence of hypocrisy. He was himself a little puzzled at the closeness of their friendship. "Why," he once asked, "should an old Bishop be so fond of a man of your profanity, unless it is that your

---

[1] An account of this prelate and his peculiarities will be found in Wks., v. p. 603. I have referred to the sermon preached by Fénelon at his consecration in chapter ii. [2] See Wks., vii. p. 291.
[3] *Ibid.* vi. p. 613. This was, of course, the poet-diplomatist Matthew Prior.

character has two sides; you are an evil genius to yourself, but true and noble to your friends?"[1]

But even Fénelon had no hope of the Chevalier's reformation, unless, indeed, the peccant bachelor became uxorious, and fell into the clutches of a masterful wife. For once the great Director acquiesces in the moral *status quo*, goes to theology only for jests about this sluggard so sunk in 'polyphagy' that Irresistible Grace itself could hardly save him,[2] and preaches a doctrine no more 'interior' than that of Horace and the *parvoque beatus*, a strict régime and many suppers suppressed.[3]

And, in return, these letters, too light and delicate of structure to bear transplanting to the *hortus siccus* of an extract, give us Fénelon in his brightest, happiest vein— Fénelon as he appeared during these latter years at Cambrai, no longer the condescending aristocrat, no longer unduly disquieted for his own or others' Perfection, no longer merely a great man, but, as his people proudly boasted, become a man both great and small.[4]

And the friendship with this officer is a pleasant appendix to St Simon's panegyrics on our hero for his never-ending kindness to the troops brought through Cambrai by the progress of the Spanish War. There the Duke paints him moving among the sick and the whole, the known and the unknown, the officers and the common soldiers, with a knowledge of the world which understood how to gain them all by treating each in his due degree, and yet a true and watchful shepherd of their souls, as constant in his ministrations to the humblest as though he had no other business in life. And he was no less careful for their bodily comfort, lodged officers innumerable in his Palace, tended the wounded among them, sometimes for

---

[1] Wks., viii. p. 234. Further details about Destouches will be found in St Beuve, Causeries du Lundi, ii. p. 15.
[2] p. 229. Irresistible Grace was a great doctrine of Fénelon's enemies, the Jansenists.   [3] pp. 43, etc.
[4] See the curious passage, pp. 70 and *ff.*, in Marchand's Nouvelle Vie de Fénelon, written in 1731 from Cambrai traditions.

many months, until their entire recovery, supplied the hospitals with costly drugs and endless streams of food and delicacies, sent out, for all their abundance, in such perfect order, that every patient had exactly what he needed. And, in return, they sang his praises even in the antechambers of Versailles; it was incredible to what a degree he was become the idol of the troops.[1]

Nor was it only to the soldiers of his own country that these benefits were extended; he had equal care for the prisoners of war confined within his diocese, so that their Generals and the Court of Brussels, the Protestants at least as much as the Catholics, the Duke of Marlborough as well as Prince Eugene, vied with one another in showing him honour, and protected his estates better than the French themselves. None of his property was allowed to be pillaged, nor the lands of those for whom he interceded, and, at his prayer, powers were granted to many French prisoners, such as no one else would have dared to ask. "In short," ends St Simon, not without a touch of irony, "much as he was loved and revered throughout the King's dominions, his fame stood even higher wherever the King's enemies were the masters."[2]

[1] St Simon, xi. pp. 60, 61.
[2] St Simon, Écrits inédits, qu. Broglie, pp. 214, 215.

CHAPTER XI

JANSENISM

> Ci-gît Fénelon, qui deux fois se damna
> Une fois pour Molinos, l'autre pour Molina.
> —*Jansenist Epigram.*

ADVERSITY had done much for Fénelon, but it had not wholly reformed him ; the peaceful beauty of his later life was still to be marred by one great blot. He had not been long at Cambrai, before he began to engage in the series of endless shufflings and intrigues, the *intolerabiles ineptiæ* of acrid argument and legal quibblings on the one side, of Jesuit perfidies and brutal acts of royal violence on the other, in which was drawing to a close the chief religious drama of the age, the Jansenist controversy of Arnauld and St Cyran and Pascal.

Jansenism was the great Catholic reaction of the century, as reflected in the sounder, stronger, conscience of the nation, an impulse not exhausted, like the reforming zeal of M. Olier, in the foundation of a single Institute or Order, nor was it even peculiar to the clergy, but spread abroad among the whole body of the people. It was a movement wholly lay and national, that drew its chief support from the middle, professional classes, but found, if not adherents, at least friendly allies everywhere, in M$^{me.}$ de Sévigné and M$^{me.}$ de Grammont at Versailles, in Bossuet and de Noailles among the Bishops, in Racine and Boileau and La Bruyère among the men of letters, as lastly in that general public, *qui se portait toujours du côté où les Jésuites n'étaient pas.*[1]

It was a call to make Christian faith and practice a

---
[1] Henri Martin, xiv. p. 606.

reality, a cry of alarm, says Ste Beuve, a closer gathering round the Cross of men affrighted at the present commonsense rationalism of the Jesuit confessionals, at the coming shadows, already visible long before hand, of that greater rationalism whose prophet was the Jesuit pupil, Voltaire. It was an assertion of the essential mysteriousness, of the *credo quia impossibile* of the Christian religion, against the well-meant efforts of the Jesuits to make it more intelligible to human reason ; it was a violent protest against the moral laxity, the weak good-nature that so easily degenerated into a shameful, guilty indulgence, of Confessors wishful to lighten every burden, to explain away every commandment by their doctrine of 'probability,'[1] till it became well-nigh impossible for man to sin, and the Jesuit showed himself worthy of his title : *Ecce Pater, qui tollit peccata mundi*.

In ancient days, said Pascal, men were not admitted to the Church until they had renounced the world, but now they enter both Church and world at the same time. And it was to those ancient days that Jansenism appealed, to the godly discipline of the Primitive Church against the "filthiness of the casuists,"[2] to the traditional rights of Bishops and priests against the growing power of Rome, to the teaching of the Fathers against the Jesuits' love of novelty, against their habit of making expediency the test of truth, of whittling down, to suit the customs of the Present, the most venerable dogmas of the Past.[3]

The Jesuit was all compromise, but the Jansenist all iron. He entrenched himself behind the oldest, sternest doctrines of Christianity, Predestination, the Fall, Original Sin, behind whatsoever most grievously revolted the pride or intellect

---

[1] Probabilism, in its extreme form, maintained that no action need be considered sinful which had been declared lawful by any recognized writer on casuistry, however new and small his authority. See Jervis, Church in France, i. p. 427, ii. p. 164.

[2] *Les ordures des casuistes*, said Bossuet, qu. Ste Beuve, Port Royal, iv. p. 67.

[3] Der Kampf (mit dem Jansenismus) sollte nicht eher aufhören als bis . . . die weltformige Praxis des Beichtstuhles der Dogmatik ihr Gesetz vorschreiben konnte. Harnack. Dogmengesch : iii. p. 628.

JANSENISM   229

of man. With his master, St Augustine, he looked out on the world as a bare, waste, formless outbound of God's Kingdom, as a sinful chaos, a shaking quagmire of corruption, in the midst of which rose, stark and lonely, the storm-swept citadel of Grace.

For Nature, like man, was under a curse, implicated in his aboriginal calamity, and thenceforward a wilderness, burnt up, rather than watered, by rivers of fire. Jansenism turned hotly on such Christian rationalists as Fénelon, who sought to argue God's Existence from the courses of the moon and stars, and bade him remember that Nature was an atheist, created, not to set forth God's glory, but to teach man his need of Redemption in Jesus Christ, through Whom alone the Universe gained a meaning, for He was the centre of all things and the goal to which all must tend.[1] And to those who, like Fénelon again and St Francis of Sales, would show a larger charity and extend some little of God's 'uncovenanted mercies' to the virtuous heathen, Jansenism sharply answered that there was no goodness without Grace, nor was Grace ever given without Faith, wherefore all the prayers of infidels were sins, and the virtue of the philosophers was vice.[2]

Yet in the very narrowness that alienated the humaner modern spirit of Fénelon lay the strength of Jansenism—for what is more inspiring than a creed which believes that it is always and everywhere fighting God's battles, since every good thought and every good deed must of necessity come from Him alone? Jesuit mildness had allowed man a part in the working out of his own salvation, had even made him the master of his fate, teaching that Grace was always given, though the will might always resist it; but Jansenism would have none of these 'sufficient Graces that did not suffice,' and boldly answered that man's will was fast bound in slavery to sin, so that only by God's irresistible

---

[1] See Pascal Pensées, Art. xiv.
[2] See the 25th condemned Proposition of Baius, and the 101st and 59th of the Bull Unigenitus.

power could he be raised again to a state of liberty and receive the freedom to live according to his own higher nature, the freedom to be good and wise.

"The Jesuit doctrine of sufficient grace," wrote Walter Pater, "is certainly, to use the familiar expression, a very pleasant doctrine conducive to the due feeding of the whole flock of Christ, as being, as assuming them to be, what they really are, at the worst, God's silly sheep. It has something in it congruous with the rising of the physical sun on the evil and the good, while the wheat and tares grow naturally, peacefully, together. But how pleasant also the opposite doctrine, how true, how truly descriptive of certain distinguished, magnificent or elect souls, vessels of election *épris des hauteurs*, as we see them cross the world's stage, as if led on by a kind of thirst for God. . . . Of certain quite visibly elect souls the theory of irresistible grace might seem the almost natural necessary explanation. Most reasonable, most natural, most truly is it descriptive of Pascal himself."[1]

Yes, just as nothing is more vigorous than a fatalist doctrine in its youth, so no faith suffers a more prompt decay. Already before the death of Pascal (August 1662) a gangrene of chicanery had set in, and by the days of Fénelon, Jansenism, as a formal creed, had come to live on controversy and chicanery alone. When their tenets were again and again condemned, Pascal cried that they must appeal from Rome to God, but his party set up 'the very gross distinction of the *fait* and *droit*, an acted lie,'[1] maintaining that the Church had an infallible right to condemn heresies in the abstract, but no special authority to say where or in whom such heresies were to be found. The Five Propositions, so-called of Jansenism, they condemned as heartily as the Pope, but the later history of the party is the history of the 'respectful silence' with which they sought to evade the question whether or no those Five Propositions were the teaching of their master's book.

[1] Essay on Pascal, reprinted in Miscellaneous Studies, pp. 64, 65.
[2] So said Bossuet. See Le Dieu, ii. p. 362.

JANSENISM

The original quarrel had ended in 1669 with a very ambiguous acceptance by the party's leaders of the Treaty of Peace of Clement IX., but the matter was reopened in 1701, chiefly by the foolish action of the Jansenists themselves, and the storm thus conjured raged with fitful violence till it was swallowed up in the greater tempest of the Revolution. In this second controversy an Archbishop of Cambrai was almost bound to take a part, placed as he was on the frontier of the Low Countries, the original birthplace and always a home of Jansenism, at the head of a clergy whose most zealous and learned members were drawn from Louvain or Douai, the two Universities where Jansen's name was chiefly held in honour.[1] But Fénelon did far more than his episcopal duty demanded; in the innumerable Charges and pamphlets that streamed from Cambrai during the last twelve years of his life, in the letters and State-papers and denunciations of suspected Jansenists to the Court of Rome, to Louis' Confessor Le Tellier, to Beauvilliers and Chevreuse and to the Elector of Cologne, Fénelon showed himself one of the most watchful and remorseless enemies the Jansenist party had ever had.[2]

Although no extreme Jesuit in doctrine—nay, by our modern eyes scarcely to be distinguished from Port Royal itself—for he accepted Predestination in its literal sense and the consequent Divine determination of the will [3]—Fénelon's

---

[1] Fénelon admitted this, Wks., iv. p. 453. Jansen (A.D. 1585-1638) was a Dutchman by birth, spent many years as Professor at Louvain, and died Bishop of Ypres in Belgium. The famous Treatise on St Augustine, which gave rise to the whole controversy, was not published till after his death.

[2] See the *Memoriale clam legendum* to the Pope. Wks., iv. p. 453, and the many letters to Chevreuse, etc., Wks., vii. pp. 368 and *ff*. To the Pope Fénelon did not spare the Elector of Cologne himself—he was *leviusculus atque incertus animi* on the great question. See Brunetière. Etudes Critiques, iv. p. 156.

[3] Predestination was the real question at issue between the parties. (1) The ultra-Jesuit party, or *Molinists* so called from the famous Spanish professor, Molina, resolved it simply into God's foreknowledge of man's actions, and held that Grace sufficient for salvation was given to all men, and that all were free to reject it. The other three great parties all maintained absolute Predestination (*i.e.* by arbitrary decree of God, irrespectively of man's merits) with varying degrees of clearness. (2) The *Jansenists*, in fact, though not in name, abolished

was, none the less, an instinctive antipathy to Jansenist thought and Jansenist practice; and this feeling, rooted in his nature, had been strengthened by an early training at St Sulpice, and by all the friendships and associations, the alliances, enmities, and ambitions, of his subsequent career. Bossuet could winnow the pure and noble grain of Jansenist virtue from out the husks of Jansenist theology, could even see in that theology itself a half-truth, a presentation of the hideous face of the Gospel,[1] to be corrected by a preaching of the whole; but Fénelon's eyes fell never on the grander, inward, spirit, only on its crabbed, and often repulsive envelope. From the heights of his own more gracious morality this aristocrat looked down upon a virtue, real and zealous and austere enough, and courageous in its resistance to evil, but harsh and unlovely and given to censure, noisily quarrelsome and overbearing, stamped on its forehead with acid vulgarity, with the mark of the middle-class Pharisee.[2]

A forerunner of the eighteenth century, Fénelon loved broad and spacious horizons, sweeping principles bounded by no narrow captious restraints. Truth, he told the Jansenist leader, Quesnel, was one and indivisible, not to be found among forced, unreal, distinctions, among Formularies

---

Free Will altogether; God abandoned the Reprobate to themselves, and saved the Elect by irresistible Grace. (3) Bossuet and the *Thomists*, followers of St Thomas Aquinas, distinguished two sorts of Graces, the 'sufficient,' given to the Reprobate, ideally enough for salvation, though certain to be practically inoperative—this was the famous grâce suffisante qui ne suffit pas of Pascal's Second Provincial Letter—and the 'Grace efficient in itself' which was given to the Elect and invariably followed by its effect. (4) Fénelon adhered to the *Congruist*, or moderate Jesuit, party. These differed from the Thomists in making the efficacy of Grace depend, not on any difference in the Grace itself, but on its "congruity" to the mind of the recipient, God so adapting, or, as Fénelon said, "seasoning" His Graces that the Elect would certainly accept them, and the Reprobate as certainly reject them. See the articles on Grace and Predestination in Addis and Arnold's Catholic Dictionary, also Hist. Litt. pp. 307 and *ff*. Fénelon's clearest statement of his own position is contained in the Letters to Father Lami on Grace and Predestination, written about 1708, and printed in Wks., ii.

[1] La face hideuse de l'Évangile, said Bossuet.
[2] See Esp. 5th Sp. Let. Wks, viii. p. 444.

accepted in a non-natural sense, or even in such a respectful silence as knew neither silence nor respect. "Yours is a terrible position, my Father, and I tremble the more for your sake the less you tremble for your own. Sooner than sign the Formulary you have fled to Holland, and the mass of your party, having signed it, thereby declares you a rebel against the Church. In return, you curse them for a crowd of cowardly, perjured hypocrites, but they do not cease to admire you, call you their oracle and the Athanasius of our days, while you are forced to bless them as your children, as the only remnant faithful to your cause."[1]

Nor was the cruel, uncompromising logic of Jansenist theology more to Fénelon's taste than the policy of tortuous subterfuge, with which it was so incongruously allied. In matters of Faith Jansenism must have all or nothing, black outer darkness or the 'thunderbolt of Grace,' but Fénelon, when he could not have the greater, was content to thank God for the less, to welcome the tepid piety of the worldling, the natural religion of the Deist, to look kindly even upon those first vague promptings towards a sense of mystery and wonder, in which religion, like philosophy, began.[2] The spirit of rationalism, he well knew, had made vast strides in France since Pascal thought it enough to bid the careless atheist bet for or against the chances of a future life, or Bossuet noted a frivolous indifference to all religion as a sign of the times more ominous even than their vice. Bossuet himself, in his later days, was secretly aware that the evil did not stop short at indifference, while Fénelon, younger and more outspoken than his whilom master, openly proclaimed that, under the stress of mad curiosity and presumption, belief in the Christian Mysteries was crumbling away, and the Church reeling helpless under the blows so repeatedly dealt her by each new godless system of error begotten of the infidel North.[3] And his prophecy was

---

[1] See the Letters to Quesnel. Wks. iv. pp. 582, 606.
[2] See esp. Wks., i. p. 134.
[3] See the Epiphany sermon, preached in 1685, Wks., v. p. 623.

being fulfilled sooner, perhaps, than he had thought for. During these latter years at Cambrai he was compelled to defend the Existence of God and the Immortality of the Soul to the Duke of Orleans, Prince of the Blood, and shortly afterwards Regent of France, while his lively correspondent, the Marquise de Lambert, wrote, with no more than a pardonable exaggeration that Christianity was become such a scandal and a laughing-stock that 'one was held to belong to the lower orders, if one ventured to express belief in God.'[1]

But, while Fénelon, in the name of Reason, went forth to meet and turn the advancing tide of incredulity, the Jansenist leaders stood coldly aloof, or drew their cassocks tighter round them, and thanked God they were not as other men. They poured scorn on Fénelon's careful deduction of His Existence from the nature of the Infinite or the constitution of the human mind, answering him in a phrase of Pascal that a man might well have excellent notions of a metaphysical First Cause, without being advanced one step along the high road of salvation.[2] Faithful to a tradition that had now become an encumbrance and a danger, they denied the competence of the intellect in matters of Faith, taught, not merely that 'the heart has its reasons, which the brain can never know,' but insisted that these were the *only* reasons for belief, that the Grace of Faith was a blind, undiscriminating instinct, ' more like the wild enthusiasm of the fanatics than the ordered creed of sober, reasonable Christians.'[3]

But these were among the least of Jansenist iniquities. Fénelon's real grievance against the party, their wholly

---

[1] Written in 1712. Wks., viii. p. 51.
[2] Pensées, Art. xiv. Pascal, it is true, does not represent the whole of Jansenism, and his attacks on Reason had scandalized the earlier generation of Port Royal. (Bouillier, Hist. de la Philos. Cartés., i. p. 432.) But Port Royal's confidence in Reason weakened gradually (*ibid.* vol. ii. p. 209)—or, as is more probable, the few real believers in Reason left no successors; and the party drifted within twelve years of Fénelon's death down to the level of the Abbé Pâris and the miracles of St Médard. [3] Wks., i. p. 129.

unpardonable sin, was that they had 'impugned even more the Justice of God than outraged the petty interests of man' by their utterances on the Freedom of the Will.[1] And his indignation was all the sharper because, in substance, they were nearly agreed; he was himself no Molinist, to ascribe man absolute powers of choice between Good and Evil: if consciousness on one side told us we were free, on the other it told us that we were dependent. And, although he held our meed of liberty to be the glory of our birth and state, a very image of the Godhead in us, above the faculty of merely choosing he placed the faculty of choosing *right*; and, arguing that our whole life was one continuous Grace, asked whence its highest power came, if not from God?[2] For our will was but a reflection of His own; He worked immediately within us, an indistinguishable partner, when we chose; our choice was His and ours alike.[3] How this should be so was a mystery insoluble—as well attempt to set it out in detail as ask a man of good and careful education to pass in review his fading memories of childhood, and determine exactly between what he had learnt from his parents and what he had learnt for himself.[4]

But for the Jansenists this was not enough. Their Predestination knew no half-truths, allowed no haggling over terms with God, but denied man's liberty in violent and insulting language, speaking much of chains and bolts, of a human will sold into thraldom to an imperious mistress, Concupiscence, and as unable to shake off its bonds as to ride post-haste without a horse.[5] God's mode of operation was no mystery to them; they held, as Fénelon said contemptuously, to the truly low and pitiful idea that He determined His creatures, not by appeals to their conscience and reason, but by awakening what was lowest in them, the selfish craving of their passions. "This party believes that man is swayed by an unconquerable appetite for pleasure, which inclines him sometimes towards the

[1] Wks., ii. p. 179.   [2] i. pp. 32, 33.   [3] ii. p. 169.
[4] v. p. 385.   [5] pp. 424, etc.

Celestial Delectation of Virtue, but far more often towards the Terrestrial Delectation of Vice. To pleasure the party sacrifices everything; it becomes our only rule of action, the soul of our souls, the mainspring of our hearts; by it the scanty band of the Predestined are led infallibly into right-doing, while the rest of mankind are flung, no less irresistibly, into the arms of sin. . . . There is a system more shameful than that of Epicurus, yet much bepraised of those who cry down the relaxed morality of the casuists! There is a system which the least scrupulous casuist would hold in horror, which defies every rule of morals, shocks even a pagan sense of modesty, which, when the time of blindness is over, will make posterity blush for those who, in their own day, knew no shame!"[1]

Fénelon's language is strained, his caricature of the religion of Pascal and St Cyran is atrocious, but for some of his anger there is worthy cause. Port Royal's frankly hedonistic language, its cynical disregard of mystery, its conception of the human will as governed by mechanical forces,

> Rolled round in earth's diurnal course
> With rocks and stones and trees,

seemed to him a wanton surrender of religion into the hands of the materialists.[2] "Now that determinism is become the fashionable opinion among our free-thinkers." he wrote, "they are delighted to gain for their own doctrine of 'the greatest pleasure' the support of a party so influential as the Jansenists. Nay, they do not scruple to take the name of Jansenist themselves, that they may the more effectually attack the Church; it costs them nothing to believe in God, if only they need not fear Him, if Hell and Liberty and Merit are swept away, and they may give free rein to the uncontrollable necessity of their passions."[3] And the Churchman's instinct did not lead him false; on the heels of Arnauld and Quesnel trod Condillac and Helvétius.

[1] Wks., v. pp. 225-6.   [2] p. 301.   [3] *Ibid.* viii. p. 112.

Yet, even had free-thinkers never been heard of, a doctrine that enslaved the will to pleasure could never have found much favour with the apostle of Disinterestedness. It is true that devotion to Saint Augustine, coupled with a desire to rout the party by exploiting their special Father in an orthodox sense, led him to speak that Father's language, till his own mind became imbued with Augustinian habits of thought; but behind the controversial Fénelon rises continually Fénelon the mystic, resolute to secure the will its lawful rights—for was it not the mother of Love, and what was the value of the child, if the mother were not free? Too rapid a thinker to care for absolute consistency, and with his master's boundless inconsistencies before him, Fénelon, in his spiritual writings, lets Predestination and Necessity drop out of sight, and builds up on the basis of 'dependent freedom' a system as austerely majestic as the Jansenist's own Irresistible Grace.

Jansenism, in its higher aspect, was the party of Divine Eternal Order, of the reign throughout the Universe of one only Law, that led captive men and all things in a chain of iron necessity, "which none could break, or slip, or overreach." But Fénelon set himself to create a conception of Order no less stringent, of Law no less Divine, though it was founded on no irresistible outward compulsion, but on willing acceptance by the heart of man.

God, he argued, as the Sum of all things, the Absolute Being, must of necessity embrace within Himself the whole of Goodness and of real Existence; His Pleasure made the moral order of the Universe, His Glory was Creation's only end. Mankind and Nature were but His playthings, bound to His service by a law which even His own power could not break, for He must Himself obey the dictates of His infinite excellence, and call that only into being, whose fulness, whose ideal perfection, was to be found within His Own.[1]

The Law was one and the same for all, though His in-

[1] Wks., i. p. 116.

struments served in divers fashions, according to their several natures and capacities; Matter was His slave, but Spirit His free dependent; Matter brought Him no free gifts, had no free choice, must blindly move or stand still at His bidding; but man, the child of Spirit, was born into a higher order, allotted a more glorious destiny: from him God asked no soulless, indeliberate motion, but conscious acts of thought and will.[1]

In himself no more than a borrowed being, a half-existence, a shadow of the True, Grace had given him the power to choose between Good and Evil, between living Reality and cheating dead Appearance, to enter, as a link, a lowly partner, into God's secular process, His eternal Order, or else to stand outside in the land of darkness, a worshipper of the empty idol, Self. For the establishment of Order within the soul was the whole of true religion; it was a casting out of the false god, and a setting up of the True, a forcing of that Self, which would fain be the centre of all things, back into such little corner of the Universe as its scanty share of Being and Perfection might justly claim.[2]

Once man had come to see things in their true proportion, once he had learned that the all-but-nothing may not bargain with the All, the reign of selfishness was ended, and the reign of God begun. Now there was no more thought of pain or pleasure, of that hireling devotion, which made the Love of God the means, and its own advantage the final end, for the soul had learnt to judge *sub specie æternitatis*, its centre of gravity was shifted from self-interest to desire of His greater glory alone, and it was now borne peacefully onwards by the sole attraction of His Love.[3]

It would have been well for Fénelon had he fought the Jansenists only along these nobler lines, and descended to no more vulgar polemic than the new edition of St Augustine, destined to show how grossly Jansenism had falsified its master's teaching, or the familiar Dialogues, in

---

[1] Wks., i. p. 117. [2] *Ibid.* p. 102. [3] *Ibid.* v. p. 275.

which, as he hoped, he had caught something of the spirit of " M. Pascal," and enlisted in the cause of truth 'an art that could fling a veil of touching gracefulness over the most abominable errors, and hold the reader's attention spell-bound, while poison poured in torrents from its pen.'[1]

But Fénelon was devoured by anxiety for his own reputation, by the belief that, for his honour's sake, and the good of the Church, he must blot out all remembrance of the Maxims of the Saints, and regain, by a superabundance of militant orthodoxy, the good-will of the Courts of France and Rome. If time had worn away the sharp edge of his longing to return to Versailles, its memories were still very far from effaced; the affairs of his diocese were trivial and easily managed; political interests had not yet absorbed him, and even books and letters and visits were no sure resource against the intolerable ennui and languor that, as he said, comes upon those who have been suddenly transplanted from busy and active surroundings to a life as slow and sedentary and monotonous as the ticking of a clock.[2] To this oppressive stillness the Jansenist controversy came as a relief and an excitement, as a welcome channel for energies, which, else, would have fretted uselessly to waste.

Nor was it altogether displeasing to Fénelon to find himself again at war with two of the old Triumvirate of Quietism, but this time under very changed conditions, with the Pope and Louis at his back. Bossuet had long been suspected of Jansenist sympathies and might now be forced to speak out plainly at last,[3] while as to the unhappy de Noailles, he was being buffeted along from party to party and from blunder to blunder, 'was wishing,' wrote the nuns of Port Royal, 'to make us change our faith as often as he changed his own,'[4] 'a man whose opinion no one cared to ask, for he would declare himself now for this side, now for that, yet was too timid, too dull, too fogged of understand-

---

[1] Wks., v. p. 227. [2] Ibid. vii. p. 419.
[3] Ibid. p. 574. Bossuet frustrated this amiable intention by dying in 1704.
[4] Le Roy, p. 255.

ing to see what either party really meant.'¹ It had been prophesied of him long beforehand that he would one day head a party without his knowledge and against his will, and the working out of his destiny was to make this newly-clad Cardinal, this favourite of Louis and Mme. de Maintenon, into the shambling, helpless puppet-chief of Jansenism.

Barely six months after the condemnation of the Maxims, Fénelon, well knowing that a new Jansenist storm was about to break, had begun to draw out for Beauvilliers a plan of campaign on the lines of that followed many years beforehand during the Protestant mission to Saintonge.² Now as then, his personal dealings were warmed by a spirit of real cordiality, by the desire, so instinctive to him, to stand well with all he came across, so that his tolerance, as even St Simon acknowledges, won him the respect and affection of every Jansenist in his diocese, even made Cambrai a haven of refuge for those outside.³ Now as then, he urged that authority could never take the place of reason, that five hundred episcopal charges were not worth a single argument, that warrants and arrests and *lettres de cachet* were the weapons of men whose cause was bad.⁴ Yet now as little as then did he shrink from the baser arts of proselytism; the names of secret supporters of the party might be discovered by pryings into letters, questioning of servants, *espionage* ; such notorious partizans as Cardinal de Noailles should be publicly ' discredited '; to all sympathizers with Jansenism, whether lay or clerical, the gates of promotion should be rigorously barred.⁵

Both in his writings and his counsels to the Government Fénelon showed a cool unbending kindness, a courteous moderation that had nothing in it either of sympathy or violence, but was a blend of Christian principle with the

---

¹ Fén. Wks., vii. p. 220.   ² See the letter to Beauvilliers. Wks., vii. p. 219.
³ viii. p. 419, xi. p. 62.   ⁴ Wks., vii. p. 574.
⁵ Thus he was anxious in 1711 to have as First President of the Parliament, or Lord Chief Justice, a sensible infidel of good morals rather than the most pious Jansenist. Wks., vii. p. 352.

gentleman's refined dislike of cruelty, and fear lest the brutal measures, beloved of Louis, should shed ill-fitting lustre round the victims. In his eyes Jansenism was a hideous moral cancer, curable only by a patient watchful surgery—not, as Louis and his advisers vainly imagined, by a policy of listless indolence, broken here and there by cruel slashing blows, such as the infamous destruction of Port Royal,[1] that struck alike at the guilty and the innocent, were never followed up, never accompanied by sounder teaching, but fitted exactly to anger the party without doing it serious damage, and to inflame the public mind against its adversaries.[2] Fénelon preached a method far more uniform, more economical of energy, more promising of good results; he would draw a sharp line of cleavage between the real members of the party and their semi-Jansenist, but still orthodox, admirers, would have a special eye to the more moderate, as, for this very reason, the most dangerous disseminators of corruption, yet would punish them only when they were clearly wrong, sparing the common folk and letting the weight of prison or banishment fall only on their leaders.[3] But he put less trust in severity than in education, in reforming the many seminaries and colleges that were become mere 'nurseries of seduction'; the best way to eradicate Jansenism from the future was to call into existence a new and better race of priests.[4]

One man alone, the wretched de Noailles, stood wholly beyond the pale of his charity. With Chevreuse and the Jesuits, especially, from 1709, with le Chaise's successor, the terrible Le Tellier, 'a man of iron, whose only god was his Order,'[5] Fénelon entered into a real conspiracy against the Cardinal, overcame Beauvilliers' reluctance to work against

---

[1] Between 1709 and 1711 the convent of Port Royal was pulled down and its cemetery violated, as 'a place which had the misfortune to incur His Majesty's displeasure.'   [2] Wks., vii. p. 381.   [3] pp. 220-1.   [4] p. 333.

[5] St Simon, vi. p. 242. Le Tellier succeeded to the Confessorship in February 1709. Fénelon's controversial spirit managed to discover 'goodness and learning' in his ally (Wks. vii. p. 311), but even Cardinal Bausset admits that Le Tellier was universally detested, and for good reason (Bausset, iii. p. 535).

the man, who, at his own brother's expense, had saved him from the loss of his places during the Quietist storm,[1] plied the two Dukes with reasons why the King should publicly renounce his beloved Archbishop, now that he was become the head and front of Jansenist offending. He intrigued against de Noailles in Rome; twice, at least, he stirred up ecclesiastical disturbances against him in France and gave his little stratagems a truly odious appearance when he denied to de Noailles' family that he had had any part in either.[2]

In truth, during his campaign against de Noailles, Fénelon showed for the last time that curious kaleidoscopic changefulness of character, that moral unsubstantiality, at which his own conscience seems to be darkly hinting when he wrote again and again in despair that 'say what I will about myself, the words seem false before they have passed my mouth.' For it is a poor and prejudice-blinded criticism that can set down all this bitterness to personal enmity; Fénelon's character bears no such easy label—in a skein so tangled the motives cross and re-cross each other continually, as they weave out their web of patternless contradictions. His desire for revenge was limited, now by Christian feeling, now heightened by intellectual arrogance or envy, contempt for one who could never hold an opinion or see a difficulty, jealous irritation that this dullard had supplanted him with Mme. de Maintenon, and become, for a while, all-powerful at Court. For years he made believe to himself and the public that he was acting out of the purest zeal for orthodoxy; he tried in sober earnest so to act, to uproot from his heart all

---

[1] According to St Simon (ii. p. 48) the King had told de Noailles that he was going to dismiss Beauvilliers and give the reversion of his places to the Archbishop's brother, Marshal de Noailles. But the Archbishop magnanimously represented that none of Fénelon's errors had been proved against Beauvilliers and induced the King to relent. De Noailles was made Cardinal in 1700.

[2] The Denunciation of the Theology of Hobart and the Affair of the Bishops of Luçon and La Rochelle. See Bausset, iii. p. 540. For Fenelon's mendacity, *cf*. Wks., vii. pp. 336 and 361, with Wks., viii. p. 66. The evidence has been gleefully collected by Le Roy, pp. 323 and *ff*.

feelings of malicious gratification at the sight of his rival standing in the place where he had stood, drinking of the cup whence he had drunk, face to face with a degradation greater even than his own, with expulsion from the Cardinalate and his see. Yet his best efforts ended in a cold and dreary charity. "Strange as it may seem," he wrote, within a few months of his death, " I even feel compassion for the Cardinal ; were I, as some imagine, to take malignant pleasure in the troubles now crowding so thickly on the Church, mine would indeed be the poisoned joys of Hell." [1]

Mere ill-will to de Noailles might be pardoned ; it was the great part Fénelon played in these crowding troubles that his countrymen have found it hardest to forgive. Does not Michelet draw him kneeling, like a guardian angel, at the cradle of the *Unigenitus*—that ill-starred Papal Bull which struck the final blow at Jansenism, though at the price of forty years of war ; nay, as Voltaire said, its very appearance ranged the whole country into two opposite camps—on the one side a hundred bishops supported by the Jesuits and the Court, on the other fifteen bishops and all the nation ? Does not Henri Martin speak of it as an infamous scandal, and a Bull more Jesuit than Christian, the work of Le Tellier rather than of the mild and virtuous Clement XI. ? And the foremost living critic of France declares this last persecution, of which the *Unigenitus* was the means, and the destruction of Port Royal the presage and the symbol, to be a crime only less big with evil seed for the future than the Revocation of the Edict of Nantes.[2]

But most significant of all is Fénelon himself, writing to tell his friends at Rome of the universal agitation caused by the Bull ; how it was said everywhere that the Pope had condemned St Augustine, St Paul, and even Jesus Christ, in that he denied the necessity of Grace, wrested from the hands of the children the Bible that had nourished their fathers, and sought to bow the consciences of Kings and

[1] Wks., viii. p. 229.   [2] Brunetière, Etudes Critiques, iv. p. 163.

peoples alike to the tyrannous injustice of his thunders from the Vatican.[1]

And it is the worst reproach against its chronicler that he saw in this national resistance nothing but 'rebelliousness and calumny and lapse from the happy simplicity of our fathers.' Fénelon, lost in abstract notions, could not look away from them to facts, could not see that Jansenist theology, hard and narrow, was but the cloak, the sectarian vestment, of a great human-catholic ideal of Duty, that Bishops and doctors, seminaries and Orders, lawyers and ladies, would never been swept away by its torrent,[2] unless they had in their creed a barrier against vice, a guide to otherworldliness, an incarnation of their national conscience. Jansenism had denied Pure Love, and on behalf of Pure Love Fénelon rushed into battle, heedless of consequences, indifferent to the character of the allies he gathered around him, little dreaming that the end of the story would be a *sic vos non vobis*, where he might labour, but Father de Tellier and his like would carry off the honey to their hive.

For Disinterestedness had no share in the victory; the downfall of Jansenism meant the triumph of the Jesuits, pending the greater future triumph of Voltaire. And Jesuitism, though, in a sense, the party of progress, was, for the most part, progress in a wrong direction; if, with Fénelon, it strove to mitigate Jansenist rigour, it also buried Jansenist love of truth under "the divine authority of things doubtful," and crushed out Jansenist manly independence under the soft viscid pressure of a bureaucratic clericalism. And in its train followed all that Fénelon most detested, a reign of sham throughout the Church, bastard learning, bastard piety, stucco morals, the spirit, not so much of Macchiavelli, as of a theological Della Cruscan Academy, that recked of florid common-place, and grew fat on sensuous imagery and little mincing devotions, on the preference above the great of the infinitely small.

[1] Wks., viii. pp. 198, 199.   [2] See Wks., vii. p. 381.

JANSENISM

And yet Ultramontanism is right in claiming Fénelon among its children. None of his countrymen, he boasted, had done more for Rome, or done it with a gladder heart;[1] none was more determined an enemy of the Gallican Liberties, that control of Papal Bulls by King and Parliament and Bishops, which tied the hands of the foes of Jansenism, and kept them in "a very servitude."[2] And he stood almost alone in defending a dogma that put the crown and seal on the clerical victory, the dogma of the Infallibility of the Roman See.

Into this latter course he was betrayed against his better judgment, partly by his own precipitancy, and partly by the feebleness of his brother Bishops. For, as he bitterly complained, De Noailles and the weaker prelates would take no definite step, but contented themselves with vague denunciations of Port Royal, in language which, as they were themselves the first to explain, was "doubtful, confused, and probably erroneous."[3] So Fénelon turned to Rome in search of a more drastic medicine—but only to find that now, as ever, all things Roman had their price, and that not even a Pontifical anathema could be purchased without concessions to the Pope. 'Little they care here,' wrote his Vatican correspondent, the French Jesuit, Daubenton, 'whether the Jansenists be put to silence or no, unless it be by establishing against them the infallibility of the Holy See. So long as you do not assert it, they will speak politely of your books, but never cordially approve them; for they hold this infallibility to be the universal weapon against all the heresies, and to them all other interests are as nothing beside the extension of their darling prerogative.'[4] For a long time Fénelon hesitated and protested. It was idle, he urged, to talk to Jansenists of a papal infallibility that they laughed to scorn, till they had learned the full significance of the prior infallibility of the Church. It was dangerous, and

[1] Wks., vii. p. 303.
[2] Ibid. p. 315.
[3] Ibid. iv. p. 463.
[4] Ibid. vi. p. 626.

destructive of all hope of Roman rule in France, to teach a doctrine which Louis XIV. and his Parliaments and ministers abhorred, holding it part and parcel of the papal claim to determine the right of Princes to their thrones. And the doctrine sounded hatefully in Gallican ears; Bossuet, the great master of controversy, had never taught it; it was held by scarce a Bishop or doctor; it ran counter to the strongest prejudices of the nation.[1]

Rome listened to all these protestations with a uniform bland indifference. The Pope, Fénelon's Italian friends told him, was satisfied with his good intentions, and knew how he must pick his words, but some of the ardent spirits around him would never be satisfied, till he had uttered the little word " Infallibility."[2]

And at the last Fénelon rose to the bait so skilfully dangled, and wrote, though under promise of the strictest secrecy,[3] his Treatise on the Authority of the Sovereign Pontiff. This had for its object the welding of all the more moderate Gallicans and Ultramontanes into one great anti-Jansenist alliance, like a coalition of Law and Order formed to resist agrarian crime, and armed with its doctrine of Roman infallibility as with a kind of spiritual Coercion Act, a suspension of the *Habeas Corpus*, that would remain forever in force.

And the mischief of the principle was not much diminished by the restrictions with which Fénelon hedged it round. His Treatise was intended for purely Roman consumption; but its ideas came back quickly, like curses, to roost in France. Mindful of Louis, he allowed the Pope no authority over the temporal concerns of Princes;[4] but the Jesuit spirit can govern kings, and does not need depose them. Engrossed

---

[1] See the Appendices to the Dissertation on the Pope. Wks., ii. pp. 56 and *ff.*

[2] Wks., vii. p. 656. Cardinal Fabroni, a great power at the Vatican, seems to have been one of these (p. 304).

[3] p. 308, and see p. 304. Fénelon was in the habit of sending private advice to Rome.

[4] Wks., ii. p. 49. Nihil sæcularis potestatis sibi vindicet sedes apostolica. Procul esto suspicio hæc infelicissima.

JANSENISM

by the idea of constitutional sovereignty in Church as well as State, he lodged infallibility in the united clergy of the See of Peter, and treated as irreconcileable extremists those who gave it to the Pope alone; but these extremists were the victors at the Vatican Council of Pius IX.[1]

And Fénelon's Treatise, utterly unknown in his own day, has proved a power for evil in the present century. First published in 1820, when the events that led up to it had long been forgotten, this *œuvre de circonstance*, this diplomatic makeshift, is still often quoted as one of the fountainheads of the new philosophic Ultramontanism. Joseph de Maistre, and Lamennais, and Louis Veuillot professed to do no more than water the seed that Fénelon had so lightly sown; and thus his tares have greatly swelled the stinging-nettle harvest which Curialism to-day is reaping in the Church of France.

[1] Wks., ii. p. 66. He is speaking, indeed, primarily of those who held the Pope infallible *ut privatus doctor*, but his words cover also the official infallibility of Pius IX.: evidens est nullam pontificiam definitionem . . . esse infallibilem, nisi accedente ipsius sedis apostolicæ consensu (p. 6). And he says again (p. 7), supremam hanc auctoritatem, non in sedente, semper mortali et interdum incerto, sed in sede immortali, et semper certa, permanere. The final authority is therefore the Apostolic See, defined as the majority of the clergy of the diocese of Rome (pp. 65, 66).

CHAPTER XII

AMONG THE PHILOSOPHERS

> Quant aux volontés souveraines
> De Celui qui fait tout, et rien qu'avec dessein
> Qui les sait que lui seul? Comment lire en son sein?
> Aurait-il inprimé sur le front des étoiles
> Ce que la nuit du temps enferme dans ses voiles?
> La Fontaine.

CLOSE as was Fénelon's alliance with the Jesuits, it was momentarily interrupted from an unexpected quarter, when, in 1712, a second of his manuscripts shared the fate of Télémaque, and was ushered by a new unfaithful copyist into the world. This was a revised edition of a youthful work, the First Part of the Treatise on the Existence of God,[1] written in the days when its author was strongly under Cartesian influence, more especially that of Descartes' great disciple, the Oratorian Father Malebranche, with whom the Society of Jesus had a deadly feud. Thus the brethren of Le Tellier found themselves in an awkward dilemma; either they must alienate their chief episcopal ally by a refutation, or else sit silent, while his book was quoted in triumph by the enemy. But in the end their diplomacy proved equal to the situation; without asking Fénelon's leave, they reprinted his Treatise with a preface by one of the cleverest of their theologians. Here the book is explained away as a covert refutation of Cartesianism; Fénelon, it is said, borrows from its arguments, not because he believes them, but simply to turn them against the Cartesian misbelievers themselves—though, to be sure, adds the Preface, it was a pity he had forgotten Spinoza—thus classing Malebranche and Descartes with the atheistic bugbear

---

[1] The Second Part, which belongs to the same period of Fénelon's life, was never finished, and was only published in a fragmentary form after his death.

MALEBRANCHE

FROM AN ENGRAVING

of the age. But alas! diplomacy does not always meet with the success it deserves; Fénelon disavowed the Preface, Malebranche appealed to his powerful friends, and eventually wrung from the Jesuits a public apology.[1]

There were many reasons for this Jesuit hatred of the new philosophy, a hatred already old in years, and responsible, jointly with the meddling spirit of the Government and the vicious conservatism of the universities, for the petty persecutions Cartesianism had undergone. The Society, strong in military virtues, has always shown a more than military unwillingness to give up its old *Mumpsimus* for the *Sumpsimus* of newer lights; its greatest writers had been scholastics, and now its corporate pride must look on in dismay while scholasticism was banished to the college lecture-rooms, and every philosophical primer in France reeked of the influence of Descartes.[2] His teaching was above all things intellectual, and Jesuits have always been suspicious of the intellect, foremost among those who prove by reason that we ought to renounce our reason—a pretended virtue flouted by Malebranche as equally consoling to the vanity of the shepherd, and to the brainless inertia of his flock. And this entire distrust of reason had made them 'probabilists' as well in metaphysics as in morals, of the opinion that 'a little Pyrrhonism sits prettily enough on the philosopher,'[3] meaning thereby that it was better to come to no conclusions at all than to arrive by the wrong method at the right results. Cartesian idealism, with its independent proofs of immortality and God's existence only stirred their bile; they made common cause against it with the materialistic freethinkers of science, men who scoffed at Descartes as a spinner of transcendental cobwebs, much as their latter-day descendants scoff at Kant or Hegel, and declared that if this new metaphysical moonshine made its way— then good-bye to all sound medicine and philosophy.[4]

---

[1] Bouillier, Hist. de la Phil. Cart., ii. pp. 276, 277.
[2] *Ibid*. i. p. 484, quoting the Jesuit Daniel.   [3] *Ibid*. pp. 572 and *ff*.
[4] *Ibid*. p. 558.

Besides, Cartesianism had a family likeness to an even more detested rationality, also of Augustinian descent. In their several degrees, Arnauld, Nicole, Quesnel, were all disciples of the new philosophy, so that 'Jansenist' and 'Cartesian' became convertible terms of Jesuit abuse; and it would be hard to say which triumph over the Oratory pleased the Society the most, the Formulary of 1678, by which the home of Malebranche was made to forswear Cartesianism, or that of 1684, wherein it, for the last time, reprobated Jansen.[1]

But even the Society was not omnipotent. It might trample on a University or Order; it could not touch the secular priests, still less that loose-knit world of Academies and drawing-rooms, in which Cartesianism, during the last three decades of the century, became an intellectual fashion. The great Condé's country-house invitations to Malebranche, even M$^{me.}$ de Sévigné's resolve to study the new philosophy, "as one learns the rules of Ombre, not so much to play oneself, as to know what the players are about," did more to quicken the progress of Cartesianism than the Cardinals and Jesuits did to hinder it, when they placed its founder's works upon the Roman Index.

There was, indeed, a kind of natural alliance between Cartesianism and the world; had not the Master written in his native language that he might have no book-worms for his judges, but men of ordinary culture and intelligence? Henceforward common-sense and metaphysics would join hands; Reason need bow no more before the formulas of Aristotle and the mysterious shibboleths of the schools; since philosophy had come to mean, as Bossuet said, 'no poring over many books, nor vast accumulation of experiments, but simply the art of knowing ourselves, whence we might rise up, step by step, to knowledge of the Author of our being.'[2] And Fénelon put the matter with still more characteristically

---

[1] Bouillier, Hist. de la Phil. Cart., ii. pp. 432, etc.
[2] *Ibid.* p. 244. See, however, Brunetière's great article on Bossuet's philosophy.

Cartesian brevity : All that a real philosopher needs, beyond a due conviction of his ignorance, is anxiety to discover what he is, and astonishment that, as yet, he does not know it.[1]

To Churchmen of the more enlightened sort Cartesianism offered a peculiar attraction. On the one hand the whole philosophy turned on its proof of the Existence of God ; on the other, that great principle once established, it meddled with no further mysteries of Faith, but treated, in the quaint language of an early disciple : *de omnibus quæ fiunt, salvis quæ sunt Dei et Cæsaris.* Not until the roving Platonism of Malebranche had disturbed this original concordat between Reason and Faith did Bossuet foresee a terrible onslaught preparing against the Church in the name of this philosophy ; for he held that its principles, rightly applied, would yield great profit to religion by convincing metaphysicians of the divinity and immortality of the soul.[2] And Fénelon found there generous satisfaction for the two halves of his nature. The prophet of education and philanthropy delighted in Cartesian optimism, in its visions of the illimitable progress of a once emancipated human mind ; the apostle of mystical ' passivity ' found his needed counterbalance in its doctrine of Continuous Creation, which taught that the world was not only made and sustained, but every moment recreated by God's Power, so that every single thing within it, excepting only the human will, was moved by Him, and Him alone.

But both prelates were careful to preserve their independence, though Bossuet treated Descartes with distant respect, and Fénelon pleaded guilty to a warmer prejudice in that philosopher's favour. He provides the dialect in which they speak, but not the inner core of their ideas ; Bossuet was scarcely a Cartesian at all, and Fénelon has forbidden us to call him so, declaring that in speculative matters he would swear allegiance to none, but appeal from Aristotle and Descartes alike to the bar of Reason, their

[1] Wks., i. p. 135.   [2] Bouillier, ii. p. 239.

common judge. If he must have a master, it should be St Augustine, whose vaster genius showed itself in every branch of metaphysics, though he treated of them only by the way, according to no settled plan.[1] And to this principle his practice corresponds; Fénelon's castle of argument is built of Augustinian stone, though quarried under the guidance of Malebranche or Descartes.

And, of the two, he was more in sympathy with his fellow-priest and fellow-Platonist than with the physics and mechanics of Descartes. Not for Fénelon was a realm of natural sciences, where man was nothing more than man;[2] though both employ the same Methodic Doubt, there is a world of difference between the coldly rational enquirer, anxious to distinguish truth from falsehood that he might see his pathway clear before him, and walk with confidence in this life, and the passionate Churchman who follows him trembling, fearful to lose his God at every step, and crying out: 'Whither do you lead me, Reason? What shall I do when all escapes me? Who will bring me out from this torment of uncertainty?'[3] Descartes studies metaphysics in the spirit of a man of business; Fénelon, like Malebranche, in the spirit of a prayer; both look to God for their light and their reason, both deride that 'figment of philosophy, the scientific temper unmoved by pride or prejudice or hurry, which trusts entirely to itself.'[4]

And yet between these two there are great differences, though Malebranche shares one leading quality with Fénelon, and is a greater artist than philosopher; Fontenelle once likened his genius to the flame of spirits-of-wine, too delicate to burn hard wood.[5] But, while both writers let their fancy stray into a certain graceful rhetoric—its use defended on the ground that, since Adam's Fall, man has

[1] Wks., i. p. 124.
[2] *Cf.* Desc. Disc. de la Méthode, and notice the habitual exaltation of *les occupations des hommes purement hommes* as against more abstract studies.
[3] Wks., i. p. 47.
[4] *Ibid.* p. 136. Maleb. Médit., i. §§ 10, 11.
[5] See St Beuve's Port Royal, v. p. 362.

been buried in the things of sense, unable to raise himself to abstract or continuous thought [1]—with Malebranche feeling keeps the second place, with Fénelon it is always striving to be first. Here, as in Education, he stands half way between the school of Descartes and the school of Rousseau, haltingly convinced of the sovereignty of Reason, yet believing far more strongly that, even in speculation, "love with a little wit works marvels"—or, as he strangely says of the search for God, *Connubialis amor de Mulcibre fecit Apellem* [2]—and therefore never far away from the Vicar of Savoy and its "rags of metaphysic floating in the sunlight of sentimentality."

Malebranche is an illustrious example of a devout Christian never afraid of his intellect, but Fénelon boasted alike his indocility in matters of thought and his feminine credulity in matters of religion. For Malebranche Faith and Reason were different dialects of one heavenly language, guides to truth of equal authority, one in their aim and mutually helpful, though wholly separate in their methods, so that it was as unlawful to reach by Faith conclusions unacceptable to Reason as to argue by Reason only in the teeth of Faith—though indeed a discord between them could never be real, but only apparent, due to the blind impatience of our judgments and to be corrected by profounder meditation.[3] But Fénelon speaks in less masculine tones. It was his pride, whenever Faith and Reason clashed, to pay no attention to this last, but 'choose God's wisdom rather than his own,' and sacrifice his feeble powers to the divine authority of the Church.[4] He could never have repeated the noble words in which Malebranche reminds men that they make on earth the same use of their Reason that they will in heaven, for Faith must pass away, but Reason will abide forever.

---

[1] The idea is St Augustine's. See Fén., 2nd Dialogue on Eloquence, Wks., vi. p. 582. [2] Wks., i. p. 135.
[3] See the various passages collected in Ollé Laprune's Philosophie de Malebranche, i. pp. 100-128. [4] Fén. Wks., i. p. 123.

And yet, though his speculations are now obsolete, and over his proofs of God's Existence the most timorous sceptic of to-day need not fear to lose his unbelief, there still breathes through Fénelon's pages a certain intellectual stimulus, a spirit of chivalrous adventure in the world of thought; he also might have been a philosopher, had not sentiment always been breaking in. When is it, he asks, that men will learn that they have only a few days to pass on earth, and cannot pass them better than in plumbing the mysteries of their state? They will go to Monomopata or Japan in search of what is not in the least worth their knowing; they will not cross the English Channel to gain eternal happiness and wisdom.[1]

Fénelon sets out across his metaphysical Channel under the guidance of Descartes. Resolute, like his leader, to leave no loophole open to scepticism, he decides to whittle away all beliefs and opinions in any way capable of being doubted, until he has reached a foundation of certainty, on which the whole fabric of positive knowledge can safely be rebuilt. And this foundation he finds in self-consciousness; I may think the whole universe a dream and a fable, I may hesitate over every truth, I cannot but be sure I doubt; and, if I doubt, I think, and, if I think, I am, for nothingness can neither think nor be: *si enim fallor, sum.*

I have, it is true, no proof of my being beyond its self-evidence, and with self-evidence I must rest content; having no other criterion than my faculties, I must make an act of faith in them, if I would avoid the shipwreck of universal scepticism. Even if they lead me wrong, I shall be excusable in following them, though I shall hope to prove their truthfulness by proving the existence of a truthful God.

Thus Fénelon has fallen into the same vicious circle as his leader: Reason is to demonstrate the existence of God, and God to guarantee the validity of Reason. And the cause of the error is a wrongly-chosen starting-point; both make the

[1] Wks., i. p. 135.

Self the first principle of knowledge, only to find that, on their own showing, consciousness of God must come before all other kinds of consciousness. For we could not even see ourselves except against the background of a greater not-self, nor know, as Fénelon says, that our own soul was one, had we no previous knowledge of the Unity of God.[1]

And thus the first defect of Fénelon's proofs is that they presuppose what they set out to justify. Only by comparing myself with a self-subsistent Being do I learn my own dependence on an outside cause ; only by showing that my finite mind could never have conceived the notion of infinity do I argue the existence of an Infinite God.

But, secondly, so long as he remains faithful to Descartes, Fénelon does violence to logic in vain. He takes for granted the existence of God, but leaves Him still external to our mind : God is not Himself within us, but only the cause of our idea of Him, the patron of that Divine Image in our reason, which Fénelon strangely calls a second God, like to the first in infinite perfection.[2] Nor is his consistency to be admired, when he swings round from Descartes to Malebranche and Augustine, and declares that no image whatsoever can represent the Infinite God, since every idea of our finite mind must needs itself be finite. Under the guidance of these more congenial masters God is now made immediately present to the Reason under the form of our Clear Ideas, Ideas no longer, as with Descartes, simply modes of thought, but given a new, Platonic, Augustinian, sense, as meaning the intuitive first principles, the axiomatic truths, mathematical, metaphysical, and moral, that lie at the root of all our judgments, and are identified by Malebranche with the thoughts of God, if not with God Himself.[3] And Fénelon, in his turn, declares them in us, but not of us, above us, but closer to

---

[1] p. 31. For a masterly criticism of the Cartesian proofs of God's Existence, see Dr Edward Caird's Essay on that subject.   [2] p. 56.

[3] See Ollé Laprune, i. pp. 188 and *ff.*, for a comparison of the views of St Augustine with those of Malebranche, but see also pp. 267 and *ff.* And *cf.* Malebranche's own explanation of their differences in Recherche de la Vérité, III. ii. § 6.

us than we are to ourselves, our inspiration when we think aright, our bridle when we go astray, a Reason eternal and invariable, not to be questioned, nor corrected, nor denied; and asks what they can be, if not the very God of Truth, illumining our inner, as the sun illumines our outer man. If I stay entangled in my lower natures, if I do not love and follow this eternal Reason, then I am not worthy of the name of man, then I am as one born blind, as the dwellers in those inhospitable northern regions, who have never seen the sun.[1]

It was in this sense that Fénelon claimed to see " God in everything, or, rather, everything in God, since I should know nothing, distinguish nothing, be sure of nothing, but for my Ideas." Not, indeed, that he quite adopted Malebranche's theory of Vision in God, which placed the two prime elements of Creation, Matter and Mind, so widely apart that neither could be influenced by the other; nay, Mind could not even see corporeal objects in themselves, but only the Idea of them in God.[2] Fénelon kept more closely to Augustine; his Ideas are Malebranche's Truths, eternal ratios between Ideas, not intellectual archetypes of material bodies; for him these last are visible in themselves, though only through a faculty lent by God. For although Matter and Mind react on one another, each in itself is blind, and God the only nexus between them; He, in recreating His work each moment, determines also the manner and circumstance of being, and directs my attention to the particular thing He would have me see, giving to me a power of understanding, to it of being understood.[3] Thus Fénelon's real difference from Malebranche is but small; whether I see the Ideas of things in God, or see the things themselves through His ordaining, the practical consequence is the same; my sight is but a passive agent in His Hand.

And each philosopher's theory of vision is the essence in

---

[1] Wks., i. pp. 27, etc., and see the fine passage in Télémaque, bk. iv. (Wks., vi. p. 424).
[2] See Ollé Laprune, pp. 238 and ff.
[3] Wks., i. p. 67.

AMONG THE PHILOSOPHERS 257

little of his system ; from belief that all things are seen in God it was but a short step to believe that all things are done by One Who, in the graphic phrase of Malebranche, 'never sits with folded arms.' "Bodies, spirits, pure intelligences, can do nothing in themselves, but are moved and enlightened by their Maker; it is He who carries out our acts of will, *semel jussit, semper paret.* He moves our arm, even when we disobey Him; since He has complained through the mouth of His prophet that His people have made Him to serve with their sins."[1] Reservations, it will be seen, are made in favour of the human will, timidly by Malebranche, more peremptorily by Fénelon; though he also holds that, in good philosophy, the accessory being follows its principal, and God is prime author of every modification in His creatures.[2]

And not only is God the cause of all things, He *is* the whole of all things. In their horror of an anthropomorphic Deity 'with hands and feet,' Malebranche and Fénelon pile abstraction on abstraction, after the manner of the Areopagite, till God recedes ever farther from our view, and we long for a touch of something more definite, were it only the grotesque Almighty of the Jesuits, a God "quite Personal and very singular, although endowed with infinite virtue,'[3] modelled, apparently, on the Pope. 'He Is,' cries Fénelon, and that is all; we need no other word. To speak of Him as infinite or perfect is to set bounds to the unbounded, to encroach upon the majesty of sovereign, universal, Being, to flatter with senseless idle terms the paltry imagination of mankind. He is all that is real in Spirit, but He is not Spirit; He is all that is real in Matter, but He is not Matter; He is all that is real in whatever other Substance there may be. Sweep away all distinctions, all

---

[1] Recherche de la Vérité, VI. ii. § 3. The reference is to Isaiah xliii. 24.
[2] Wks., i. p. 32.
[3] See Bouillier, i. p. 578, quoting Father Hardouin, the eccentric, famous for his attacks on the authenticity of Virgil. But, as M. Bouillier shows, there was method in Hardouin's madness, and his real object was to discredit the authenticity of St Augustine and such other Fathers of the Church as happened to be obnoxious to the Society of Jesus.

differences of creatures, and there remains only the Universality of Being, the perfection of Him who is all things, in and for Himself.[1] . . . When I remember that Thou, O Lord, art all that is, my Reason faints, engulfed in Thee; I do not know what I become, all that is not Thee is gone, scarce doth a shadow of myself remain."[2]

Fénelon, lapped in sensuous enjoyment of his rhetoric, does not seem to have noticed whither he was drifting, but Malebranche's intellectual sight was clearer. After suppressing all individual thought and action, well-nigh all individual existence, he begins to ask himself whether any personality whatsoever is left to man, whether our Ideas are really distinguishable from the Divine Reason, our being from the Divine Substance—whether, in short, he is not falling into the grave of Pantheism, already dug by 'the wretched Spinoza'[3] under his feet. And certainly there was good reason for the fear. However different the spiritual significance and colouring of their language—and imaginatively speaking, no two men were further apart—from the purely speculative standpoint it is otherwise: this Catholic priest, who transfigures the Universe into God, is all but reproducing in another guise the naturalism of the Jewish philosopher, who translated God into the Universe; for coats have a knack of being the same, whether we turn them inside out or outside in.[4] It was not logic, but the Book of Genesis, that arrested Malebranche in mid course; while tempted to believe that his Substance was eternal, he suddenly remembers that that cannot be—else God would have left His creatures without their most essential mark of dependence, the knowledge that they have not always been.

But, in thus speaking as a divine, Malebranche does not forget that his divinity is 'geometrical,' and takes his stand beside Spinoza as a prophet of the Universal Reign of Law.

---

[1] Wks., i. p. 69.   [2] *Ibid.* p. 45.
[3] 'Le misérable Spinoza.' The words are put into the mouth of Jesus Christ. Ninth Meditation, § 13. See Ollé Laprune, pp. 361, 388.
[4] See Dr Martineau's Ethical Theory, i. pp. 223-225.

His God is not the blind, capricious tyrant men would think it fine to be ; our earthly sovereigns may not exercise the wretched right of whimsicality, and how much less their Sovereign Lord![1] *Deus est summe constans in suis operibus;* with Him is "no variableness nor shadow of turning"; the Absolute God and sum of all things, He may speak only in universals as grandly simple as His attributes, must work always in a manner worthy of Himself, by laws as general as unchanging, ordered, not with a view to the passing needs of time, but only in the interest of eternity. Often these laws are fraught with evil consequence to us, and our selfishness would have Him change them; yet He may not break in on their established harmony by particular decrees, for He loves His Wisdom more than His Work, and of that Wisdom order is the very essence[2]—

> He is the reaper, and binds the sheaf,
> Shall not the season its order keep?
> Can it be changed by a man's belief?
> Millions of harvests still to reap . . .
> He stoops not either to bless or ban,
> Weaving the woof of an endless plan.

But the two philosophers soon part company over the nature and purposes of God. Spinoza can give no explanation of the Universe beyond that it *is*; his God is the harsh step-mother Necessity, "the Mosaic conception of the One God of Israel wedded to the Lucretian conception of the one and inflexible nature of things."[3] Malebranche acknowledges a Divine Purpose with the orthodox divines— "God must have created the world for the Church, and the Church for Jesus Christ, to find in Him a Victim and High Priest worthy of the Divine Majesty."[4] Spinoza had denied to God all will, on the ground that Infinite Perfection is not like a man, to wish for something that it has not got;

---
[1] See the passages collected by Ollé Laprune, pp. 218 and *ff.*
[2] Traité de la Nature et de la Grâce (ed. 1684), p. 64.
[3] Sir F. Pollock, Spinoza, p. 134; and see pp. 319 and *ff.*
[4] Traité, p. 15.

orthodoxy gives Him an arbitrary freedom of good pleasure, expressed as Providential Ordering; Malebranche tries to make room for the two conceptions side by side, not seeing that they cannot be content with separate empires, but, if they are to co-exist at all, must be united under a higher synthesis, as some "stream of tendency, not ourselves, that makes for righteousness." Thus his whole system becomes a crash of gentle discords; leaving God arbitrary freedom to create or not create, He binds Him by an iron law of Order once He has created, and thus tends to make Order not the essence, as Spinoza holds, nor, as orthodoxy, the legislative enactment, but the judge of God, 'a kind of pagan Destiny, supreme over gods and men alike.'[1] Nor does he save the position by allowing God the one initial act of choice; qu'il dise de bonne foi, cries orthodoxy, que Dieu n'avait qu'une seule chose à faire, qu'il l'a faite, et qu'il s'est épuisé,[2] an adjuration to be compared with the famous saying of Pascal, that Cartesianism made one well-directed kick from God send the world spinning on its axis for all time.

Moreover, through this back-door of Order return those anthropomorphic conceptions of God, which Malebranche is usually so eager to cast out. Not only must He, the infinitely wise workman, do all things in the most perfect possible way, as an earthly workman should, but Malebranche goes for his scale of perfection to human experience, and decides that the most perfect method is the simplest: is not the best machine the most economical of energy, and does not a crowded statute-book argue haphazard legislation?[3] If, therefore, God determines to descend to what His critic, in utter scorn for the Contingent, calls 'the low and as it were humiliating office of Creator,'[4] He must call into existence the best of all possible worlds, and govern it by the simplest and most general laws, both in the realm of nature and the realm of Grace.

---

[1] Fén. Wks., ii. pp. 72, 92.   [2] p. 77.   [3] Traité, p. 59.
[4] La qualité basse, et pour ainsi dire, humiliante de Créateur. — 19th Meditation, § 5.

Inasmuch, however, as our actual world is imperfect indeed, Malebranche calls theology to his aid, and refuses to consider it except as 'bathed in the reflection of an infinite glory' through the Incarnation of the Word. Inasmuch as God can only work by general laws, Malebranche sets up a hierarchy of secondary powers, physical laws and laws of nature in the natural world, angels under the Jewish Dispensation, and, under the Christian, Jesus Christ, to apply those general laws to particular effects. Yet it is little enough that they can do; though there are miracles these are rare, and due, not to any interruption of God's Order, but to occasional supersession of the Laws of Nature by the Laws of Grace. But over these last, also Order presides; too many souls must not be saved 'lest the Mystical Temple grow unwieldy through being made spacious in excess.'[1] Not, indeed, that there is Predestination in the usual sense; Malebranche's Heavenly Architect cares only for the whole, not for the particular stones with which He builds; the choice of souls is left to Jesus Christ, considered as a kind of glorified man or 'Word come down,'[2] and endowed with capacities less than infinite, so that His mind moves, like our own, among particular things, thinking now of this man, now of that, and therefore unable to remember all. . . . For Charity is wholly swallowed up in system; God's very Essence is His Order, man's only task to cherish and obey it, bowing, if need be, to a scheme of salvation, of which his own eternal happiness forms no part.[3]

Long before Malebranche reached this point, Fénelon had started back in alarm. So much Cartesianism as seemed to be of service to religion he kept, it is true, to the end of his days, but on the graver matters where Faith and Science were drifting apart, he declared unhesitatingly for the Church. Of Spinoza, whom he refutes without understand-

---

[1] 14th Meditation, § 15.
[2] Une sorte de Verbe déchu, says St Beuve, P. R., v. p. 431.
[3] See Fénelon's criticisms. Wks., ii. pp. 110, 111.

ing, he speaks with truly ecclesiastical bitterness; he was as impious as extravagant, head of a sect, not of philosophers, but liars, a dealer in that *physique métaphysiquée* which Plato had long ago condemned in Aristotle.[1] Malebranche he calls an eminent thinker and divine led away by the profane wisdom of this world, and undertook, though never published, a Refutation of the book on Nature and Grace, which has been already mentioned as written in his youth under the eye of Bossuet.[2]

From Bossuet, too, comes much of its spirit, a logic more serried than is usual in Fénelon, a strong uncompromising grasp of theology, that refuses to let Malebranche have his way, and coax its dogmas into conformity with his requirements. His fundamental assumption that the world only becomes worthy of its Maker through its union with the Word is declared an opinion utterly unknown in the Church, that makes the Incarnation the cause of God's love for man, instead of its "incomprehensible demonstration and prodigious effect," nay, it implies—since Redemption only follows after sin—that He never could have loved mankind, had it not been for Adam's Fall.[3] And the prophet of Disinterested Love of God has little to say to the prophet of Disinterested Love of Order, except that he has united two odious extremes, limitation of God's Charity on the one hand, and on the other, of His right to predestinate.[4]

It is over this question of Order that the real battle takes place. If God must always take the most perfect course, how, Fénelon asks, can He be free to create or not create the world, when existence is certainly better than nonexistence? Why did he not make it infinitely perfect and eternal? Why, when simplicity is so much prized, is it as complex as it is? Would not one single atom have been enough, if all its lustre comes from the Word? And he points out the anthropomorphic conclusions at which the great enemy of anthropomorphism arrives. God is not

---

[1] 24th Dialogue of the Dead. Wks., vi. p. 268.   [2] See above, c. i.
[3] Wks., ii. pp. 121 and *ff*.   [4] *Ibid.* p. 142.

an infinitely wise Workman, obliged to choose general, rather than particular, laws, that He may do things with the smallest possible expenditure of effort: effort is with Him a word unmeaning, and thrift the virtue of poverty, not of wealth immeasurable—nay Fénelon will agree with Bishop Berkeley that "splendid profusion should not be interpreted weakness or prodigality in the Agent who produces it, but rather be looked upon as an argument of the riches of His Power."[1]

And in the course of these attacks on Order Fénelon gives a new answer to the underlying question: Is virtue one and the same for God and man? In the Treatise he had answered that it was, and ranged the great axioms of morality among our other Clear Ideas; in the Refutation he does not hesitate to say No. God is indeed bound by laws of His own, but these have nothing in common with us, creatures of His arbitrary will: how can our finitude share with his Infinity, or weigh in a scale of better or worse One beside whom the lowest atom and the highest angel are equal nothingness? And, as emotion more and more asserts her empire, Fénelon passes from philosophy to Quietism, from the mild First Cause of Malebranche to the Destroying Spirit of Jewish Prophecy, and bids men remember its figure of the potter and his wheel; he moulds clay, he breaks it, and none may ask the reason of his acts. 'But God has no need, like this vile workman, to ply a trade; not only has He formed His clay, but made it; it is nothing but for Him. Whether He moulds or breaks it, He is wise; He does what He will, and what He wills is always good; His is the right and His the power.'[2]

As in the moral, so in the physical world; there also Fénelon will allow no iron rule of Order to limit the autocracy of God. General laws of a sort, it is true, there must be, since, without presupposing some kind of Uniformity in Nature, Fénelon admits, that we could neither act nor think,

[1] Principles of Human Knowledge, § 152, qu. Pollock, p. 232.
[2] Wks., ii. p. 89.

still less could he himself have written those pages on the Argument from Design, wherein a disciplined Universe is pictured as the slave of man—the sun his candle, the earth his nursing-mother, birds and beasts and plants and fishes created for his use.[1] None the less, Fénelon denies all scientific value to the Laws of Nature. Malebranche, he holds, went grievously astray in making them the supreme example of Almighty Power; they are no more than a veil of ordered regularity, made to hide His constant workings from the eyes of sinful man.[2] Not in the General, but the Particular, is His Hand revealed, not in the rule, but its exceptions.

For these exceptions are His Providence, "the continual government that directs to an end things which seem fortuitous,"[3] whether they be the unforeseen element in our own lives, that, as Bossuet says, somehow always makes us do more or less than we meant, or the result of some seeming accident from outside, like the cannon, 'charged from all eternity,' which killed Turenne.[4] Or again Bossuet will show its workings on a larger canvas, as in the famous Sermon[5] where he explains the Great Rebellion against Charles I. by God's desire to give Princess Henrietta to the Catholic Church. 'The laws of her father's kingdom being a stumbling-block to her salvation, He swept that kingdom utterly away; for, such is the value of a soul, that He will put all heaven and earth in travail to bring forth one of His Elect.'

Fénelon has not this last splendid audacity; his Providence is of all attributes of Divinity the tenderest and most merciful, keen not to wreck one soul for the profit of another, but to provide the common benefit of both. Only in the far-off realm of Universal History[6] does he dwell on

---

[1] Treatise, pt. i. c. ii. *passim*. [2] Wks., ii. p. 100. [3] p. 109.
[4] See Mme de Sévignés letter of 31st July, 1675.
[5] Oraison Funèbre de Madame, Duchesse d'Orléans, daughter of Charles I. and sister-in-law of Louis XIV.
[6] See the Epiphany Sermon preached in 1685 before the ambassadors of the King of Siam, then supposed to be about to introduce Christianity into his dominions (Wks., v. pp. 618-622).

the terrible operations of God's Hand, knowing no better aid to Faith than the spectacle of mighty empires swept from the path of the Messiah, the Jews, who rejected Him, scattered to all the winds of heaven, the Roman Empire, drunk with the blood of the martyrs, delivered over to the barbarians, wandering hordes of brutal idolaters, unworthy even to be called a people, yet destined now to find a God they never sought, and build up in His Name a civilization and a State. And yet the Epiphany Sermon lacks the note of triumph of Bossuet's great Discourse: we may rejoice, Fénelon says, at the conquests of religion, at the Cross planted in a new hemisphere larger than the old, at the missionary zeal which bears the Gospel to lands that Alexander's lust of conquest never reached—yet in rejoicing we must also tremble; the vocation of these Eastern peoples may betoken the secret reprobation of ourselves; they may be called to raise a new Temple on our ruins, as the Gentiles on the ruin of the Jewish, and the Church of France be what the Churches of Antioch and Alexandria are become, or like the African land of Augustine, still smoking from the thunderbolt of God.

And through all Fénelon's spiritual writings runs this strain of melancholy. The whole human race is painted falling into decay before our eyes,[1] a hundred new worlds rising on the ashes of the age that saw our birth; we are the shadow of a dream, "a wretched crowd of changing things "—

> None other than a moving row
> Of visionary shapes, that come and go
> Around the sun-illumined lantern, held
> In midnight by the master of the show.

Nor may we know the part we play in the drama of our own world's history. Its great events are like the letters of a giant alphabet, so huge that they defy our feeble sight; we may, here and there, spell out a single one, but not till

[1] See in particular a fine passage in Wks., vi. p. 150.

the world has run its course, may we hope to read the whole of the message, and cry, with God's map rolled out before us, that He alone is just and wise.[1]

And so Fénelon passes from the Shadow to the Substance, to chant the praises of the Changeless and Eternal, Him whose Name is the Name revealed to Moses in the desert: *I am that I am.* To us the highest attribute of Divinity might seem not Being, but Becoming, a quickening, fructifying breath of life, *ein ewiges lebendiges Thun—*

> Umzuschaffen das Geschaffene
> Damit sich's nicht zum Starren waffne:
> In keinem Falle darf es ruhn—

but the Age of Louis XIV. thought otherwise, and Fénelon, in his conception of the Deity, was a true child of his age. Its massive harmonies and love of stable, orderly magnificence speak in his stately chapters on the Unity, Eternity, Incomprehensibility of God, as the Creed from which those terms are borrowed inspires the triumphal march of his sentences, exulting in the mystery they preach and in forcing it on other minds, heavily laden, yet not bowed down, with resonant metaphysical jargon, great echoing epithets and clanging reverberations of one central word, as when their writer cries to God: *Plus on vous contemple, plus ou aime à se taire, en considérant ce que c'est que cet être qui n'est qu'être, qui est le plus être de tous les êtres, et qui est si souverainement être qu'il fait lui seul être tout ce qui est.*[2]

Yet in the very splendour of the rhetoric lay its danger. Fénelon, who could never touch without adorning, and never adorn without extravagance, exalts the majesty and unity of God till the mind is dizzied by a truth beyond all speech or thought, all affirmation or denial, and sinks, as Fénelon sank himself, into "a view wholly obscure and indistinct and general," the philosophical accompaniment of Quietist passivity, or else into some vague dilettantism of the Infinite, that

[1] Wks., i. p. 42.   [2] *Ibid.* p. 84.

asks not for law or creed or gospel, nor yet for Spinoza's grandly sombre rationality, but only for the luxuries of sentiment, and a God to tingle through its nerves.[1] Are we so far from Faust's confession of his faith to Margaret when Fénelon cries: 'Not in the multitude of Thy perfections do I best conceive Thee. The more I separate and distinguish, the more I weaken and diminish Thee, the more I weaken and confuse my sight. This crowd of attributes is not my God, these parcelled out infinities not the Infinitely One. How poor, multiplicity, thy seeming abundance! Numbers promise unity, and give it not; composite notions fall to pieces in my hands; thoughts, with me one moment, vanish irrecoverably the next—who will bring me out from these things that smell of nothingness? Myself a bundle of such vanities, I must divide Reality to grasp it, and confess that Indivisible Unity is beyond the reach of multitude.'[2]

But the youthful extravagances of the Treatise must not be taken too seriously. *Combien la rime*, asks the Logic of Port Royal, *n'a-t-elle engagé de gens à mentir?* and none knew better than Fénelon that the same danger waits on metaphysical préciosité. Here, even more than elsewhere, his later writings are a recantation of past errors; the very Maxims suddenly descry behind the tremulous heresies of Molinos the dreaded countenance of Spinoza, and urge that to separate God's Being from His Attributes is to pass from Christianity into Deism, and thence into "a kind of Atheism, where creature and Creator are made one."[3] And how much more Christian, and how much more really indicative of his thought, are those later letters to the Duke of Orleans, wherein Fénelon, laying aside all metaphysical pretence, speaks simply as a priest, to warn the royal Deist that there is such a thing as mock humility, and that reckless exaltation

---

[1] See two brilliant pages of M. Lanson's Bossuet (pp. 428, 429), where Fénelon's Quietism is deduced from his philosophy. But, as I have tried to show in chap. vi., Quietism had only a very shadowy connection with metaphysics.
[2] Wks., i. p. 76, and cf. p. 84. [3] Maximes des Saints, p. 192.

of the majesty of God is often the first step to bowing Him politely from the universe. 'Two conceptions of the Godhead lie before you—the one of a Ruler good and vigilant and wise, who will be loved and feared of men, the other of a First Cause so high that He cares nothing for the souls He made, for their virtue or their vice, their disobedience or their love. Examine well these two conceptions, and I defy you to prefer the second to the first.'[1]

[1] Second Letter to Orleans, i. § 10. Wks., i. p. 105.

CHAPTER XIII

THE LETTER TO THE ACADEMY

He comes to understand how it is that lines, the birth of some chance morning or evening at an Ionian festival, or among the Sabine hills, have lasted generation after generation, for thousands of years, with a power over the mind, and a charm, which the current literature of his own day, with all its obvious advantages, is utterly unable to rival.—J. H. NEWMAN, "Grammar of Assent."

TÉLÉMAQUE once published, Fénelon, since his accession to the episcopate, had remained 'a bankrupt on Parnassus.' Only within a few months of his death was this silence broken by a Letter on the Occupations of the French Academy. The Letter's title masks its real importance; in the guise of a mere academic programme, it is Fénelon's answer to the chief literary problems of his age, more especially in relation to two controversies then proceeding, the so-called Quarrel of the Ancients and the Moderns, and the wider, more perennial, battle between the Classic and Romantic schools.

The first of these, the Quarrel of the Ancients and the Moderns, had raged intermittently during nearly the whole of Fénelon's lifetime. In the larger sense it was a struggle between the exclusive worshippers of Greece and Rome and those who held all earlier literature to be only a preparative, first steps toward that summit of supreme inimitable perfection, reached only in the age of Louis the Great. It was an argument for and against the reality of progress, in poetry, in science, in the arts, a war between the Protestants and Catholics of literature, Reason setting itself up against Authority, the judgment of the street against æsthetic canons, inventiveness against prescriptive right; it was the Modern belief that each generation stands upon the shoulders of its fathers, opposed to the Ancient *quod semper, quod ubique, quod ab omnibus*.

And, in this larger sense, the question is, of course, unanswerable. No single formula of progress can govern the whole realm of knowledge; *gyrans gyrando*, circling in spirals, goes the spirit, alike in literature and life. There are fields where the Greek remains our master, other fields where he is less than a child; the sciences increase each year in wisdom and stature; of the arts, some go forward and some go back; music does not share its laws of growth with sculpture, nor does the art of healing rise and fall with eloquence. It is impossible to be wholly ancient or wholly modern; because Euripides is greater than Racine, we need not abandon Harvey for Galen [1] on the circulation of the blood.

But to these greater interests in their quarrel the combatants on either side were blind; seldom, even in controversy, has been seen such grim determination to abide by detail, to be decoyed away from no side-issue, from no vexatious triviality of criticism. In Fénelon's day they had reached the very *nadir* of the struggle; then they found their chief enjoyment in the travesty of Homer, rallied round his ghost on either side, the Ancients to 'reconcile' his 'teaching' with the Scriptures, to discover in the Iliad 'the most profound philosophy, the most sublime religion,' [2] the Moderns to demonstrate that, without judicious pruning, neither his taste nor his morals were fit for ears polite.

Such a judicious critic had appeared in a friend of Fénelon, Houdar de la Motte (A.D. 1672-1731), an amiable worldly poet of no vast talents, though champion of the Moderns in the last great battle of the war. His translation of the Iliad was indeed a challenge to the Ancients'

---

[1] As Dean Swift had done in the Battle of the Books, the greatest utterance of the English Ancients. Harvey was a special embarrassment to them. See Hawksworth's ed. of Swift, i. p. 270. Fénelon, however, does not deal with the scientific aspect of the matter, and believed in Harvey. See Wks., iv. p. 462.

[2] See Fén. Wks., vi. p. 648.

camp, for he had 'considerably shortened it,' though without sacrificing anything of its character or its action, had 'glided by a free translation over the great defects' which made more faithful rendering impossible in French, at times had even 'ventured to depart entirely from the text.'[1] In short, he prided himself on having brought Homer up to date, on forcing the Father of Poetry to speak the language that he must have spoken, had it been his happy fortune to live at the beginning of the eighteenth century. And as Fénelon said, there remained only one question to determine: Ought Homer to yield up to La Motte the bays he had worn for five-and-twenty hundred years; or was his improver only half a poet?[2] Into such a debate Fénelon's sense of the ridiculous would have forbidden him to enter, were it not that Télémaque was being busily quoted as an argument on either side and La Motte had personally appealed to his protection. At first he tried hard to divert the poet's energy to safer channels. 'Genius like yours,' he wrote, 'should not content itself with mere translation of the works of others, but must furnish some original master-piece which future ages will, in their turn, translate.'[3] La Motte, however, proved deaf to this delicate suggestion, and a lesser man than Fénelon would have found himself confronted by an awkward dilemma—either to give official approval to this fatuous caricature of Homer or to wound the feelings of his friend. But the Archbishop of Cambrai was not a diplomatist for nothing, and the letter to the Academy is the proof; there an ironical balance is held between the Ancients and the Moderns; La Motte and his party are inundated by a shower of double-edged compliments, their admissions are courteously over-valued, their principles turned to their own confusion. 'The Ancients,' said Fénelon, 'have their faults, yet are still not unworthy

---

[1] See his letter to Fénelon in Wks., vi. p. 650.   [2] Wks., viii. p. 220.
[3] Wks., vi. p. 649. The whole La Motte correspondence has been analysed at length by M. Rigault (Querelle, pp. 391 and *ff*.) whose chapter on Fénelon is invaluable.

of our imitation ; I hope that the Moderns will learn to surpass them by turning their own arms against themselves.'[1]

For, play as he might with La Motte and his Homer and proclaim himself never so much a peace-maker, Fénelon was in reality far from indifferent to the greater interests of the quarrel. Tear off the cloak of politeness, and he will be found at heart an Ancient of Ancients, his Letter an olive branch shot from a catapult, an Eirenicon only in masquerade. From beginning to end, it is full of that 'Back to the Greeks' which was the corner-stone of its author's gospel of taste; its one panacea for all literary diseases is 'the amiable simplicity of the dawning world.'

And this love for the Greeks determines Fénelon's relation to the most illustrious writers of his century, Corneille and Racine, Molière and Boileau, the group we now call the Classical School. Like every Ancient, he was, of necessity, in some degree a Classicist, for Classicism, above all things, meant belief in the essential unity of literature, in the existence of one unchanging code of perfection, one absolute standard of good and evil, by which all prose and poetry must everywhere be judged. For this code was not the peculiar inheritance of one age or people, but was held to be implanted in the breast of every nation, an almost divine Intuition of Taste, categorical, universal, as the Moral Law; though it was chiefly made manifest among the Greeks and Romans, by them developed into a system, and handed down for the guidance of the modern world. Its postulates were the most generally acknowledged of literary virtues, clearness and symmetry and moderation, fidelity to Nature and good sense ; its ideal was the Reign of Law, as contrasted with Romantic lawlessness, with that contempt for rules, that reign of passion and individual fancy, to which we owe our Shakespeare and our Faust. In Classic eyes the two schools of literature stood to one another as Greek to mediæval art ; Fénelon himself will compare the

[1] Wks., vi. p. 641.

Romantics to a Gothic cathedral, all windows, tracery and mouldings, all decoration and pretentious artifice, strength passing itself off as unsubstantiality in massive archways resting on a slender pillar, in granite columns hacked about like cardboard, all really fashioned to endure for centuries, yet seeming free as sun-beams, light as air. "But true good taste," he cried, "eschews these meretricious glories. Our poems should be wholly free and simple, yet gracious and majestic, patterned on those stately Doric temples where there is no superfluous ornament, nothing bold, nothing capricious, nothing ill-proportioned, but all that is necessary to the support or covering of the building takes on an air of highest elegance by reason of its natural grace. . . . He that has never felt the force of this unity, the beauty of this order, is like a dweller in the cave of Plato who has never seen the noonday sun."[1]

Yet Fénelon, even the Fénelon of Télémaque, was never one of those Classicists of the strict observance who swore by Boileau and the Art Poétique. Like him, indeed, they looked back to the Greeks and Romans, but looked with very different eyes; they found in antiquity a governess, but he a nursing-mother; he sought to breathe the very air of Hellas; they drew an Ordnance Map of Greece. They stood to Homer as a Church-system to the Scriptures, as Fénelon's own ill-fated Maxims to St Bernard or St John of the Cross; their imitation tended to become a pedantry, their reverence for rule a fetish and a bondage, that placed the difficult above the beautiful, and made the writing of a poem a discipline of useless torture.[2]

And of these failings in his brethren Fénelon himself was well aware. His Letter to the Academy all but retracts allegiance to them, appeals from the degenerate new to the old, the real, Classics, from Corneille's 'wordy rhetoric' to Roman simplicity, from Racine's academic sighs to the sad earnestness of Sophocles, even to the limpid grace of Terence from Molière's 'galimatias of metaphors.'[3] Nay, he

[1] Wks., vi. pp. 623, 648.   [2] p. 626.   [3] pp. 634, 637.

carries this criticism of his own contemporaries beyond all reasonable bounds; to every word of praise for Racine's beauties or Molière's greatness as a comic poet, he adds a paragraph of blame. 'No new thing can be good,' was his definitive literary judgment; modern Classicism was, from first to last, a corrupted following of antiquity, mawkish and artificial in its sentiments, and in its language turgid and obscure.

The extravagance of this verdict needs no comment. Corneille may not have been an Æschylus, nor Molière a second Aristophanes, but it is preposterous to do as Fénelon does, and utterly condemn them, simply because they could not reach the peculiar excellences of their models. Their critic has forgotten his own wiser saying that countries vary in their literatures just as climates vary in their fruits, that it is as vain to look in Lapland for the arts and wit of Sicily as to expect from Normandy or Flanders the grapes and figs of Languedoc.[1] And he misconceives the principle on which French Classicism was based; for Corneille and Racine claimed, not so much to imitate, as to continue, the work of their masters, to adapt old themes to modern needs: their periwigged Cæsars and Iphigenias in high-heeled shoes did not pretend to be a life-like portrait, but were Antiquity dressed up, tricked out in furbelows and flounces, till she was fit to make her curtsey before the Court of Louis XIV.

But it was just this prim decorum, this powdered academic elegance, that angered Fénelon the most. The child of a decaying civilization and prophet of its greater decadence, he longed to make away with these inveterate forms, these more than nauseous complexities, yearned, as, most of all, such men must yearn, after the depth and freshness of an earlier, more unconscious age, the vivid exactness of Homer or Horace, "the single words and phrases, the pathetic half-lines of Virgil, giving utterance, as the voice of Nature herself, to that pain and weariness, yet hope of better things, which is the experience of her children in every time."[2]

[1] p. 618.   [2] J. H. Newman, Grammar of Assent, p. 79.

But Classicism was, of all literatures, the most complex and the most professional, filled, as it seemed to him, with wearying artifice, with barren self-approving cleverness, with that hard-hearted brilliancy of wit, which is no more than half-won beauty.[1]

And, as he thought, the chill pretentiousness of Classic form reacted on the substance of the Classic poem: such glittering, unsubstantial icicles without were the sure index of a frozen grandiosity within. 'Study the Court and only know the Town,' was Boileau's rule, and Classicism had obeyed him; it chose its subjects at Versailles, and passed by with averted head the humbler realities of men and things. Here was no Homer, master of a child-like detail, no Virgil to breathe life and passion into everything, even into dying animals and trees and flowers, no rustic homeliness transfigured by emotion, no care for landscapes painted in a single graphic word. Claiming to be a world-wide literature, the School of Racine must be wholly rational and abstract; writing for all ages and according to the accumulated wisdom of the past, it might cumber itself with no detail, nothing transitory or concrete, valued Nature, the ever-changing, only as a back-ground, language as a mathematical symbol, the token of an inner thought, dared break in upon the laws of literary harmony, established for ever by an ecumenical Reason, with no fitful sally of an individual passion; its business was with human nature in its noblest, most universal manifestations, painted *en beau et en grand*.

But 'the buskin must not alter nature.'[2] Fénelon had begun to feel—what later writers have expressed more strongly—that Classicism did not fulfil this portion of its mission, but to an unrealized dream of 'universality' had made great sacrifice in vain. Its masters failed just where Shakespeare had succeeded; they had set out to paint the whole of human nature, and human nature mocked their widest canvas: in place of man as he ever was and ever

[1] Wks., vi. p. 633.   [2] p. 635.

will be, they offered only a class, a view of civilized society —Corneille, said Gœthe, has always given us great men and Racine always men of rank.[1] And to Fénelon, above all men, this continual harping on

> la majesté des rois
> Au-dessus du mépris, comme au-dessus des lois [2]

was detestable, since, with advancing years, had come increasing repugnance to all pompous exclusiveness; now, far more than in Télémaque, he placed the simple above the marvellous, the common before the surprising, Titian's green valleys watered by a limpid stream above rich parterres and fountains in a marble basin. Nay, even coarseness found some pardon, if it were only vigorous and well-expressed; Fénelon could enjoy those village-feasts of Teniers, which Louis XIV., the King of Classicism, had made haste to banish from Versailles. "Nothing on earth," "he cried, is bettered by its rarity; the beautiful thing does not lose, but gains, in beauty, when it is made accessible to the whole human race."[3]

For Fénelon, in the Letter to the Academy, has not forgotten the politics of Télémaque. Even in literature he is a philanthropist, keen to promote the greatest happiness of the greatest number, to secure 'a Sublime so simple and familiar that all may understand it.' Like the true king's, the author's mind must be a mirror of self-sacrificing duty; all the hard labour must fall to him, all the pleasure and advantage to the public. He must never dazzle, never be obscure, never seem more clever than his readers, but must take his stand upon their level, and lend them, though without their knowing it, the wit they have not got. He must remember that, like the king's, his is a high and noble mission; that orator alone is worthy of a hearing who makes his pleasures serve his thoughts, and makes his thoughts serve truth and justice; poetry is only 'more serious and

---

[1] Wilhelm Meister's Lehrjahre, bk. III. c. viii.; and see the admirably common-sense remarks on Classicism in Mr Oliver Elton's Augustan Age. c. iii.
[2] Corneille Médée, II. iii.   [3] Wks., vi. p. 628.

more useful than the vulgar think it,' when it is employed to sing the praises of virtue and religion.[1]

And, as in Télémaque ideals, impossibly high, were imposed upon the people from above, so Fénelon in literature, though not without a smile, invokes the authority of the French Academy. Its interminable dictionary was to be finished; there was to be an official Grammar and an official Rhetoric, a Treatise on the Art of Poetry, on History also, and on Tragedy and Comedy. Not that Fénelon exactly wished his brethren to claim infallibility in matters of taste, and legislate by Prætorian Edict; the Academy was to govern as he himself would have governed, to lead the public taste by flattering it, never to take two steps forward at one time, nor move at all, unless it was followed by the multitude. And perhaps even this persuasive influence would not have been ascribed to a body whose leisurely wisdom had already long been the subject of popular jest, had not Fénelon thought it the only instrument capable of accomplishing the most instructive of his desired reforms, the Project for Enriching the Tongue.

For Fénelon, of all great literary artists, was perhaps the most ungrateful to his native speech; never does his Greek and Latin prejudice stand out more clearly than in his destructive analysis of French. It was, he said, a medley of all sorts of languages, neither grand nor harmonious nor free nor varied; it did not lend itself to verse or to imaginative transports; it was fast bound within the iron rules of grammar. Everywhere the parts of speech came by in one monotonous procession—first, the subject of the sentence, leading an adjective by the hand, next, with an adverb tightly clinging to it, came the verb, and, not far behind, one beheld the accusative, labouring up to take its place.[2] And within the last hundred years, all was gone from bad to worse; men had straitened and impoverished their tongue under pretence of making it more pure. Many words were cast out and few brought in; the old nervous

[1] pp. 622, 625. [2] p. 627.

racy language of the sixteenth century was gone; syntax had banished sentiment and vividness and force.[1]

And Fénelon's remedies were as characteristic as his complaint. Verse was to be, as far as possible, abolished, inversions of order to be freely used, synonyms to be multiplied, expressions found for ideas that had none, old terms revived again, new brought from near and far, and much was hoped from a *callida junctura* of compound words. But a task so delicate was not for the people; half-conscious as he was that language is a living organism obedient only to the laws of convenience, that over its speech, at least, the people, *populum late regem*, is sovereign, Fénelon dared not entrust his reform to the caprices of the drawing-room or the market-place; towards its accomplishment the Academy must lead the way, be always ready to forestall the public, and issue its Letters of kindly Denization to each clear or sweet-sounding alien word.[2]

For Fénelon was no leveller in matters of language— Fénelon who had found Molière guilty of vulgar buffoonery in his farces and 'smelt a little of the air of Paris,' even in the aristocratic chit-chat of Versailles. His was a plea, not for greater lawlessness, but for greater beauty, an appeal on behalf of a vanishing picturesqueness, of that *vieux langage qui se fait regretter*, so bold and harmonious, so free and varied, so charged with delicate suggestiveness and passion, so necessary, also, to the perfecting of his own peculiar excellence, the 'poetry without rhyme or metre that is a living fiction painting nature,' in musical imaginative prose. It was a plea often maladroit enough—as witness his love of tortured inversions and sesquipedalian compounds—and hopeless even if well directed, in that it asked men to stem the whole current of their century, and give back to a language, daily becoming more cold and rational and abstract, the vividness and warmth of imagery it was rejoicing to have left behind. Yet the soil on which he sowed was not entirely barren; Time brought Fénelon his revenge when

---

[1] pp. 617-625, and the letter to La Motte on p. 653.   [2] p. 618.

THE LETTER TO THE ACADEMY

in his own country there arose a generation which knew not Classicism, when Lamartine and Victor Hugo restored his principles to honour and hailed the author of the Letter to the Academy as the chief poetic genius of his age.

Distinct from the rest of the Letter, and a more original departure, stands Fénelon's chapter on the art of writing History. In his conception of the study he belongs to the second, or predominantly literary, School, which intervened between the byegone annalist, lover of isolated facts and dusty disconnected dates, and our doughty modern Samsons of the Muniment Room, the heralds of that approaching Age of Documents, which is to divorce the writer from the man of research, and render History independent of historians. In Fénelon's eyes a history was a work of art, ' with something in it of the epic poem ' ; lively narration was worth more than scrupulous exactitude, clearness and order more than lively narration—in the good history, like the well-built city, each street and gate should be visible from the central square.[1]

But Fénelon was a scholar as well as an artist, and, if his first requirement be symmetry, impartiality is the next. The true historian must be of no age or country, neither a patriot nor a satirist, neither an apologist nor a flatterer ; his own opinions, feelings, personality, must be undiscoverable in his work. Morality will be there, but facts, not he, will be its teachers ; his intelligence will point out origins and disentangle mysteries, but woe betide him if he turn it to unlawful uses, if, with Polybius the theorist, he lower history into an anatomical design, or, like Tacitus, into a theatre for his own imaginative cleverness, seeing profoundest wisdom in an accident, and lending all the airs of statecraft to an irresponsible caprice.[2]

But, in this jealous limiting of the personal element, the historian fares no worse than those he writes about ; Fénelon was no believer in the courtly maxim that the world's

[1] p. 639. [2] p. 641.

history is the history of its greatest men. 'Interesting as may be the traits and sayings that shed light on the character of a single person, it is,' he says, 'a hundred times more interesting to study the progress of a nation.'[1] As one who hoped to reform the world by Institutions, the author of Télémaque would give a special eye to the circumstances of their origin and growth; as a child of his century, he could not see—and herein lies his difference from the truly modern historian—that Institutions are not everything, that they are no more than the lawful offspring of Ideas, and that the truest history is the history of these same Ideas, scattered abroad, as germinating seed, in the diffusive conscience of a people.

[1] p. 640.

FÉNELON

FROM AN ENGRAVING AFTER VIVIEN

CHAPTER XIV

BURGUNDY AND POLITICAL REFORM

Nisi Dominus ædificaverit domum, invanum laboraverunt qui ædificant eam.—
Ps. cxxvi.

IT is a thankless task to follow Fénelon back from discussions on the art of writing history to his dreary connexion with history in the making, to the elaborate schemes, worked out so carefully with Chevreuse and Beauvilliers, which were to prepare his old pupil, the Duke of Burgundy, for a kingship that never came. Begun so soon as the first blush of his Court disgrace was over, this political correspondence widened a little with every year, as Fénelon's influence gradually increased, and culminated in 1711 and 1712, during the few months that Burgundy was heir-apparent to the throne.

It was a gloomy period, overshadowed by the last and gloomiest of Louis' wars, the War of the Spanish Succession, undertaken in the hope of performing the impossible, of gaining the whole of that vast and heterogeneous empire for Louis' grandson, Burgundy's next brother, the Duke of Anjou. Against him was arrayed a Grand Alliance of all the Powers who dreaded the time when the Pyrenees might no longer be: the Empire, ready with its rival candidate, the Arch-Duke Charles, Prussia and most of the German States, together with the two great maritime enemies of France, Holland and our own country, furious with Louis for having recognised the Old Pretender as King of England, on the death of James II. (Sept. 1701).

Even if the French King's hands had been cleaner, and he had restored by a strict observance of treaties "that belief in his honour, which it was so important to reestablish," [1] the War of Succession would have been a crime, for France was exhausted by her former wars, and Spain, from the first, was utterly helpless, " a mere dead-weight, a corpse, able to do nothing for herself, and sure to crush the men who tried to lift her." [2] And Louis, at the very height of his power, borne up by a long succession of victories, could ill have endured the strain of a war, whose theatre shifted from Calabria to Ghent, from Gibraltar to the Danube, and required, in the one year 1708, no less than eight of his armies in the field.

But now, except in Spain itself, where the battles of Almanza (1707) and Villa Viciosa (1710) secured the peninsula for Philip of Anjou, the tide of fortune, under Marlborough and Prince Eugene, was flowing steadily against the French. Blenheim (1704) taught Louis that no man might call himself great or happy before his death; Ramillies (1706) lost Spain her possessions in the Netherlands, Turin (1707) the Milanese; in the next year her Neapolitan kingdom fell without a struggle, and Louis was driven to sue for peace. But peace was refused, and in 1708, the old King, girding himself up for a mighty effort, despatched the Duke of Burgundy to command the army in Flanders.

With the appearance of his old pupil in the field, Fénelon's more personal interest in the war began. He had always been anxious that the Prince should serve, and Burgundy had already gone through the insignificant campaigns of 1702 and 1703 with some small credit to his name and great advantage to his character. But between 1703 and 1708 matters had altered immeasurably for the worse; then France still could boast that for more than half a century she had not known what it was to be defeated; now her forces were utterly demoralized, and the army of Flanders worst of all. There, says St Simon, there was, at best, no question of victories, only of orderly retirement to the frontier; the troops were ill-

[1] Fén. Wks., vii. p. 150.   [2] *Ibid.* p. 149.

paid, ill-provisioned, ill-equipped; disasters without end had taught them to believe in the incapacity of their generals as a matter of course, so that they never troubled to make a stand, but looked on themselves as vanquished before an engagement began.[1]

Yet Burgundy had a worse misfortune than the weakness of his army; often as Louis XIV. blundered in his choice of men, he never made a more fatal error than when he named the Duke of Vendôme Chief of the Staff and virtual leader of his grandson. Beside these two fire and water were congenial elements; the Prince had grown up mild and devout, over-scrupulous, almost ascetic, in his ideas of military discipline; the General was one of the most profligate cynics in the kingdom, and allowed his men all the license that he took himself. Burgundy was timid and irresolute, a man of books and many precautions, well grounded in the theory of warfare, but lacking in resourcefulness and presence of mind; Vendôme was a great winner of victories and the idol of the common soldier, brave with the light-hearted courage that never has and never will be beaten, but reckless and indolent, with no settled plans, no care for detail, believing all he wished to believe, and treating the whole art of war in the spirit of a gambler, ready to sacrifice everything to a whim, and treating the enemy's hand of trumps as a personal insult to himself.[2]

Between these two there could be nothing but discord, 'deliberations more like a tumult than a sober Council of War,' perpetual bandying to and fro of the supreme responsibility, first to Vendôme, hampered by Burgundy and his staff of mediocrities, next to the Prince, checked, in his turn, by Vendôme's laziness and jealousy of his rivals. Divided counsels lost them the great battle of Oudenarde (11th July), kept them inactive while the enemy invested Lille (12th August), and, once invested, thwarted all serious effort

[1] v. p. 439.
[2] See Fénelon's excellent and very fair analysis of Vendôme's character. Wks., vii. pp. 273, 275, etc.

to relieve it. When Burgundy, at the end of November, was recalled to Versailles, the town of Lille had already fallen; after a few more weeks of heroic defence, the citadel also surrendered, and the great barrier fortress between Paris and the Netherlands was wholly in the hands of the enemy. Vendôme would have been for ever disgraced, had not his friends thrown the greater blame on Burgundy; "as for our Little Prince," cried Fénelon, "his reputation has been damaged incalculably; not a soul has a word in his favour." And Saint Simon, though an admirer of Burgundy, is more luridly dramatic; "it was thought disgraceful not to load the Prince's name with abuse, even within the precincts of the royal Palace."[1]

Against this universal verdict there is no appeal. The villain may be reinstated—not so the scapegoat; for him there is no hope, save in the reader's prerogative of mercy. And few are more deserving of his mercy than this unhappy young strategist of twenty-five, expected, though without great military aptitudes, to withstand, in Marlborough and Eugene, as powerful a combination of genius as is known to military history, knowing that he had been sent to the front to keep in check the recklessness of Vendôme and to repress the license of his soldiery, yet well aware that he had scarce a friend in the army, that all, from Vendôme down, hated and despised him for his strait-laced morals, that his carefulness was sneered at as a love of detail, and his most necessary precautions as an ill-placed fear, that absurd and impossible schemes were deliberately prepared for his rejection, in order that it might be told in every market-place and tap-room in the country how the experienced and capable General was being thwarted by an ignorant and cowardly young Prince, on whose youthful shoulders head-long impetuosity and desire for glory would more fittingly

---

[1] St Simon, vi. p. 90. It is fair, however, to add that Mme. de Maintenon's letters, written during this autumn, by no means bear too heavily on Burgundy, although the Prince was far from being one of her favourites. See Geffroy, ii. pp. 177, and *ff.*, esp. p. 200.

have sat[1] . . . The excuses for Burgundy are neither few nor trifling; the pity is that they do not cover all.

For they leave unanswered the grave indictment of weakness of character brought against Burgundy by Fénelon in the letters written to him at the seat of war. There, with an almost cruel faithfulness, leavened, however, by infinite tact, by many reminders of the usefulness of humiliations to spiritual health, of criticism to a Prince who would win the love and affection of his subjects, Fénelon set down, not as coming from himself, but 'simply in the manner of a historian,' the principal charges generally brought against his pupil. First, his incapacity as a commander, his alternate feeble defiance and still feebler trucklings to Vendôme, his irresolute precautions and unstable resolves, his wish never to fight except with a full certitude of victory, his preference of his own unworthy familiars, men whose personal courage, even, was doubted, over the counsel and companionship of the most distinguished officers. Nay, Fénelon was afraid after Oudenarde, that he would be led into following the advice of these creatures, not out of poltroonery so much as weakness, and remove his precious person from the army, 'as though a field of battle were a pic-nic, to be deserted at the first sound of danger.'[2]

And in the army he had made himself neither popular nor respected, was seldom seen on horseback, did not know his officers by sight, but shut himself up in his tent to read and pray, wasted his time on little childish amusements, even talked too freely over his wine. And, worst of all, he degraded religion in the eyes of the Libertines by his narrow and timorous devotions, scrupled to spend a night in the guest-house of a convent, and would not risk a battle, lest he should send many souls post-haste to Hell. "Your piety," wrote Fénelon in despair, "tries to govern an army like a nunnery, and wears itself out on little trifling details, while it neglects everything that is essential to your honour and to the glory of the arms of France."[3]

[1] See St Simon, v. pp. 440 and *ff*. [2] Wks., vii. p. 267. [3] p. 282.

It is possible that this exceeding bitterness was inspired by a pang of self-reproach. " I hear that you feel annoyance at the education which I gave you," he says in one of his letters ; and certainly more than once the pupil's scruples are a distorted reproduction of the master's teaching. Sometimes the scruple was not even distorted ; it was unjust in Fénelon to reproach the Prince with unwillingness to defend his grandfather's conquests, for fear they should have been unjustly gained, when he himself had 'trembled for the King's salvation,' on account of the number of places taken in his former wars, and held the surrender of some of them at Ryswick the finest act in Louis' life.[1]

Nor can Fénelon well have ignored how often popular outcry coupled his own with his pupil's name; the modern critics, who make Fénelon and Burgundy the text of their sermon on the evils of a too religious education, were forestalled by the soldiers, who cried out " Télémaque ! " as their commander passed by, or by the gutter poets who flooded Paris with such rhymes as these—

> Acknowledge your pupil, my lord of Cambrai
> When Lille is blockaded, he's far from the fray,
>   In action takes never a part.
> His face is so doleful, his mien is so sad,
> That—answer me—is not the sanctified lad
>   A Quietist after your heart ?

Yet this charge of excessive religiosity has often been indiscriminately and unfairly pressed. Burgundy was no follower of M$^{me.}$ Guyon, nor was his back 'brave with the needle-work of noodledom'; his was a religion all terrors and scruples and sick-room austerities, the melancholia of a miniature Pascal. He had never outgrown the nervous disorders of his childhood ; the old passionate irascibility was still alive, though generally bridled by a strong output of his will, at times even, converted into a calmness, wholly unnatural and apathetic, as witness the patience—less

[1] p. 158.

worthy of St Louis than of some Robert the Saint or tonsured Merovingian—with which he bore Vendôme's gross and utterly unwarranted aspersions on his personal courage.[1] He was still moody and peevish, tactless and undignified, would sit and dream for hours in a corner of M$^{me.}$ de Maintenon's drawing-room, till the world treated him like a sulky child, or as if he were some poor harmless crazy being, to whom no one need trouble to show respect.[2] But to this universal dislike and contempt he was perfectly indifferent, shut himself up in his study, happy among his books and Government reports, though even there he reasoned too much and did too little, had not the patience to get to the heart of a difficult matter, but gambled away his time and energy on 'vague speculations and sterile resolves.'[3]

Nevertheless, as Fénelon well knew, under this outer crust of 'shocking defects' lay the elements of a truly noble character, an unfailing sense of duty, a powerful intellect, though of a kind better suited to a man of letters than a man of affairs, together with that truly God-given moral instinct, which turns always towards the Good and the True. It was Fénelon's great merit to have discovered these higher possibilities in Burgundy, as it was his misfortune to find no better remedy for his weakness than that of forcing strength of character on him from without. *Ce qui lui faut*, he wrote, *c'est du nerf dans l'esprit, et une autorité efficace.*[4]

But this wished-for authority was not to follow and assist Nature, conformably to the wise precept of the Education of Girls; rather was it conceived of on a false analogy drawn from the Maxims of the Saints. Criticism, represented by a watchful Triumvirate, of which Chevreuse and Beauvilliers were the working members, but Fénelon himself the movement and the life, was to do for Burgundy what the mystical process did for the soul; as the Saint, by shaking off the bonds of the creature, rose naturally and

---

[1] St Simon, vi. p. 57, and see Henri Martin, xiv. p. 499.
[2] Fén. Wks., vii. p. 237.   [3] *Ibid.* p. 332.   [4] *Ibid.* p. 371.

inevitably to God, so Fénelon hoped that Burgundy would attain in a moment to free and vigorous manhood, once others had purged him of his childish indolence and passion. Never for a moment did he see that his means and his end were in flagrant contradiction, that manly independence of thought and will is something more than mere absence of childishness, more than the mushroom offspring of a night; he plied his two lieutenants with orders to 'enlarge, sustain, redress,' the Prince's mind and ' take it in turns to tell him the truth,' pressing into his service the Duchess of Burgundy (a charming and devoted wife, though more of a Eucharis than an Antiope), even $M^{me.}$ de Maintenon and the King.[1] From this benevolent Inquisition no act of Burgundy's life was safe; though fast approaching his thirtieth year, his studies, amusements, opinions were all minutely controlled; a whole army of precautions surrounded his first reading of Pascal, to keep him clear from the taint of Jansenism; nor did Fénelon scruple to interfere in matters yet more personal, and regulate his behaviour to his wife.[2] Well might $M^{me.}$ de Maintenon declare that, if the Duke of Burgundy had his defects, it was not for lack of honest counsellors!

And for a time it seemed as though these labours would have their reward. In April, 1711, God, "often most merciful when He seems to strike most cruelly," took away the wretched Dauphin at a sudden blow, and left Burgundy heir-apparent to the Crown. The change of outward dignity was great, but the inner, personal, change was greater; with the death of the father disappeared the most blighting influence on the life of the son. For the Dauphin, utterly vacuous and insignificant in himself, had been the friend of Vendôme and all the most profligate nobles at the Court, the rallying point of the frivolous, of all who sneered at Burgundy for his tactless virtue, or dreaded the conscientious zeal of a Prince, for whom no sweeping reform was too drastic, no petty ecclesiastical detail too small, who was

[1] pp. 239, 310, 335, etc. [2] pp. 243, 335, 362, etc.

BURGUNDY AND POLITICAL REFORM 289

pledged at once to redress the miseries of the common people and to force on the Court a stricter observance of Lent. The Dauphin alive, it was easy to scoff; the Dauphin dead and the King over seventy, the world made haste to humble itself before its coming master. Louis himself caught something of the general feeling, and, although the most jealous of autocrats, and hitherto most intolerant of the thought of a successor, broke through all the traditions of his reign, and admitted his grandson to a share in the royal authority.[1]

In the glories of their master Beauvilliers and Chevreuse shared to the full, but the greatest change of all was in the position of Fénelon. The late Dauphin had hated him almost more than he hated Beauvilliers; the new Dauphin begged for his recall from exile as the one supreme favour, beside which all others were as nothing.[2] The prayer was not granted, though Louis showed some signs of relenting, and all those courtiers who had not yet made their advances became busy with letters and visits to Cambrai, ' scattering a few grains of seed in the future.' Fénelon's Palace was besieged by every officer of distinction on his way to or from the Front, till it seemed more like the residence of a Governor of Flanders; and already there was joy at Rome, and consternation in the Jansenist camp, at the thought that the great Ultramontane might soon be sitting in the seat of Richelieu, as Cardinal Prime Minister of France.[3]

And, on Fénelon's own side, neither ambition nor philanthropy was allowed to sleep. Now, more eagerly than ever, he watched such ' scraps of government ' as came before him in his frontier-diocese, and posted Reports on the state of the country to Father Le Tellier and Chevreuse, some parts of which, after careful selection, were laid before the King himself.

[1] St Simon, viii. pp. 431, 434.   [2] Fén. Wks., vii. p. 702.
[3] See the letter from Roslet, de Noailles' agent in Rome, quoted in Le Roy, p. 410, *note*.

His letters all centre round the War and its appalling evils. 'It is intolerable,' he cried, 'that a struggle, entered upon only for a point of honour, should be still continued, when it brings us nothing but disgrace. We have no money, no soldiers, no commanders; only a miracle keeps us alive; France is like an old rusty machine, that still spins round from the impetus given it long ago, but will break in pieces at the first collision. It is not for us to talk of national pride or honourable conditions of surrender; we must lower our heads and sue for peace, for the whole Kingdom is one great beleaguered city—all of us are prisoners of war—we are at our Caudine Forks.'

Fénelon's words are strong, but they are borne out by his own experience. He had been forced to turn his Palace and Seminary into a hospital, for the wounded were crying in vain for food and medicines and care; year after year he had thrown open his granaries to the starving, for 'men would not fight, unless they were fed, and, sooner than die, they had taken to pillage, till the country folk dreaded them more than the enemy.' Only a timely advance from his own archiepiscopal revenues had saved the garrison of St Omer from going over in a body to the enemy, as other regiments had done; 'everywhere there was mutiny, everywhere streams of deserters, the best fortified places tumbled like a pack of cards.'

But, even more than for the soldiers, Fénelon's heart bled for their innocent victims, the peasantry who could no longer 'live like men.' The Arctic winter of 1708 had killed their cattle and their fruit-trees; their horses were seized and worn to death in the Government service; one harvest after another had failed, completely; the little that was left them was taken by the troops. And worse than the marauders were the Government officials, able to keep pace with the King's demands only by cheating and cozening on every side; they were no longer men of authority, but 'a band of Gipsy pilferers, the heralds of a universal bankruptcy.' Yet the King and his Ministers shut their eyes, and kept on taking, careless whether anything was left to take or no ; Louis abandoned none of his superfluous expenses, but ruined the country without consulting it, in order badly to carry on a useless war.¹

For Fénelon laid the whole blame on Louis' shoulders, laid it with a passion which was not all philanthropy, with a merciless vindictiveness which shows that in him the disappointed courtier was not wholly dead, nor satisfied to wreak his vengeance only on de Noailles. All of his charges have their truth, yet more than one of them is cruel and unreasonable, at a time when Louis' courageous firmness under disaster was winning the praises even of St Simon, and "rightly earning for him that title of ' The Great,' which flatterers had bestowed so prematurely."² The critic at Cambrai was less pitiful ; we hear no more of Arc Louis of the Letter to the King, a Prince of just and noble temper, corrupted by an evil education, no more of the Idomeneus of Télémaque, generous, wrong-headed, and repentant ; in the private correspondence with Chevreuse the King is drawn without disguise, a miserable, selfish, obstinate, old man.

His tyranny, once the most prompt and efficacious of governments, was become the weakest and the most behind-hand, busily occupied in doing to-day what should have been done two years ago, and hopeful of accomplishing two years hence the work that should have been begun to-day. Yet, as the sick man shrinks from the violent remedies that are his only cure, so Louis' pride would hear of no reform ; even now this formalist, to whom religion meant an anthem or a chaplet or the harrying of the Jansenists, dared think himself a holy King, tried by adversity like righteous Job, or punished like David for the sins of his youth. Even now, he did not see that peace was only the first necessity, that behind lay the need of finding bread for a starving people, of setting bounds to

¹ See pp. 159, 160, 321, etc.
² St Simon, xii. p. 152. On Louis' retrenchments, see Geffroy, ii. p. 208.

the luxury that had eaten away the heart of the nation, to the tyranny that was the cause of all its ills.[1]

And so from the selfishness of the grandfather Fénelon appealed to the conscience of the grandson, drew up with Chevreuse his Tables of Chaulnes, or plans of Government reform, and, for Burgundy's own use, a breviary of royal virtue, the Questions for Self-examination on a Sovereign's Duties—two writings meant to actualise the 'great and holy maxim,' often on the Prince's lips, that Kings exist for the sake of their people, not peoples for the sake of Kings.[2]

Yet Fénelon is not seen at his best in these excursions into practical reform. A would-be reconciliation of facts and fancies, they halt irresolute between the two, lacking alike the bold unhesitating sweep of Télémaque and the fiery energy of the Letter to the King. They are a reminder to the political idealist that *le contact de la réalité souille toujours un peu*, a warning that, if he once desert Utopia for the Statute-book, the glory of his inspirations will vanish, the glamour of his dreams will fade, before the hard dry light of day.

Not that their author was always in the clouds; there are times when he rises to a really high degree of statesmanship. Thus Burgundy, although in law and fact an autocrat, was not to stand aside in lofty isolation, the Solon or Lycurgus of a new Salentum, but must associate his people with him in the Government, and call back from the limbo, to which his selfish ancestors had banished them, the Representative Assemblies which, in times past, had often bent the Sovereign to the national will.[3] Local Councils, Provincial Estates, States General, could all return, though only with a consultative voice; and Fénelon in his special advocacy of the smaller bodies, is one of the first to utter that cry for decentralization of the Executive, which, ever since, has been loud in the mouths of French reformers.[4]

---

[1] Fén. Wks., vii. pp. 323 and *ff*.   [2] See St Simon, ix. p. 225.
[3] Fén. Wks., vii. p. 90. The States General had not sat since 1614, and were not convoked again till 1789.   [4] p. 183. See Broglie, pp. 322 and *ff*.

Yet if many of Fénelon's projects show the hand of the generous and large-minded reformer, whose sleepless humanity had noted the horrors of the press-gang, and felt for the deserter and the galley-slave, there are also traces, not a few, of the moonlight economics of Salentum. In time of peace the King must live of his own, and, if he went to war on some point of purely dynastic importance, he must pay for the luxury out of his private revenues, together with such subsidies as his people might vote him 'out of pure affection.'[1] Inasmuch, too, as the profession of Informer was detestable, yet some kind of Secret Service a necessity, Burgundy would choose his spies among the most honourable gentlemen in the kingdom, sure that the duty would be best performed by those who found it odious and repugnant.[2]

And Fénelon falls into other errors more unpardonable. The recall of the Huguenots, timidly proposed by Chevreuse, meets with no response from the master, but much is said of plans for the extermination of the Jansenists.[3] Or he stood aghast at that breaking up of the feudal organization of Society, which had been the chief merit of Louis' reign, and resented, almost in the spirit of St Simon, the royal policy of humbling the greatest nobles of France before a mob of middle-class Ministers, of kneading every rank and every station into one *vil peuple en toute égalité*.[4] Colberts and Louvois' he would utterly abolish—the King must be his own Prime Minister, aided only by his Councils of State; the aristocracy must lay aside their vexatious privileges and their idleness, and take their rightful place at the head of the nation. Commerce and the Bar might be thrown open to them, but there must be no mingling with the people; now, more than ever, the doors of the Peerage must be closely guarded, and *mésalliances* in either sex be checked.[5] . . . Alas! it was not for Fénelon to see that many a Pisgah is beset with mirage, that often the gorgeous vision of the

---

[1] p. 89. [2] p. 97. [3] p. 184.
[4] St Simon xii. p. 54. [5] Fén. Wks., vii. pp. 187, 188.

Future is no more than the dressed-up phantom of the Past.

Nor had Burgundy the practical wisdom or breadth of mind necessary to correct the errors in his master's perspective. Excellently as he could discourse on the "understanding of the human heart as the best way of bringing men to justice,"[1] real knowledge of men was not to be looked for in a Prince, of whom his Jesuit Confessor proudly records that he was not content to possess the mere substance of modesty, but must make public profession of his virtue by a demeanour that put to the blush the most irreproachable ladies.[2] And it was in vain that Fénelon had warned him against trusting entirely to any one man.[3] Although in fourteen years they had only met twice, the spell of the master's fascination was as strong as ever; Burgundy would often bid his wife choose between three courses of action, "the good, the better, and the perfect way, which last would assuredly be M. de Cambrai's."[4]

None the less, it may be doubted whether the living Télémaque ever really understood his mentor. Little as he spared the King in private, Fénelon always respected the claims of outward decorum, but Burgundy once caused a grave court-scandal by blurting out that France's present miseries were the heaven-sent punishment of her past transgressions. And it was in vain his master told him that toleration for others is an excellent virtue, which sometimes departs from the letter of a rule, that it may keep more closely to its spirit.[5] The Prince's virtue hardened into an almost Jansenist austerity, refused to go in State to the theatre, 'because the best theatre for a Dauphin's energy was the improvement of the provinces,' and threatened to burst on the Court with headlong reforms, which, as Fénelon said, the greatest prudence and precaution could scarcely have effected.[6]

---

[1] See Proyart's Life of Burgundy, ii. p. 232. [2] *Ibid.* p. 207.
[3] Wks., vii. p. 86. [4] Proyart, ii. p. 140.
[5] See Bausset, iv. p. 97. [6] Wks., vii. p. 343. See Geffroy, ii. p. 190.

And, if the Prince had succeeded his grandfather, it is to be feared that this pragmatical righteousness would have worked mischief on wider fields than Versailles, that the wine of Télémaque would have been let evaporate, while its lees were distilled into careful statute, that the conclusion of the whole matter would have been monkish austerity on the throne, surrounded by a governing aristocracy, a violent revival of the days of St Louis, to confront the dawning age of Voltaire.[1] Often enough it has been asked whether Burgundy and his master might not have saved the crown of the Bourbons, but all our finger-posts point to one answer: Télémaque excepted, Fénelon's best political service to his country was his devotion to her wounded, starving soldiers, and Burgundy, hailed before his death as *omnium consensu capax imperii*—was more fortunate than Galba.

[1] See Henri Martin, xiv. pp. 557 and *ff*.

CHAPTER XV

THE END

A tout prendre, c'était un bel esprit et un grand homme.—St Simon.

PROVIDENCE had other destinies for France than the rule of a Prince 'already ripe for a blessed Eternity.'[1] In February, 1712, Burgundy died, carried away by a sudden epidemic, together with his wife and eldest son, before he had enjoyed the Dauphinate a year. And with him fell all Fénelon's worldly interests and aspirations of reform. "God's wrath with us," he cried, "is not yet stayed; He has destroyed all our hopes for Church and and State. He formed this young Prince; He prepared him for great things, He showed him to the world, only at once to take him away. I am overcome with horror, and sick to death without an illness; all my links are broken; there is nothing left to bind me to the earth."[2]

For one moment, indeed, the flame of philanthropic energy flickered up, to urge the immediate formation of a Council of Regency, in preparation for the time when the old King must die, and his Crown pass to Burgundy's surviving son, the child of five, who, three years afterwards, became King Louis XV. For Fénelon had foreseen a danger worse than the War or Jansenist plots or national insolvency; unless Louis, during his lifetime, would bring such a strong Council into working order, a Regency of autocratic powers would fall, at his death, to the Duke of Orleans, a battered dissolute cynic and fouler copy of our Charles II., on whom the popular hatred fastened

[1] St Simon, ix. p. 227.   [2] Wks., vii. p. 374.

every kind of crime, from incest to the poisoning of Burgundy.¹

The scheme was bold, its execution was impossible; for, even if Louis had been capable of persuasion, none of the old Court agents were left to persuade him. Father Le Tellier could think of nothing but the *Unigenitus* and the Jansenists, while from Beauvilliers and Chevreuse, since Burgundy's death, all life and vigour had departed : "the very joints of their soul were loosed." So Fénelon allowed himself to be disarmed by the princely sceptic's sudden interest in Christianity, and entered into a correspondence with him on the first principles of religion, in the hope, if not of effecting his conversion, at least of securing his future aid against the Jansenists.²

And there were lesser signs in plenty to warn Fénelon that his race of worldly ambitions was fully run. He had arranged to marry his favourite nephew, Gabriel, to a young lady of position, but her father, on Burgundy's death, broke off the match—" for which," wrote the courtier-prelate, " I cannot blame him; to do so would be to announce myself a misanthrope. All we can do in this world is to avoid such pitfalls ourselves, and not condemn too sharply the shortcomings of our neighbour."³

Nevertheless, although the plan of marriage failed, Gabriel soon fettered his uncle's attention on himself in a more painful, but not less salutary, fashion; Fénelon almost forgot his grief for Burgundy when a wound, received by the young officer at the engagement of Landrécies in the previous year, broke out afresh into a dangerous malady. Every comfort that love could devise, or money buy, was placed at the invalid's service; he was lodged at Cambrai in the 'little grey room,' that opened out of the Archbishop's own, and to him were addressed, during the two years of his slow and wearisome recovery, some of the tenderest and

¹ Wks., vii. pp. 189-193.
² This is the probable meaning of the mysterious passage in St Simon, x. p. 287. ³ Wks., viii. p. 53.

most beautiful letters that ever came from Fénelon's pen. Here is no more of those counsels of Polonius, which jar a little in their earlier correspondence: half-jestingly as he might write, as "having to get rid of somehow the stuff left over from my Lenten sermons," Fénelon treats only of the highest themes, the mystery of pain, its value as an explanation of the deepest problems of existence, the sufferer's need of borrowing, not from a heaped-up store of human courage, but from that heaven-sent gift of patience, which is lent only for the day. And through the mystical jargon that still remained with him, as a scar to remind us of his byegone conflicts over the Maxims of the Saints, pierces the deepest and most spiritual affection—" I love you," he wrote, "for yourself, and not for my amusement, with a love that now you cannot understand, though some day God will make it clear to you. I love you for His sake, and not for mine, even as I would have myself all in all to you through Him."[1]

And of Fénelon's last three years in general Ste Beuve's gracious comparison is true; they are like the close of a genial winter, big with promise of a coming Spring. Not for him, was old age the state at which he had so often shuddered in the Past, as a time when reason grows dim and virtue lax, when humours and disquietude gain all the strength the mind has lost, till they become our only sign of life.[2] Fénelon's grey hairs were no burden, but a glory; as he drew rapidly nearer the tomb, the earthlier parts of his nature crumble away—

> The soul's dark cottage, battered and decayed,
> Lets in new lights through chinks which Time hath made.

His life, indeed, still ran its ordinary course. Though now little more than 'a skeleton that walked and talked,' he had still many episcopal duties to perform; the Peace of Utrecht brought no peace to him, who had more than six

---

[1] Wks., vii. pp. 458, etc.   [2] 108th Sp. Let. Wks., viii. p. 532.

THE END

hundred parishes to visit. And there were new nephews and grand nephews to entertain—the *follet bambin* of Beaumont's sister, Mme de Chevry, who "ate and played and laughed and chattered all the livelong day," or Chevreuse's little grandson, the Comte de Montfort, "on whom, had I been younger, I should have had great designs," who rose to be Cardinal and Archbishop of Sens, and, dying just before the outbreak of the Revolution, brings down the Fénelon tradition within a generation of living memory.

But already Fénelon was gathering up his robes, as though impatient to be gone. All good friends, he told Destouches, some little time after the death of Chevreuse (November 1712), should make up their minds to die together, or, better still, like Philemon and Baucis, one should become an oak, when he sees the other changing into a poplar.[1] And when Beauvilliers, some months later (August 1714), followed Chevreuse to the grave, Fénelon felt that his own time was nearly come. "We shall soon find again him whom we have lost," he wrote to the widowed Duchess; we come a long step nearer to him every day. It is only the imagination and the senses that miss their object; he whom we can no longer see, is closer to us than before; we meet him continually in our common centre, God. As for me, who was deprived of seeing him for so many years, I talk to him, I open my heart to him, I seem to find him in God, and, although I wept bitterly at the news of his death, I cannot feel that I have lost him."[2]

The prophecy was not long in being fulfilled. In November 1714, Fénelon was returning from a visitation in the country, when one of his horses shied at a wind-mill, and almost overturned the carriage. At first it seemed as though he would recover from the shock, but in the evening of New Year's Day, 1715, he was attacked by "a sharp fever of unknown origin," whose fatal nature soon became

---

[1] Wks., viii. p. 195.   [2] *Ibid.* vii. p. 390.

apparent. During the next few days, says his secretary,[1] the Bible was read to him continually, and, at his special request, the end of the fourth, and the beginning of the fifth chapter of the Second Epistle to the Corinthians were several times repeated. On the morning of the 6th of January he dictated a letter to Father Le Tellier, wherein, speaking as one who had received Extreme Unction, and was about to appear before the Judgment Seat, he declared that he had nothing but horror for the religious novelties imputed to him, and had received the condemnation of his Maxims with the most absolute submission. Further he protested his gratitude and attachment to the King, of whom he asked two graces, though neither for himself nor for his family—the first, that he would appoint to Cambrai a prelate good and pious and firm against Jansenism; the second, that he would allow the Cambrai Seminary to be entrusted to Sulpician Fathers.[2]

During the rest of that day and night, continues the secretary, his agony was terrible, and we recited to him the passages from Scripture that show how the sufferings of this present time are not worthy to be compared with the glory that shall be revealed in us. In the evening M. l'Abbé de Fénelon, M. de Beaumont, M. le Marquis de Fénelon and others, came to receive his blessing, together with his servants and a few of his friends in the town. M. l'Abbé Le Vayer, Superior of the Seminary, received the blessing for the Seminary and diocese, and then began to read the prayers appointed for souls in their last agony, adding some sentences of Scripture appropriate to his condition. Soon after five o'clock in the morning of the 7th January, after remaining about half an hour without any sign of life, he fell peacefully asleep.

Thus Fénelon died, and was buried in his Cathedral, and on his tomb was graved the legend: Non mutus cinis spirat adhuc splendetque, præsulibus perpetuum decus, in-

[1] Bausset, iv. pp. 431 and *ff.* [2] Wks., viii. p. 283.

taminatus Christi discipulus, forma factus gregis. There let us leave him, choosing for our own last tribute the words he once wrote of Charlemagne, that if among such splendid talents and virtues some weaknesses are mingled, these may serve to remind us that we are dealing, not with the vague, impossibly perfect hero of a story, but with the chequered courses of a living man.

FINIS.

A CHRONOLOGICAL TABLE OF THE PRINCIPAL EVENTS OF FÉNELON'S LIFE, VIEWED IN RELATION TO THE GENERAL HISTORY OF FRANCE

Political History.	Fénelon's Life.	Church.	Literature.
Ministry of Mazarin. The Fronde (1648-1653). Coalition of France and Cromwell against Spain (1654-1658). Peace of the Pyrenees (1659). Louis marries (1660). Mazarin dies (1661).	1651-1663. Fénelon lives with his parents at Fénelon.	Spread of Jansenism. Pascal's Provincial Letters, 1656. Bossuet begins preaching in Paris, 1659, and becomes famous immediately.	Last plays of Corneille. Moliere's plays, 1659-1673. Racine, 1663-1677. Boileau's Epistles begun, 1669. La Fontaine's Fables published, 1668, 1678. M$^{me.}$ de Sévigné's Letters. La Rochefoucauld's Maxims, 1665.
Administration of Colbert. War of Devolutions breaks out (1667). Peace of Aix-la Chapelle (1668). The Dutch War (1672), ending with the Peace of Nymwegen (1678).	1663-1666. Fénelon at Cahors University. 1666-1668. At the Collége du Plessy. 1668-1678. At Saint Sulpice.	First period of Jansenist controversy ends with Peace of Clement IX. (1669). Bourdaloue begins preaching. Bossuet Preceptor to Dauphin (1670-1679). He writes the Discourse on Universal History.	Pascal's *Pensées*, (published in a very inaccurate form), 1670 Malebranche's *Recherche de la Vérité*, 1674. [Spinoza's *Ethics* were published just after his death in 1677.]
France seizes Strasburg (1681). Death of the Queen and of Colbert (1683). Louis marries M$^{me.}$ de Mainten^{on} (1684).	1678-1689. Superior of the New Catholics. Fénelon makes acquaintance with the Beauvilliers and Chevreuses. He writes the	Bossuet made Bishop of Meaux (1681). Drafts Four Articles of Gallicanism at Assembly of Clergy, 1682.	Malebranche's *Treatise on Nature and Grace*, 1680. Malebranche's *Meditations* (1683).

303

FRANCOIS DE FENELON

Political History.	Fénelon's Life.	Church.	Literature.
Revocation of the Edict of Nantes (1685).	** *Refutation of Malebranche*, the *Education of Girls*, and part of the * *Treatise on the Existence of God*, also preaches the *Epiphany Sermon* (1685) and writes the ** *Dialogues on Eloquence*.		
Formation of the League of Augsburg (1686). English Revolution (1688).	Missionary in Saintonge (1685-1687). Makes acquaintance with M$^{me.}$ de Maintenon and M$^{me.}$ Guyon.	Condemnation at Rome of Molinos, 1687.	La Bruyère's *Caractères*, 1688.
Outbreak of War of League of Augsburg captained by William of Orange. Revolt of the Cevennes (1689). Battle of the Boyne (1690). English naval victory of La Hogue; French victory of Steinkerk and capture of Namur (1692). French victory of Landau (1693). Recapture of Namur by William III. (1695). Peace of Ryswick (1697).	**1689-1695. Preceptor to the Duke of Burgundy.** Fénelon writes the * *Fables*, the * *Dialogues of the Dead*, and begins *Télémaque*. 1693. He writes the ** *Letter to the King*. 1694. The Commission of Issy. **1695-1715. Archbishop of Cambrai.** Finishes the * *Dialogues* and *Télémaque*. Publication of the *Maxims of the Saints*. Fénelon is banished to his diocese (1697). 1699. The *Maxims* condemned by the Pope. Publication of *Télémaque*.	Gradual recrudescence of the Jansenist controversy. It becomes acute in 1702.	Racine's *Esther*, 1689. Racine's *Athalie*, 1691. Voltaire born, 1694. Bayle's Dictionary published (1697).

CHRONOLOGICAL TABLE 305

Political History.	Fénelon's Life.	Church.	Literature.
Beginning of the War of the Spanish Succession (1701).	From 1701 till the end of his life Fénelon writes incessantly against Jansenism. He also writes various political papers for Chevreuse.		
Battle of Blenheim (1704). Ramillies (1706). Burgundy takes the field; Oudenarde (1708). Malplaquet (1709).		Death of Bossuet (1704).	
	Fénelon writes the ** *Treatise on the Authority of the Sovereign Pontiff* (1710).	Le Tellier succeeds Père La Chaise (1709) and brings about the final destruction of Port Royal (1711).	
Death of the Dauphin (1711); Burgundy succeeds to the title.	Fénelon writes the ** *Questions for Self-Examination on the Duties of a King*, and draws up with Chevreuse the ** *Plans of Government*.		
Death of Burgundy (1712); French victory of Denain.	Publication of the * *Treatise on the Existence of God* (1712).		Jean Jacques Rousseau born (1712).
Peace of Utrecht (1713).	Fénelon writes the ** *Letters on Religion* to the Duke of Orleans (1713). Fénelon writes the ** *Letter to the Academy* (1714). Fénelon dies (1715).	The Bull *Unigenitus* issued (1713).	

NOTE.—A single asterisk distinguishes those of Fénelon's writings which were only incompletely published in his lifetime; a double asterisk those which were not printed till after his death.

A LIST OF THE MORE IMPORTANT BOOKS DEALING WITH FÉNELON.

Except where otherwise mentioned, all references to his writings are made to the enlarged reprint of the Versailles Edition of his Works, published by Leroux, 1851, 1852. Similarly all references to Bossuet are made to the Besançon Edition of 1840, and all references to St Simon to the edition produced by Chéruel and Regnier in 1873.

BIOGRAPHIES.

Cardinal Bausset, Histoire de Fénelon, revue et augmentée par l'Abbé Gosselin, 1850.
Emmanuel de Broglie, Fénelon à Cambrai, 1884. (See the review by Brunetière in his Histoire et Littérature, vol. ii.)
Paul Janet, Fénelon (in Grands Écrivains series), 1892.
Crouslé, Fénelon et Bossuet, 1894. (Reviewed by Mahrenholtz in *Romanische Forschungen* for October, 1896.)
Mahrenholtz, Fénelon, Erzbischof von Cambrai, Leipzic, 1896.
See also article on Fénelon in Faguet's Dix-septième Siècle, and the articles by Brunetière on Fénelon and Bossuet in the Grande Encyclopédie Lamirault.
Proyart, Vie du Dauphin, Père de Louis XV., 1819.
Geffroy, Mme. de Maintenon, d'après sa véritable correspondance, 1887.
Lanson, Bossuet, 1894.
Rebelliau, Bossuet, 1900.
Haussonville, Articles in the *Revue des Deux Mondes* for February, April, June, 1897.

WORKS.

Histoire Littéraire de Fénelon, by the Abbé Gosselin. It is prefixed to most editions of his Works, but also separately published.

Toleration.

Essay by Bishop Boulogne of Troyes, reprinted in Fénelon's Works, vol. x.
Douen, L'Intolérance de Fénelon. The second edition (of 1875) is alone valuable.

Education.

Rousselot, Histoire de l'Éducation des Femmes en France, 1883.
Von Sallwürk, Fénelon und die weibliche Bildung in Frankreich, Langensalza, 1886.
Gréard, edition of Fénelon's Éducation des Filles, 1890.

Mysticism.

Inge, Christian Mysticism, 1899.
Bigg, Christian Platonists of Alexandria, 1885.

LIST OF MORE IMPORTANT BOOKS

Rousselot, Les Mystiques Espagnols, 1869.
Strowski, Saint François de Sales, 1898.
Tissot, La Vie Intérieure, 1894.
Joly, La Psychologie des Saints, 1898.

Heppe, Geschichte der quietistischen Mystik, Berlin, 1875.
Scharling, Molinos (tr. from Danish), Gotha, 1855.
Guerrier, Mme. Guyon, 1881. (Reviewed by Brunetière, Nouvelles Études Critiques, vol. ii.)

Gosselin, Analyse de la controverse du Quiétisme, in Histoire Littéraire.
Bonnel, La Controverse de Bossuet et de Fénelon, 1850.
Deharbe, Die Volkommene Liebe Gottes, Regensburg, 1856.
Baudry, Dissertation sur la controverse de B. et F., reprinted in the ninth, or supplementary volume to Migne's Edition of St Francis of Sales, 1864.
Dean R. W. Church, Occasional Papers, vol. i.

Spiritual Letters, etc.

Sainte Beuve, Causeries du Lundi, vols. ii. and x.
Naville, Christianisme de Fénelon, Lausanne, 1873.
Merlet, Edition of Fénelon's Epiphany Sermon, 1880.
    See also the article on Fenelon in Caro's Nouvelles Études Morales, and the preface by Bishop Hedley to the St Anselm's Society Translation of the Spiritual Letters.

Télémaque and the Letter to the Academy.

Sainte Beuve, Port Royal, vol. vi.
Rigault, Histoire de la Querelle des Anciens et des Modernes, 1859.
Lotheissen, Geschichte der Französischen Litteratur im Siebzehnten Jahrhundert, 1884.
Degove, edition of Fénelon's Letter to the Academy, 1891.
Boulvé, De l' Hellénisme chez Fénelon, 1897.
Lanson, Histoire de la Littérature Française, 1898.

Jansenism.

Sainte Beuve, Port Royal.
Brunetière, Études Critiques, vol. iv., art. "Jansénistes et Cartésiens."
Le Roy, La France et Rome de 1700 à 1715.
    And see the pages on Jansenism in Harnack's Dogmengeschichte, vol. iii.

Philosophy

Bouillier, Histoire de la Philosophie Cartésienne, 1868.
Ollé-Laprune, Philosophie de Malebranche, 1870.
Brunetière, "La Philosophie de Bossuet" in Études Critiques, vol. v.

Politics.

Henri Martin, Histoire de France, vol. xiv.
Paul Janet, Histoire de la Science Politique.
Lady Blennerhassett, Französische Reformgedanken, in Deutsche Rundschau for May, 1885.

INDEX TO PROPER NAMES

AGUESSEAU, Chancellor d', qu. 33, 126, 176.
Albano, Cardinal, afterwards Pope Clement XI., 10, 173, 243 and *ff*.
Amiens, Vidame d', 217, 218.
Areopagite, Dionysius the Pseudo-, 89 to 95, 109, 257.
Augustine, Saint, 52, 90, 198, 229, 237, 238, 243, 250, 252, etc.

BARRE, Poulain de la, 56.
Bayle, 177.
Beaumont, the Abbé de, 212, 213, 300.
Beauvilliers, Duke of, 41 to 45, and Fénelon, 48 to 50, 124, 143, 145, 149, 160, 171, 213, 216, 231, 240 and *ff*, 299.
—— and Burgundy, 72, 75 and *ff*, 84, and *ff*, 281, 287 to 289, 297.
Beauvilliers, Mme. de (wife of preceding), 44, 213, 299.
Bernard, Saint, 90 to 96, 104, 116, 119, 120, 221.
Béthune, Duchesse de, 121, 124.
Blanco White, on Télémaque, 195.
Boileau, 194, 195, 227, 272 and *ff*.
Bossuet, his relation to Fénelon, 15, 17, 72, 132-177, 214, 215, 239.
—— compared and contrasted with Fénelon, in bodily health, 7; in views of Toleration, 17, 20; in social position, 31; in eloquence, 36 and *ff*; in views of women, 67; of education, 73; of mysticism, 92, 150 and *ff*; of Quietism, 113, 118, 119, 140, 153-155, 158; on duties of a King, 183; on circulation of the Scriptures, 208; on Jansenism, 227, 230, 232; on war against infidelity, 233; on philosophy, 249 and *ff*, 262; on Providence, 264.
—— his criticisms on Fénelon's character, 149, 159, etc.; on Télémaque, 8, 192, 193; on Dialogues of Dead, 79; on his diocesan administration, 206.
Bossuet, the Abbé (nephew of preceding), 145, 162, 165-167, 173, 175.

Bouillon, Cardinal, 145, 164-169, 172, 173.
Bourdaloue, 25, 36, 37, 134, 145.
Burgundy, Duke of, afterwards Dauphin, 72-79, 81-86, 224, 281-289, 292-296.
—— and Télémaque, 178-180,' 183-186, 189, 190, 193.
Burnet, Bishop, 157.

CARTESIANISM, *see* Descartes.
Casanate, Cardinal, 167, 173.
Chanterac, the Abbé de, 165-176, 209.
Chevreuse, the Duke of, 41-45,
—— and Burgundy, 75, 85, 281, 287-289, 297.
—— and Fénelon, 126, 132, 142, 143, 160, 171, 213-217, 231, 241, 293, 299.
Chevreuse, Mme. de (wife of preceding), 44, 146.
Clement of Alexandria, 88, 89, 119, 120.
Clement XI., Pope, *see* Albano.
Cologne, Joseph, Elector of, 20, 224, 231.
Corneille, 3, 116, 272-276.
Cosimo III. of Tuscany, 167.

DAUBENTON, Father, 245.
Dauphin (Father of Burgundy), 73, 288, 289.
Dauphiness (wife of preceding), 73.
Descartes and Cartesianism, 60 and *ff*, 165, 213, 248 and *ff*.
Destouches, the Chevalier, 224, 225, 299.

EUGENE, Prince, 226.

FÉNELON, Antoine, Marquis de (uncle of Fénelon), 10, 12, 14, 15, 41, 72.
Fénelon, Bertrand de, 5, 6.
Fénelon, Gabriel, Marquis de (grand-nephew of Fénelon), 30, 213, 218, 219, 297, 298, 300.
Fleury, the Abbé, 55, 60, 65, 75, 82.

309

Francis of Sales, Saint, 16, 83, 92 and *ff*, 116, 122, 128, 144, 229.

GODET DES MARAIS, Paul, Bishop of Chartres, 133, 138, 145, 147, 150, 172, 214.
Grammont, Mme. de, 219-221, 227.
Guyon, Mme., her opinions, 107-113, 115.
—— her early life, 121-124.
—— her relation to Fénelon, 112, 126-141, 149, 158, 163, 165, 170.

HARLAI, Archbishop, 15, 134.

INNOCENT XII., Pope, 148, 168-170, 173, 176.
Issy, Conferences and Articles of, 135 and *ff*.

JANSENISTS, 3, 4, 11, 227 and *ff*.
—— and education, 57, 60, 70.
—— and mysticism, 145, 157, 165.
—— and Fénelon, 157, 239-247, 289, 293, 297, 300.
—— and philosophy, 234 and *ff*, 250 and *ff*.
Jesuits, 11, 228 and *ff*, 241 and *ff*.
—— and Quietism, 115, 145, 164-168.
—— and philosophy, 248-250, 257.
John of the Cross, Saint, 91 and *ff*, 103, 128, 151.
Jurieu, 22, 26, 157.

LA BRUYÈRE, qu. 34, 35, 39, 117, 124, 227.
La Combe, Father, 121-123, 132, 163.
La Chaise, Father, 50, 146.
Lambert, Mme. de, 70, 234.
La Motte, Houdar de, 270-272.
Laval, Mme. de, 31.
Le Dieu, the Abbé, 209-212.
Le Tellier, Father, 178, 231, 241, 243, 297, 300.
Louis XIV., 2-4, 20, 24, 44-51, 73-76, 83, 239-241, 276, 281.
—— and Fénelon, 135, 136, 146-149, 160, 162, 166, 167, 170, 172, 179, 213-215, 289, 296, 300.
—— criticised by Fénelon, 2, 48-51, 77, 81, 179 and *ff*, 184 and *ff*, 281, 282, 286, 291, 292.
Louville, Marquis de, 75, 76, 81.

MAINTENON, Mme. de, 15, 24, 45-48.
—— and Fénelon, 30, 48-51, 125, 126, 129-139, 142, 146, 149, 160, 170, 205, 214, 240, 242, 288.
Maintenon, Mme. de, and education, 53, 54, 60-62, 68, 70, 81.
Maisonfort, Mlle. de la, 130-134, 149.
Malaval, 107-109.
Malebranche, 15, 248-264.
Marlborough, 226.
Mazarin, Cardinal, 81, 184.
Molière, 8, 53-56, 272-274, 278.
Molina, Louis, S. J., 227, 231, 235.
Molinos, Michael, 107-113, 118, 155, 267.
Montbéron, Mme. de, 221-223.

NOAILLES, Louis Antoine de, successively Bishop, Archbishop, and Cardinal, 135-138, 142, 147, 150, 165, 166, 172, 214, 215, 227, 239-245.

OLIER, 10-13, 227.
Orleans, Elizabeth of the Palatinate, Duchess of, 33, 155.
Orleans, Duke of (son of preceding), afterwards Regent, 8, 234, 267, 268, 296, 297.

PASCAL, 39, 105, 228, 229, 233-236, 239, 260.
Pellisson, Cardinal, 26, 197.
Peterborough, Lord, 203, 224.
Port Royal, *see* Jansenism.
Prior, Matthew, 224.

QUESNEL, Father, 232, 233, 236, 250.
Quietism, 106-113, 263, 267, 268, 286.

RACINE, 227, 272-276.
Ramsai, Chevalier de, 224.
Rémusat, Mme. de, 54, 70.
Renan, Ernest on Télémaque, 198.
Rousseau, compared and contrasted with Fénelon, 16, 49, 57, 66, 106, 180 and *ff*, 185, 199 and *ff*, 253.

SAINT PIERRE, Bernardin de, on Télémaque, 180.
Saint Simon, on Fénelon, 5, 22, 33, 83, 127, 144, 190, 206, 209, 216, 225, 226.
—— on the King, 2, 45, 291-293.
—— on the Huguenots, 24.
—— on Burgundy, 74 and *ff*, 82, 281-285, 292, 296.
—— on Mme. de Maintenon, 125.
Saint Sulpice, 10-13, 232, 300.

INDEX

Scudéry, Mlle. de, 55.
Sévigné, Mme. de, 1, 2, 25, 47, 59, 72, 227, 250, 264.
Spinoza, 115, 248, 258-262, 267.
Stuart, James, Pretender to the English Crown, 224.

TAULER, 93, 114.

Teresa, Saint, 91-95, 101-104, 128, 152.
Tronson, 10, 12, 32, 72, 135-139, 142.

UNIGENITUS, the Bull, 243 and *ff*.

VALBELLE, Bishop, 176.
Vendôme, Duke of, 283.

PQ 1796 .S3 1970
ST. CYRES, STAFFORD HARRY
  NORTHCOTE, 1869-
FRANCOIS DE FENELON